REGIONAL BEHAVIOUR

Dedicated to my parents Christos and Sofianna

Regional Behaviour

Political values and economic growth in European regions

DIMITRIOS C. CHRISTOPOULOS
University of the West of England, Bristol, UK

Ashgate

Aldershot • Burlington USA • Singapore • Sydney

Published by
Ashgate Publishing Limited
Gower House
Croft Road
Aldershot
Hampshire GU11 3HR
England

Ashgate Publishing Company
131 Main Street
Burlington, VT 05401-5600 USA

Ashgate website: http://www.ashgate.com

British Library Cataloguing in Publication Data
Christopoulos, Dimitrios, C.
    Regional behaviour : political values and economic growth
    in European regions
    1. Regionalism - Scotland 2. Regionalism - Greece - Crete
    3. Elite (Social sciences) - Scotland 4. Elite (Social
    sciences) - Greece - Crete 5. Scotland - Politics and
    government - 20th century 6. Crete (Greece) - Politics and
    government - 20th century 7. Scotland - Economic conditions
    - 1973 - 8. Crete (Greece) - Economic conditions - 20th
    century
    I. Title
    320.9'411

Library of Congress Control Number: 00-134841

ISBN 0 7546 2016 6
Printed in Great Britain by Antony Rowe Ltd, Wiltshire

Contents

List of Graph and Tables

Preface

I have been fascinated by the emergence of 'politics of identity' on the European political landscape. I thought it would be exciting to explore whether the agents of change, typically political and business elites, are somehow affected by issues of identity. Is interaction between elite groups affected by their sense of identity and does interaction between elite groups in itself affect regional growth prospects?

In the framework of the European Union a number of policies have been devised for regions in order to facilitate their balanced economic development. An attempt to coordinate these policies can be linked to the fact that European regions are increasingly interdependent as integration takes root and European Union policies become increasingly more relevant to this interaction. I believe that the importance placed by the academic literature and by the European Commission on regional planners and their actions has to an extent obscured the importance of regional elites in this process. This volume attempts to redress the balance, and does so by means of a series of interviews with business and political elites on the effects and prospects of further economic integration as well as administrative and political autonomy.

I am comparing Western Scotland and the west of Crete focusing on the wider regional political and business elites within these regions. My assumption that the interaction of regional elites with each other can be, at least partly, responsible for competitiveness differentials between regions underlies most of this analysis. I attempt a comparison of elite attitudes within regions and between regions. Particular attention is placed on the effect their aspirations to autonomy have on their interaction. I have been able to discern and identify a relationship between regional elite attitudes on devolution and their perceptions of business prospects in a region. I have also identified a relationship between the attitudinal concordance among a region's elite groups and regional growth prospects. Furthermore, I have identified certain value groups for which attitudinal concordance appears significant to elite cooperation. Ensuing conclusions do not necessarily have predictive value but, by identifying attitudinal patterns among regional elites, can provide an insight into the transforming effect of European integration and modernity on European regional civil societies.

Acknowledgements

The 'learning process' inherent in this research exercise has been extremely positive as it has led me to ever more refined, intricate and dare I say exciting investigations. This volume, as the product of a research and scholarly exercise that spans a decade (1988–98), I have to qualify with the acknowledgement of my accomplishment being at best modest. Awareness of the limitations, weakness and applicability restrictions of this research make for the frequent references to validity. The measure of my limited accomplishment does not reflect however on the incredible support I have received from my family, academic advisors, colleagues and friends.

I am also grateful to the John Latsis Group for providing me with generous financial assistance between 1989 and 1991.

Academically I have to primarily acknowledge the assistance of the supervisor to my PhD dissertation Paul Heywood. He copiously and consistently provided me with support that extended well beyond the 'call of duty'. I would not have finished this thesis without his assistance. Almost all of the academic and administrative staff at the Department of Politics in the University of Glasgow have at some point provided me with encouragement and support. I owe a particular debt of gratitude to Stephen White for consistent academic and personal support and for providing me with an example of academic excellence to follow in my academic future. Bill Miller has also been instrumental for my academic development assisting on a number of problems of methodology and providing me with a great number of refined insights on research approaches. James Kellas has frequently offered insights in to the Scottish political system and copiously proofread early drafts. John Peterson, Chris Berry and Michael Lessnof have also been a source of constant inspiration. They have been very approachable and their suggestions I have valued greatly.

I wish to also thank and acknowledge editorial and personal support from Stephen Herbert who was kind enough to review most of this volume always making valuable suggestions, he has been the most instrumental and effective reviewer of my work. Linda Blanshay, Ricardo Gomez, Clare McManus and Ian Murray have also provided me with very helpful comments on sections of this volume. Comments and suggestions during a number of conference papers proved very valuable and I would like to acknowledge comments by Charlie Jeffery, Michael Keating, Shari Garmise, Peter John, Elizabeth Bomberg, Hans van den Berg, Paul Heywood, Kleomenis Koutsoukis, Donatella DellaPorta, Martin Rhodes and Martin Bull. Also significant support I have received from Peter Lynch, Mark McAteer, Dimitrios Konstadakopulos and Geoffrey Pridham.

A great number of friends in Glasgow provided me with invaluable personal support and insights into Scottish custom and tradition. I have to specifically mention George and Jane MacMillan of MacMillan, Christopher Vine, Russel Clark-Jones, Paul Hampton, Ursilla Brown, Patricia Craig, Nadine Carmichael and Clare McAllister.

During the same period a great number of family and friends provided me with personal support. Ioanna and Vassilis Nicolaidis, John, Joseph and Edward McNelis as well as Panagiotis Pollalis, Giorgos Giannis, Nicos Giannis, Vali Lerouni, Spiros Plaskovitis, Katerina Zafiropoulou and Eleni Liakoura.

I would also like to thank all the participants in my survey for trusting me and sharing with me their opinions and perspective on a great number of potentially 'sensitive' issues. A great number of senior local government and EC administrators, business executives and academics in personal interaction/ interviews helped me orient the survey to the questions that mattered.

Finally, I owe a debt of gratitude to my mother Sofianna and my father Christos for their unwavering emotional support and financial backing through the many years of my student life. They have made life choices so much easier for me by pointing-out that 'one can only fail by not realising their potential'.

List of Abbreviations

AWH	Alternative working hypothesis
CSF	Community support frameworks
EAGF	European Agricultural Guarantee Fund
EC	European Community
EEC	European Economic Community
EIB	European Investment Bank
ERDF	European Regional Development Fund
ESF	European Social Fund
EU	European Union
FT	*Financial Times*
GDP	Gross domestic product
GRP	Gross regional product
IMPs	Integrated Mediterranean Programmes
LDC	Less Developed Country
LIC	Low income country
MNLs	Multinational enterprises
TNLs	Transnational enterprises
SMEs	Small and medium-sized enterprises
SRC	Strathclyde Regional Council
WH	Working hypothesis

Chapter One

Elites in the Regional Context

Can the behaviour of key actors at the regional level be partly responsible for differentials in the performance of regions? That question relating to the possibility of ascribing to wider regional elites a specific role as paragons of growth in regions underpins most research and scholarship in this volume. Regional behaviour for the purposes of this exposition refers to the behaviour and attitudes of elite groups at the regional level. The definition of region accepted here is that of a territorially defined administrative area. An account of the problems of definition for regions is given by Kimble (1951) who questions how meaningful it is to accept the regional concept and Gilbert (1960) who suggests integrating the physical and economic notions of the concept of a region. Furthermore, in the case of Scotland it has been convincingly argued that the wider geographically defined region has the characteristics of a nation (Kellas, 1989). In this volume, unless otherwise stated, I refer to nation states as nations and all their subdivisions as regions.

Interest in regional development within the context of European integration is linked to the possibility that an integrated European market can lead to economic agglomeration at core regions that would further hamper the competitiveness of the weakest peripheral regions. At the same time the sheer size of anticipated market transformations, could mean that any market changes will be very difficult to counteract once in place.[1] Regional inequality goes in tandem with the bleak possibility of great economic disparities that breed hardship and offend our sensitivities on social equity. They are characterised by a chronic under-utilisation of resources. It is not therefore surprising that the EU and the consisting national governments are so preoccupied with regional development and welfare. I am not suggesting, of course, that concern with regional development is on the ascendant in all member states. Regional development efforts in the UK for instance have been characterised as inconsistent since the beginning of the fourth Kondratieff cycle in the late 1940s (Prestwich and Taylor, 1990). A complicating factor to this picture is provided by the attempt since 1979 to redefine the welfare state in Great Britain (Pierson, 1991), as the 'Conservatives have stressed decreased intervention by central government and placed much more emphasis upon national economic growth' (Prestwich and Taylor, 1990, p.160). The Labour government has attempted to reconfigure that agenda since 1997 with devolution of regional development powers to the Scottish Parliament and the Welsh Assembly. It has also deconcentrated some decision making power to the ten English Regional Development Agencies, without however following it up with an endowment of the requisite financial resources or autonomy.

Accepting the fact that European Member States are, most of the times, too small or ill-equipped for a comprehensive evaluation of regional problems and adoption of appropriate assisting measures, is one of the reasons behind the prominent position of European regional economics in current academic literature.[2] Furthermore, the increase of trade and the integration of world financial markets has made mutual interdependence a feature of policy planning. The abolition of state subsidies and the limitation of financial instruments available to member states is one more reason that regional policy has to emanate (or at least be coordinated) at the European Union level. The trend towards globalisation of world production and distribution patterns, further affects inter-regional disparities in Europe.[3] A final consideration is of European regions' integration into the European economic system, which means that (relevant to their degree of integration) any slumps in their performance become crucial for the rest of the EU. The potential impact regional actors' behaviour can have, as a distinct factor of regional development and competitiveness, justifies a preoccupation with attitudes of regional elites.

Within this framework[4] I have looked at the interactions and attitudes of elite groups in two peripheral European regions, the West of Scotland (former Strathclyde) and the West of Crete (prefecture of Chania). The goal has been to detect the existence of an influence on regional economic performance from regional elite attitudes and elite interaction. I have, given particular attention to the similarity or divergence of elite attitudes within regions. I have effectively hypothesised that the degree of 'concordance' between the business and political elite subgroups could be directly correlated with past performance of a region. It is possible that a more exhaustive study could determine the degree to which regional elite concordance can be correlated with a measure of anticipated regional performance.

The role of regional elites as distinct and identifiable actors in European regions has not received particular attention in Social Science literature (exceptions include Leonardi and Garmise, 1992; Putnam, 1993; Dupoirier, 1994), although it is the case that certain regional elites perceive their goals as distinctly different from those of state-national[5] elites (Council of Europe, 1990; Morata, 1992; Newman, 1994). This could be viewed in tandem with the creation of a 'third level of governance' within European regions (Harvie,

1994), the emergence of a 'variable geometry state order' (Keating, 1992, p.60) or of 'multi-level governance' (Marks, 1993; Keating and Jones, 1995). The relevance and implications of these developments to a transformation of elite interaction at the regional level I will examine in the concluding chapter of this book.

Elites in the Regions

Behaviour of regional elites is inferred primarily by a concentration on regional elite attitudes.[6] This is standard practice among behavioural approaches in the social sciences (See Inglehart, 1990; Van Deth and Scarbrough, 1995). At a secondary level a set of semi-structured interviews with key informants has been employed to infer actual behavioural patterns and interaction among elite groups. If regional prospects can be assumed to be linked to elite actions and (by inference) to elite interaction, the behavioural patterns of regional elites become all the more important. My presumption of a sound theoretical basis for interpreting elite relationships was an inducement to attempt an investigation of elite interaction, rather than of wider political and business interactions. Theory, however, is far from settled on issues of elite interaction while it is apparent that investigating within elite interaction (i.e. interaction between elite subgroups in a region) is not tantamount to an investigation of power relationships, a common theme in elite studies. To complicate things further, attitudinal convergence or divergence (concordance or discordance) cannot be equated, without caution, with a sharing of values. While, a sharing of values, between two elite groups, does not necessarily imply that there will be higher interaction.[7] Higher frequency of interaction, on the other hand, cannot be equated with more effective or productive interaction, which leads to a need to define the 'quality' of interaction between elite groups. To avoid circular reasoning it is adequate for the purposes of this work to say that the 'quality' of elite interaction is tangential to the hypotheses underpinning the present exposition and will only be mentioned when it further elucidates particular outcomes. So the 'quality' of elite interaction will be discussed as a factor that can be distinguished from the frequency or effectiveness of that interaction. No theoretical definition of 'quality' can be offered however beyond suggesting that a sharing of values among elites presumably leads to a sharing of objectives, such as regional development. A discussion of the importance of 'core values' within a policy network framework by Wright (1991) points to their importance in determining agenda setting and network membership.

In order to define which elite groups to look at it will be of interest to look at certain aspects of the general debate relating to the study of elites. Of particular interest are definitions of elite functions and inter-elite interaction. Questions of whether elites exist as coherent groups, elite transformation as well as the mechanisms by which elites disseminate (distribute or share) power are some of the initial questions considered. Finally, the theoretical issues of relating to the investigation of elites are also directly relevant to a number of methodological issues of elite surveys.

Who are the Elite?

In order to establish a theoretical framework for this analysis, several problems had to be taken into consideration, the most significant of which was to identify a sample. Of particular significance was to take account of: a) the comparative character of the research questions; b) that surveying had to be intensive and cross-sectional rather than extensive and longitudinal; and c) the ability to identify exclusively and interview successfully an elite sample. I proceed here with a rudimentary definition of regional elites that acted as a basis for identifying a sample.

A number of references in the literature, analysed below, make it clear that it is almost impossible to have a watertight definition of who belongs to a regional political or business elite. A definition, to a degree arbitrary, had to be employed so that political and business elites could be selected. I use as a starting point theories by Pareto, Mosca and Lasswell.[8] Pareto's notion of a 'governing class' which shares the spoils of power with those who defend and sustain it (Finer, 1966, pp.77–81), ties in with the ideas of Mosca who attests that 'in every political organism the existence and functioning of a ruling class is necessary' (Mosca, 1972, p.249). According to Mosca 'in all societies ... – two classes of people appear – a class that rules and a class that is ruled'[9] (Mosca, 1939, p.50) or in Meisel's analysis of Mosca 'the history of all societies has been, is, and will be, the history of dominant minorities' (1962, p.v). So, in both Pareto's notion of clientelistic power sharing and Mosca's notion of 'dominant minorities' I can trace ideas that can be useful to the contextual setting of regional elites.

C. Wright Mills in his notion of 'power elites' incorporates 'local elites' as those 'who possess more than do others of whatever there is locally to possess; [while] they hold the keys to local decision' (Mills, 1956, p.30). He sees their role as subservient to the power elite of the larger urban centres.[10] Lasswell, on the other hand, defines elites as the influential. 'The influential are those who get the most of what there is to get ... those who get the most are *elite*' (Lasswell, 1950, p.3). He further identified power elite participants to possess among other things, a sense of a territorial community (Lasswell, 1965). Territorial identity among regional elites is by definition exclusive and presumably acts as a cohesive force for regional elites distinguishing them 'against' all others, while it aligns their interests with those of their region of identification. This notion can be instrumental in understanding territorially identified and landlocked elites, such as the regional elites.[11] Lasswell's notion of 'influential' actors is employed here in the selection of regional elites.

I proceed to examine the power context within which regional elites operate as it is essential in understanding the limits of their actions and scope for interaction. From the multiplicity of local elite groups my interest has been with those most relevant to regional growth. I encountered a number of problems in identifying them not the least of which were theoretical. I had to take account of Ivor Crewe's opinion that approaches to elites 'suffer from trying to make reliable statements about elites without first formulating a satisfactory theory of power' (Crewe, 1974, p.14). The exercise and dissemination of power by elites is a theoretical consideration with relevance to this research, as a frequent referral to clientelistic and patronage networks reveals. Articles by Clapham (1982) and Gellner (1977) cover the issues relating to the dissemination of power, particularly relevant to Mediterranean clientelism. I will in a number of occasions use clientelistic interpretations of elite interaction to explain findings that apply particularly to the Cretan elite groups. An interesting distinction between the elite groups in the two regions could be based in the existence of clientelistic networks in the case of Crete and patronage networks in the case of Strathclyde.

To further understand the notion of elite interaction it is interesting to examine notions of leadership developed by Wiatr (1973) and Fiedler (1971) which point to changes in the structure of modern society.[12] Wiatr (1973) refers to informal leadership, which can be functional, differentiating it from the formal leadership of elites. He further argues, that political elites exist only when a minority has much greater power than the rest of the community and there is a barrier of entry to the political field by non-elite members. Fiedler (1971) refers to the effect that followers have on leaders, arguing that to a great extent situations form leaders, so that leaders are not independent of the will of their followers.

European elite interaction has received particular attention in the context of policy networks analysis and the existence of multi-level governance

(Rhodes and Marsh, 1992; Marks, 1993; Rosenau, 1992). The impressive volume of the relevant literature points to an expanding interest in the role of sub-national actors. A discussion within the policy network context is of inherent interest to an examination of the 'hollowing out' of the state (Jessop, 1996) within the context of an emerging 'variable geometry' in European polity. The limitations in applying a policy network approach here stem from the generality in the conception of policy networks that diminishes from their explanatory value.[13] It can be argued that if you will look for policy networks you will find them.[14] So, although I will not use a 'policy network' approach in identifying the elites surveyed, a number of the interpretations that will be offered will derive directly from 'policy network' explanations.

Any attempt at interpreting elite interaction has to take account of the neo-corporatist perspective according to which 'elites collude and collaborate rather than compete' (Dunleavy and O'Leary, 1987, p.143). It has been further argued that 'state and economic elites are so interpenetrated by each others' concerns that no sensible boundary line or balance of influence can be drawn' (Dunleavy and O'Leary, 1987, p.185), while 'political and economic elites ... have shared interests in managing their complex environments, which facilitates cooperative elite bargaining' (Dunleavy and O'Leary, 1987, p.197). Within this framework I also consider two very distinct possibilities. In the first instance 'in Britain the unitary structure of the state and the extent to which local government functions have to be centrally handed down by statute ... severely constrains the possibility of a viable local corporatism' (Cawson, 1985, p.146). The more severe centralism of the Greek state would suggest that similar limitations to local corporatism would apply in the Greek regions. Secondly, it has been argued that 'countries locked into state corporatism at an earlier stage of development are likely to find it much more difficult to evolve toward ... a consensual solution' (Schmitter, 1979, p.41) which points to the possibility that in Crete state corporatism further inhibits the development of local corporatism. As is the case with the policy networks perspective some of the interpretations offered with the analysis of data later on are associated with the neo-corporatist paradigm.

There are also various alternative elite definitions to the ones I have employed, whose assumptions and simplifications do not lend themselves to this analysis but which can however enhance our conceptual understanding of elite interaction. Contemporary Marxist analysis of 'class fractions' I found both inadequate and without the explanatory value sought in a theoretical framework that is primarily concerned with elite attitudes and elite interaction. Poulantzas has provided an interpretation of Marx's writings dismissing aspects of the analysis by Mosca, Weber, Mills, Michels and Pareto. He argues that 'certain distinct classes, ... often appear in the social formation dissolved and fused with other classes, as groups (autonomous or not) of other classes' (Poulantzas, 1973, p.77), these he calls 'fractions'. A systematic critique of Poulantzas arguments on 'class fractions' is provided by Crewe (1974).

An alternative theory that diverges from the basic 'elite theory framework', is that of 'technostructures' by J.K. Galbraith (1967). I find the arguments portrayed in this and later work by Galbraith relevant to contemporary elite structure, but lacking, again, in explanatory power. It is indeed relevant to my hypotheses whether a technostructure has forced the entrepreneur to disappear, the business to be indifferent to which party is in office and whether ideological considerations – between Left and Right – have been made irrelevant.[15] The extent to which there is a difference between industrialising economies and post-industrial economies and if indeed the technostructure influences the formulation of policy while at the same time remaining distant from political decisions and choice, are issues relevant but not instrumental to this analysis. However close to the theoretical framework of this work, Galbraith's approach cannot serve as a basis for the present exposition, particularly since it would offer a limited explanatory value in a comparative study of societies that are in different stages of development. A similar argument is put forward by Lasch (1995) in the *Revolt of the Elites*. Lasch suggests that managerial elites disengage from their societal obligations a condition that leads to an intensification of social divisions. The prominence of multinational corporations and the internationalisation of world production patterns are to blame, while democratic institutions are weakened in the process. This is a view of disengaged and socially disinterested elites that is not compatible with my assumption of regional elites as those identifying with and caring most for their region.

And finally, an interesting element of the theoretical debate considers whether, unitary elites actually exist in Western democracies. Focusing in particular on the process for change within elites Burton and Higley (1987) attempt an investigation beyond the basic parameters of elite group identity[16] basing their arguments on Weber's concept of political actors. They also argue that present scholarly debates are characterised by a '"conceptual swamp" in which the elite concept has no agreed-upon meaning and no clearly perceived theoretical utility' (Burton, 1987, pp.237–8). This is an ongoing debate often based on semantics, without a necessarily clear direction. A consideration for the process of elite change, that stems from it, is relevant to attitudes I am investigating. But it should also be obvious that such change, could only be gauged by a longitudinal analysis, which is not attempted here.

Interaction Among Regional Elites: The European Context

The most exciting recent development in the examination of European elites is an interest on regional elites. Work by Dupoirier (1994), Leonardi and Garmise (1992), Keating (1991,1995), Harvie (1994) and Putnam et al. (1993) all point to the emergence of regional or sub-national elites in the framework of the European Communities and Union. In the long term, according to Keating, we will see the emergence of a 'differentiated state order' as a result of a breakdown in the 'tidy hierarchical order of continental, national, regional and local authorities' (Keating, 1992, p.60). The end result could be envisaged as a 'variable geometry state order'. Keating believes that civil society becomes important as 'national governments have been weakened, so the powers they can lend subnational governments are less potent' (1992, p.56). It has also been argued that there is a shift in identities from the national to the local and global.[17] 'The post-Westphalian state creates a new balance between subnational and other identities within the state, traditional nation-state loyalties and the wider sphere of international obligations' (Linklater, 1996, p.98).[18] The transfer and re-orientation in identities from the nation state is examined by Keating (1996a) in his discussion of the 'invention of regions' and Smith (1996) in his discussion of the re-imagining of regional identities, that in his view, have to be considered as concentric. Christopoulos and Herbert (1996), drawing from Gould and White (1986) offer the idea that identity in contemporary European regions can be visualised as 'concentric and fluid', with identification at the local, regional, national or supra-national level overlapping and in constant flux.[19] The timing of the series of interviews conducted, before the completion of the Single Market and the Treaty of the European Union, partially alleviates the need to consider the influences of modernity on European regional identity (as covered by Rosamond, 1995).

In this framework, the hypothesis could be explored whether elite behaviour, normally influenced by an overlapping but hierarchical allegiance to different levels of European civil society (local, regional, state and European), under the influence of modernity, will in the future be unattached to traditional territorial allegiances. Assuming that this is a valid hypothesis this will have a direct impact on elite 'consciousness' in Europe. In such a scenario regional elite behaviour should be re-evaluated. A case in point is if, for instance, local elites' allegiance does not follow a hierarchical pattern but, for instance, 'skips' a level. This would be exhibited if a Scottish nationalist identifies more with Europe than the UK.[20] It is also possible to consider elite identity as 'separated' (not to use the term alienated) from their local community, as elites may be active on a regional, national or international level without exhibiting allegiance or identifying with any of those levels of polity.[21]

Actors Relevant to Regional Growth

Selecting the business and political elites as most appropriate for the attitude survey that underpins this work is concurrent with a preoccupation with regional growth. It was important to investigate two elite groups in constant interaction and possible interdependence.[22] The research also attempts to identify, those groups most responsible for the successful implementation and dissemination of national and European regional policies. While having made the assumption that the regional political elite will be aware – if it is not indeed the vehicle for – the aspirations of the regional population.[23] Discussion of regional aspirations is also deemed relevant to issues of autonomy and nationalism, themes consistently explored at interviews. It is also rational to assume that the regional business elite will be more able to assess the prospects[24] their region has, particularly in relation to European integration and the Single Market. A growing literature on concepts like the 'local entrepreneurial milieu' (Rasmussen, 1992), the 'innovative milieu' (Campagni, 1995), the 'local context' (Johanisson and Spilling, 1983) explicitly or implicitly cite the significance of regional elite actor collaboration and identification with their region as factors of regional development.

In the survey used I have aimed on the wider business elite, without attempting to target the most powerful or those among them that would be considered 'business leaders' or opinion formers. There is an ongoing debate on the effectiveness of using any senior businessman/woman (defined by size of business they control), or assessing business attitudes by interviewing 'business leaders' or 'business representatives'. I do not believe that business people elected in Chambers of Commerce represent the attitudes and business preoccupations of their electoral college more than any elected office holder or politician represents the attitudes of their electorate, which is to say elected officials do not necessarily hold 'representative' opinions. For an alternative approach see work by Garmise (1996).

An elementary assumption here is that elite and leadership relationships apply to the whole elite cohort with similar effectiveness and as concisely as with business elites involved in the higher echelons of decision making.[25] In the case of the political elites I have attempted to identify in the data analysis those among them with a 'reputational' or functional eliteness although positional eliteness was the deciding factor in selecting to interview them. The series of pilot interviews that preceded the survey identified a number of key political figures in each region to be perceived as more influential than others. So, the political samples contain both functional and positional elite members, since I applied no measure to exclude those that by their interview or reputation I could determine were not powerful. A minor bias towards functional political elite members has to be acknowledged however, as I have made a particular effort to interview key figures (by reputation or position) within the political institutions I examined.

To place my work within the European context, it is interesting to note that most expositions on the institutional workings of the European Community and Union, take account of elite attitudes as a determinant of their behaviour. I first take account of Holland's reservations with the functionalist school which 'by stressing elite roles in the control of capital they neglect the extent to which "elite perceptions" on political issues such as European integration can be contradicted by the class role which the same elites need to pursue' (Holland, 1980, p.98). It is indeed probable that this 'class role' of elites can be instrumental in understanding their attitude and behavioural patterns. A possible 'contradiction' between elite actions (determined by their class interest) and elite attitudes (as their beliefs) towards Europe comprises a limitation of any attitudinal approach to the understanding of European integration.

Issues of 'personnel circulation' and 'social circulation' could pertain to the selection of political elites surveyed but relevant data are notoriously difficult to access. Welsh (1979, pp.24–7) has defined 'personnel circulation' as the turnover rate in elite membership; 'social circulation' as the degree to which an elite's social background changes, 'representativeness' as the degree to which the elite represents attitudes of the general population and 'inter-lockingness' as the overlapping membership in high ranking bodies of the political and other societal organisations. Lasswell gives an explanation for interlockingness between elite groups according to which 'forms of power and influence are agglutinative: those with some forms tend to acquire other forms also' (1952, p.97). The issue of 'representativeness' applies mainly to sampling of the business elites.

A framework of analysis, based on methodological considerations of researching elites, is provided by Moyser and Wagstaffe (1987) who note that ad-hoc choices have to be made in choosing procedures, while a comprehensive approach to the study of elites appears in the volume edited by Hertz and Imber (1995). Issues of 'elite autonomy' and the contrast between class and elite theory is covered by Etzioni-Halevy (1993). Theoretical considerations with empirical analyses of elite studies can also be found in Goldstone (1975) and Pahl and Winkler (1974), while a very interesting quantitative approach is taken by Ziegenhagen and Koutsoukis (1992).

More recently interest has been centred on viewing business and political elite relations within policy network analysis. In particular, the volume edited by Marsh and Rhodes (1992) on policy networks has been seminal, while important contributions on the analysis of social/political networks include Knoke (1990), Scott (1991) and Wasserman and Galaskiewicz (1994). A most interesting addition to this literature includes sociometrics in decision making network analysis (John and Cole, 1996). Policy network analysis is not used in the analysis in the present volume, due to limitations imposed by the character of the survey, but as mentioned earlier will supplement interpretations employed in the concluding chapter. Overall, the multiplicity and diversity of theoretical definitions and the difficulty in identifying and interviewing those key actors that for reasons of expediency we call regional elites, make it imperative to employ both quantitative and qualitative tools of inquiry.

And What About Methodological Validity?

The dreaded question (and therefore for most people a tedious one) in most methodology evaluations is: why and how are the methodological tools used relevant and valid?

It becomes apparent from the examination of the literature that certain questions of elite interaction, on which the growth pattern of regions depend, are not satisfactorily covered in present academic discourse. Investigating some of these by conducting research on elite attitudes in European regions, is a valid way for examining the impact on regions of elite interaction and how this interaction is (or could be) affected by European integration.

Issues investigated and analysed in the following chapters lend themselves to a cross-regional attitudinal study, as they are selected for their communality of significance across Europe (i.e. attitudes to the European Common Market). In broad terms one industrially declining and one agricultural-industrialising region of the European Community are investigated, while the local political and business elites are targeted for the survey.

Attitudinal data referring to the interaction patterns between the elite groups of each region as well as variations in replies between elite groups are employed to investigate the hypotheses constructed. Referring to limiting factors of this investigation I must point to the small size of the targeted population which

restricted my options in selecting an interviewee sample.[26] A limit to resources
further limited the time I could spend on the field collecting information and
conducting interviews. The varying response rate and degree of cooperation
among the different elite groups – when requesting interviews – restricted
testable propositions further.

A major part of the survey consists of a qualitative element which is used
in both the interpretation of results and the qualification of the exploratory
tests conducted. As with most elite, personal interview surveys, a great wealth
of information becomes available to the interviewer. This information consists
of interviewee qualifications in digressions from their replies, which was
encouraged and recorded beyond their replies to the structured part of the
questionnaire. It was felt that by recording these replies the questions they
gave to the quantitative part of the questionnaire could be clarified. It was
also felt that issues to which they reacted, could give an indication to issues to
which they held strong opinions. It has been my goal thus, to use respondents
qualifications as extensively as is feasible. To this end I employ a 'linked data
analysis' technique which focuses on the qualitative content of elite surveys
by using a quantitative basis as the structure from which all qualitative data
are analysed. The benefits of an integrated collection of both quantitative and
qualitative data in a 'linked data' format is covered by Miles and Huberman
(1994, pp.40–48) This technique can be considered as a form of data
triangulation since data of two different types are analysed concurrently. The
fact that this data originates in the same source however and has been collected
employing the same medium in part limits the validity of the technique. For an
excellent assessment of the triangulation of qualitative data see King, Keohane
and Verba (1994). A more comprehensive analysis of validity limitations and
the methodological framework employed can be found at the relevant appendix.

Notes

1   For a concise case on the necessity of European regional policy see Tsoukalis (1991, chs 2
    and 8) and Vanhoove and Klaasen (1987).
2   A seminal work on the European Economy is by El-Agraa (1990) premised on earlier
    work on *International Economic Integration* (El-Agraa, 1982). The literature on European
    regional economics is extensive including prominent work by Despicht (1980), Pinder
    (1983), Molle and Cappelin (1988), Hardy et al. (1995) and Vanhove and Klaasen (1987).
3   Economic globalisation has to be understood in a relative context. Krugman (1991 and
    1995) has pointed to the limited extent of truly global trends of what Hutton (1996) has
    called 'globaloney'.

4 Original data analysed here comprise part of my PhD research and subsequent thesis at the Department of Politics, University of Glasgow, viva voce in February 1997 supervised by Paul Heywood and examined by Michael Keating, James Kellas and Stephen White.

5 The use of the term national elites in the case of Strathclyde and Crete refers to the respective nation state elites of Britain and Greece.

6 In the 'ecological fallacy theorem' and the 'individualistic fallacy theorem', Alker (1965, pp.102–5) points to possible misrepresentations that can arise out of an attempt to infer a relationship among individuals to hold for collectivities and vice versa. I have qualified all inferences made of attitudes in respective regions with validity limitations and have not attempted to infer a relationship between institutions from a presumed relationship among the individuals I examine.

7 Empirical work on inter-elite interaction within the framework of policy networks by John and Cole (1996) points to a weak but significant correlation between a sharing of values among actors and frequency of network relations (networkability).

8 An excellent comparative analysis of Pareto's and Mosca's work was edited by Meisel (1965).

9 However, more sophisticated notions of the relationship between the ruler and the ruled have to be considered, as the demarcation line between the rulers and the ruled are not always clear and the channels of power between them can be considered interactive.

10 Mills' study (1956) focuses on American elites, with subsequent limitations on references that can be made in the contemporary European context.

11 Certain regional elites' strife for administrative autonomy can be linked to what Harvie (1994) and Keating (1996b) term 'bourgeois regionalism', under which economically advanced regions propelled by a regional bourgeoisie, seek to create political and administrative structures that would favour economic development.

12 Another important contribution to the understanding of leadership is the one by Riker (1986).

13 An effective proponent of policy network interpretations is Peterson (1995). The approach can be very helpful in examining EU policy making and the interaction between a number of different policy arenas. It can also be effectively employed in the interpretation of decision-making patterns among elite actors, as demonstrated by John and Cole (1996).

14 And indeed has been suggested by Kassim (1994), Michael Keating and Charlie Jeffery (in the context of the 1996 ECPR 'Policy Networks' workshop in Oslo) that the concept can be used most effectively as a methodological tool rather than a theoretical paradigm.

15 The role of the Scottish Office, in the case of Strathclyde, may be a mediating factor on the effect of 'technostructures' in the region. Galbraith's model would hold more explanatory power in interpreting the role of entrepreneurial rather than of local government elites.

16 These basic parameters are the so-called three Cs and include elite group consciousness, cohesion and conspiracy.

17 A more comprehensive account of the interplay between the local and the global can be found in Sassen (1991), Swyngedow (1992) and Amin (1994).

18 I am considering the influences of modernity (post- or radicalised) in the concluding chapter. According to Giddens modernity 'would not be a world that 'collapses outward' into decentralised organisations but would no doubt interlace the local and global in a complex fashion' (1991, p.178).

19 This theme is more fully explored in the concluding chapter of this book, ch. 8.

20 Which points to the inherent problems with campaigns for 'independence in Europe' as the one attempted by the SNP (1992).

21 The constant reference to 'eurocrats' in popular media points to an assumed allegiance of Commission bureaucrats to 'Europe' or to their own 'caste', in defiance of their national or ethnic background.

22 The distribution of economic and political power as the sources of 'social order' and 'economic order' are analysed by Weber (Gerth, 1991).

23 There is an implicit assumption here of higher 'representativeness' of local vs national elites without however testing that particular hypothesis, although there is extensive reference on the impact of regional identity on the concluding chapter.

24 Assessing business prospects is not tantamount to economic prospects in a region. Politicians could argue that having a wider (macro) perspective they are best able to judge economic prospects.

25 Samuel Brittan identifies reasons for difference in replies on an attitudinal survey of economists and politicians in that, 'practical politicians find it more difficult to think in terms of assumptions and hypotheses' (Brittan, 1973, p.30). This consideration together with reservations expressed in later survey work (Brittan, 1990; Rickets, 1990) has to be taken into account since they provide evidence that variance of attitudes among elites may be due to differences in perspective among elite groups.

26 The terms 'interviewee' and 'respondent' are used interchangeably. The terms 'informant' and 'form filler' as used by Bateson (1984) where thought insufficient descriptives for the participants of the present survey.

Chapter Two

Regional Actors: Catalysts of Regional Growth?

In the *First Periodic Report on the Regions of Europe* (Commission, 1981) the only section with any projections about the future is related to the labour market, signifying the importance given to the human factor by the researchers in the European Commission. In the *Second Periodic Report* as well (which is by itself a more 'mature' approach to regional problems) again the main parameters investigated had to do with labour supply and demand while a reference is made to labour force qualifications (Commission, 1984).[1] There is no apparent connection of business or political behaviour in the regions with regional development however. Admittedly the Reports try to cover the 'social and economic situation of the regions of the Community' by giving an account of the major employment, productivity and regional product disparities. They are incomplete though – to the extent that they try to make policy suggestions – without considering the effects of entrepreneurial disposition. Extensive infrastructure is not a sufficient precondition to guarantee private investment and consequent development. Of course, from the perspective of a civil servant, the periodic reports may be instrumental in identifying the problems, without however attempting to identify the catalysts of regional interaction namely regional actors.

Entrepreneurial ability and its significance is more openly discussed and given a centre stage by authors like Molle and Cappelin (Molle, 1988).[2] Although their views can be considered controversial they indicate an interest in this particular field of research.[3] Molle and Cappelin expand on the impact of Community policies in Europe centred on the distribution and movement of labour. As Economic Geographers their particular interest is with the distribution of employment effects across space. Their contention that long term economic cycles are responsible for total production levels leads them to the conclusion that the long term cycle is responsible for unemployment as well.[4] This runs counter to the mainline economic principles of business cycles and employment levels. So, they believe that their focus on the long-term cycle and long-term trends of employment allows them not to abide by the restricted concept of short-term economic cycles. The authors' particular perspective does not allow them to investigate interaction patterns within the work force or the influence of particular agents on unemployment levels.

Economists like Robson, Christiansen, El-Agraa and Pelkman touch upon the subject of relations between business with economic development and more rarely with the issue of politics and economic development, but they seem to avoid tackling the two issues together. At the same time they avoid expanding on the relevant analysis of agent influences that will take account of their interaction. Since they do not touch upon the subject at a national level we cannot expect them to cover it on a regional basis either. It should not be forgotten however that economists categorise business behaviour as a basically microeconomic issue and regional development as a macroeconomic one. Consequently most economists due to 'scientific conditioning' would avoid mixing both perspectives.

Robson, for instance, covers the impact and importance of Transnational Enterprises only from the perspective of resource allocation and equity considerations. His analysis on a regional level does not refer to the importance of a positive business climate for the Transnationals to function efficiently (Robson, 1984, pp.165–8).

Christiansen, on the other hand, makes a good study of location decisions on a regional level with business behaviour in perspective. His findings support the proposition that a major part of location decisions are made in the same way by regional actors in different countries. Although his study is limited in perspective he comes up with three rules on locational decisions:

a) decisions are made on the highest level possible;
b) small firms react more efficiently to changes in their locational environment; and
c) only very large firms use 'rational' model-oriented procedures for selecting sites (Christiansen, 1981, pp.224–5).

I believe these estimates by Christiansen to support my contention that there is a relationship between behaviour of regional actors and development. In particular it seems that locational decisions are determined by the perception the manager/entrepreneur has of economic space surrounding him or her. The ability of small firms to react better to changes in the locational environment (see b) above) could be interpreted to mean that smaller firms have the advantage of a more agile decision making process; while the fact that large firms use 'rational' procedures (see c) above) must be associated with the ability of multinationals (or aspiring multinationals) to have a global perspective possessing relatively unbiased maps of opportunity. In other words, big corporations are mainly influenced by 'rational' return on investment rules, while entrepreneurs within SMEs (small and medium-sized enterprises) are bound by their maps of business opportunities and therefore biased. Effectively this bias could be a major competitive advantage of regions, facilitating the development of small enterprises, and being an 'inexhaustible' source of entrepreneurial capital for the regional economy. Regional entrepreneurs unlike multinationals are more likely to have a permanent commitment to a region.

Disequilibrium theory assumes rational decisions by businessmen, investors and migrant workers who calculate opportunities and act accordingly. As David Pinder argues 'businessmen and investors possess "mental maps" of spatial opportunity that deviate markedly from reality' (Pinder, 1983, p.30). Pinder draws on theories developed by Hirschman, Myrdal and Friedmann in explaining that entrepreneurs do not evaluate objectively growth regions, are biased towards advanced regions and overestimate the benefits in some growth regions. All these lead to a distortion of their views on available opportunities elsewhere. The media or proximity of entrepreneurial capital to development regions, or business associates are likely to bias the opinion of entrepreneurs.[5]

It has also been argued that much depends on the ability of decision makers to filter biased information and analyse it effectively (Gold, 1980; Gould and White, 1986). Thus indicating that balanced growth is directly relevant to attitudes of important actors toward particular regions. Pinder also contents that 'strategies designed to improve international balance will be incomplete if they focus on economic considerations alone. Attention must also be given to overcoming the psychological barriers to development in lagging areas' (Pinder, 1983, p.32).

I now turn to the effect those 'biased' regional actors can have on regional economies within Europe.

Political Actors in European Regions

Nevin comes to recognise the importance of political actors in efforts of regional development by pointing to the need of politicians to alleviate regional problems in the short term. He does not however distinguish what is the effect of regional politicians nor does he see the possible importance of a positive business climate created by regional government. Furthermore, he sees entrepreneurs who 'displace the flexible prices and free markets of earlier stages of development, by administered prices' as a reason for regional imbalance, leading therefore to the market distortions responsible for regional inequality (Nevin, 1990, p.329). Although this is an admittedly negative view of entrepreneurial role it shows the preoccupation of the author with the role actors can play on the regional level. Furthermore, this view can only be sustained for entrepreneurs that are able to monopolise a market, a development that can only seem possible if an entrepreneur has a big market share or acts in collusion with his competitors. In a world of small and medium sized enterprises and multiregional competition it is difficult to imagine such a development.

It is possible that economic analysts fail to take account of those characteristics that separate one region from another and which can be seen to have an impact on the regional productive environment. The perennial discussion of identity by political scientists could be what economists miss out when they examine regional growth. For instance, in his analysis, Nevin equates national problems in a customs union with regional problems within a nation (Nevin, 1990, pp.335–41). This has the detrimental effect of altering the perspective of his exposition. He takes as given that national units (his new regions) will – or can – represent the interests of their own regions in the European Community. He, in other words, presupposes that analysing the behaviour of national governments and industries at the Community level is assimilable to an analysis of regional government actions. He does make one interesting remark in that context: 'generalisations concerning the regional impact on existing enterprises are on shaky ground ... [because] the range of productive performance within any given country ... is at least as great as that between countries' (Nevin, 1990, p.329). Effectively he recognises the limitations of economic analysis on a national level to fully account for their economic problems and provide solutions. He warns that once a common market exists it is difficult to separate industry on a regional or national basis with no reference to basic distributional statistics for industries' best and worst performers. Generalisations will be meaningful (i.e. identifying an industry as labour or capital intensive) only on a very wide basis (i.e. European Union level). The importance of this realisation lies basically in interpretations of regional data and policies in aid of regions. A region demonstrating low productivity in one industry may have a thriving public and ailing private sectors. This being an unusual event it may not be immediately identified by a simple review of the data. This fact acts as a further impediment to meaningful analysis of regional integration by conventional economic analysis.

Pelkmans addresses the issue of regional policy conducted 'from above' which would have a negative influence on the 'supply of entrepreneurs'. He poses the question: 'is the supply of entrepreneurs exogenously given, independent of the business climate?', to answer ' a favourable business climate with sufficient freedom for new initiatives and new entry is likely to exert a strong positive effect on the supply of entrepreneurs' (Pelkmans, 1984, p.274). He goes on to attack over-involvement of the government for among other reasons that 'political commitments may create an atmosphere where cost increases go unpunished', he believes that 'neither Governments nor firms can 'pick winners' individually' therefore advocating a balanced involvement by both (Pelkmans, 1984, p.274). Pelkmans further suggests that regional policy is conducted on political arguments and for electoral reasons; it ends-up distorting the market by compensating for locational disadvantage helping to maintain 'key' and 'essential' industries which would not have survived in free competition (Pelkmans, 1984, pp.44–54 and pp.271–5).

There seems to exist a dichotomy of interest between political and economic goals of regional policy. This, I believe, is evident from the fact that it can be to the advantage of national politicians – who frequently have a short term perspective – to distort market operations to ameliorate regional problems, instead of promoting economic solutions that benefit the regions in the long term. In short, national politicians seem to favour the solutions with the least political cost. That is a good reason to investigate behaviour of regional politicians to whom – hopefully – regional welfare extends beyond the next elections. I believe regional politicians' commitment 'evident' by the fact that it is a small percentage of them that will be able to pursue a political career on a national or supranational level. Therefore their 'bond' with local government should identify them more with their region. Furthermore, in regions with autonomous aspirations, politicians associated with that goal, will correlate a political career in the national arena with stronger representation of regional interests.

In a report on 'The Economics of 1992' (Emerson, 1988), representing the semiofficial view of the European Commission on the direction of the European Common Market, the issue of business climate or managerial capacity is not tackled on a regional level. Naturally, an issue emerging as having paramount importance for further integration was the training of European managers. It is evident that managerial capacity and business initiative is considered essential but regional differences are omitted as one of the sources of regional variation. Furthermore, the entrepreneurial milieu and the relationship between business and political actors are not given adequate consideration.[6] So, although regional economic variations are considered one of the major policy arenas, posing a significant challenge to the competence of the EU, causes of regional disequilibrium are not fully gauged if the main reference to business actors in the regions relates to their training.

On a major research project funded by the European Commission there is an attempt to address issues related to regional competitiveness by surveying business elites at a European Community wide level (Nam, 1991a and 1991b). This research effort, although of invaluable assistance as an indicator of prevailing business attitudes in Europe does not attempt to present the point that regional business elites are in themselves important for regional competitiveness, nor does it attempt to identify regional elites' interaction as one of the reasons behind regional competitiveness. The focus of that survey, on industrial production firms which are typically medium or large, produces a further bias towards large national or multinational operators.

Towards an Explanation of Regional Actor Involvement in Regional Development

Political scientists come to interesting conclusions when they try to tackle the issue of regional policy. It is more 'natural' for a political scientist to associate economic considerations with political motives. So Nigel Despicht asserts that 'government policies toward regions have been inspired by national problems' and 'European regional policy is acceptable if European-scale action helps to solve national problems better' (Despicht, 1980, p.40). A limitation in his perspective can be linked to its typical 'integration from above' format where significant regional actors are only those having 'aspirations for autonomy' such as the Basques or the Scots (Despicht, 1980). It is possible that the visibility of other regional groups is less prominent but I contest the view that regional actors with less radical views than, say, the Basque separatists are less significant for their regions' economic development. In Despicht's defence, regions or their integration were not very high on the political agenda of the 1970s and it was hard to foresee the importance they would assume in EC planning by the 1990s.

Another political scientist, Barry Jones, demonstrates the importance of regional political actors by focusing his discussion on regional interest groups and their power to lobby effectively. He warns that:

> The regions are parts of highly developed, integrated political systems. Regional interest group attitudes and the procedures which they have evolved are conditioned by the fact that they operate within the constitutional framework of

their respective states, according to the rules and conventions of their parliaments and the organisational structures of their national political parties and pressure groups (Jones, 1985, p.243).

In other words, regional actors do not function autonomously of national political influence. In this work Jones does not determine the extent to which they divert from national, to support regional interests however. Forecasting a possible future for European regions, Jones, believes that 'the more the regional and other interests organise to lobby the Commission in Brussels' the more centralised the EC will become which will result in 'regional and peripheral interests [to] ... be subordinate to the needs of the Community as a whole' (Jones, 1985, p.245). So, Jones sees two forces namely the 'proprietorial interest expressed by the national Governments' and the 'consolidation of power in the Commission' (Jones, 1985, p.245) as seriously threatening the chances of European regions to autonomous decision-making. His contentions seem consistent and point to subsequent developments in the European political scene that have however taken a slightly different turn than what Jones predicted. One of the possible scenarios for the development of Community institutions presupposes that regional autonomy and decision making will be enhanced, by the process of Community integration, so that this 'new third level' of government at the regional level will counteract centralised legislative and executive powers of the Community. Under this scenario the national units will be the only ones to suffer loss of sovereign power.[7]

The view has also been expressed that regional units become increasingly players on their own right, while regional politics and lobbying attain a different focus. According to Boisot, 'what we are witnessing in this evolution is a shift in the nature of regional strategy from one which could be described as a game against nature to one that is more appropriately labelled a game against adversaries' (1990, p.394). According to this perspective, regional authorities lobby Brussels directly, competing with other local authorities for ERDF or other funds and preferential treatment on regulations or allocation of resources. This would signify the emergence in Europe of regional players in their own right. Such a development would be more significant for regional authorities like Strathclyde, which financed a representative office in Brussels, while it can be argued that by its mere existence such an office created a higher awareness about European issues among the Strathclyde local political elite.[8]

It can be of course counter-argued that the emergence of regional actors as players in the European arena is a chimera. The European Union budget is just over one percent of the collective GDP of member states. Most research detects only incremental effects of regions in EU policy making (Bomberg, 1994; Van der Knaap, 1994; Jeffery 1995). The concept of 'Europe of the Regions' has been derided while an alternative concept of 'Europe *with* the Regions' (Borras-Allomar et al., 1994; Hooghe, 1996) has been offered as a more accurate assessment of future relations of European institutions with regional government. It is also evident that lobbying in favour of a region is more effective with the intervention and collaboration of a 'home' nation state (Mazey and Richardson, 1993). Furthermore, it has been suggested that it is not the allocation of resources that drive regions to a European representation but the need for information and of a reassertion of their regional identity (Marks et al., 1996).[9]

The degree to which regions will proceed from being integral parts of nation states to outright inter-regional competition with one another, is the subject of an ongoing academic debate (Hardy et al., 1995; Ohmae, 1995) which is still at its early stages.[10]

Finally, to produce a complete account of forces affecting European region-alisation it is important to mention those that support the 'emancipation' of regional units within national and European institutions as a political conviction. Most prominent is the Federalist Intergroup in the European Parliament. According to the Federalists, consolidation of political power in the EU cannot but get balanced with more autonomous decision making from the European Union regions.[11] The question then arises whether regional actors are able to benefit their region more effectively than actors at the national level.[12]

It is obviously very difficult to make a distinct separation of decision making on the regional level that is not directly related to the national or supranational level.[13] Hence the need to examine regional autonomy and its relation to business and political behaviour.

Regional Autonomy and Economic Development

There would be a limited scope in discussing the relationship of autonomy to regional development if all operations and decisions on growth and development were taken at a national or supranational level. On a cursory overview this would appear to be the case for both Scotland and Crete. It is my contention, however that regional elites are able to influence decisions at a national and supranational level,[14] while policies devised at the national and supranational level are subject to lobbying from those regions with the strongest and most determined regional elites.

On the other hand, in a free trade area, with transportation costs becoming marginal for most products,[15] the concept of economic autonomy has an inherently restricted meaning.[16] Within the globalisation of production and consumption patterns, the EU regulatory framework becomes quintessential for regional competitiveness. I contend here that one of the most important assets of a region's productive environment is the attitudinal concordance of elite actors.

I will also argue that, although the major fiscal and monetary decisions are taken in the centre[17] – be it Europe or nation state – there exists an inherent ability for manoeuvre of regional and local government. This power is often more than just an ability to bend rules and amend decisions taken at the centre. It is one of my hypotheses that regional government can create a conducive business environment,[18] and therefore be instrumental in creating the 'attitudes' that can be beneficial to the people of their locality.

It will, furthermore be interesting to examine whether the politicians of a region accommodate the businessmen of a region, within the process of 'policy networks' or the existence of neo-corporatist arrangements among local elites (Schmitter, 1979, 1982; Cawson, 1985, 1986; O'Sullivan, 1988).[19] In the context of examining European regional prospects, it has also been suggested that the emergence of public-private partnerships in European cities and lagging regions can be associated with the 'generation of dynamic development strategies' in the 1980s which, however, cannot by themselves be a sufficient condition for development (ERECO, 1993, pp.44–6).

At this point it is good to remember that it is still an open question whether businessman or politicians are in a better position to assess the economic predicament of a region better. 'Policy-makers have presented themselves as possessing spatially unbiased views which give rise to an appreciation of the suboptimal resource use characteristic of regional systems in disequilibrium'; in other words, politicians in designing regional policy claim they can correct 'the inaccurate mental maps possessed by industrial decision makers' (Pinder, 1983, p.66). In assessing the role of politicians it should be borne in mind that policy making for the regions cannot be considered separate from the seasonality of the political 'game' and the party political scene.

I assume that regional politicians (in contrast to national ones) could create the necessary equilibrium for two main reasons. First, they must feel more accountable to their region, if only because of the immediacy afforded by a smaller electorate. Secondly, they must be more receptive and better aware of the needs of their region possessing a more accurate 'mental map' of their area.

The development of services in European regions can be a case in point. Sven Illeris (Illeris, 1989) argues that the service industry cannot operate without the existence of infrastructure but at the same time the existence of infrastructure alone is by no way a guarantee of the development of services. The two must go hand in hand. Obviously for the most promising sector of growth for the Community regions (Commission, 1984), the question does not become one of just providing the infrastructure funds but creating those attitudes that will make possible tapping into the latent human resourcefulness in every area.

The creation of new service firms depends decisively on the presence of entrepreneurs (Illeris, 1989, p.103). What is characterised as the 'entrepreneurial type of human resources' (Illeris, 1989, p.104) is considered essential for innovation and firm creation. The frequency of creation and degree of success of new firms depends to a great extent on the social and cultural background of the entrepreneurs. Local and regional authorities can therefore be instrumental in creating those conditions that will cultivate and encourage innovative skills and assist in the marketing of new products.[20]

To go back into examining politicians and policy makers relevance to the development of a region it is relevant to examine possible effects of regional planning on a region. It has been suggested that the 'competitive advantages of a region or firm are less determined by what happens to be their "natural endowment" and are to a large extent the result of deliberate strategies reflected in investment in productivity, people and R & D' (Emerson, 1988, pp.180–81). European Commission researchers, in other words, believe that planning can be a sufficient counter balance for lack of endowments. Although 'investment in people' is a vague enough concept to include the creation of a positive innovation climate, I believe there exists a failure of elevating this concept to the importance it deserves.

Researchers working for the Commission, in the same report on the effects of market integration believe as well that eventually there will be an even pattern of development 'between dynamic centres and lethargic peripheral areas' (Emerson, 1988, p.181), seeing the latter as lagging in basic technological infrastructure and vocational training. More recent analysis suggests that globalisation of production will eventually lead to convergence of real incomes while core-periphery disparities will be eliminated in the long term (Krugman and Venables, 1994). This analysis is premised on an assumption of constantly diminishing transport costs.

On the other hand, it is generally accepted that distributive effects from infrastructure improvements are small, when they take place on all regions at the same speed (Rietveld, 1989); that as 'US experience has shown ... public work projects, chiefly because of their long delays in implementation fare badly as economic stabilisation instruments' (Burns, 1987, p.240), and that international capital investment is directed towards locations with already existing qualified labour. From these premises I conclude that it has to be indigenous investment efforts that can trigger an adequate process of development. As indigenous investors I also consider the institutional ones since 'the structure of the region's "production environment" may ... be more decisive than the abilities of the entrepreneur' (Lambooy, 1986, p.160) or as W. Stohr claims, a prerequisite for innovation in the regions is the interaction of among others 'risk financing ... and locally rooted decision making functions' (as quoted in Vanhove, 1987, p.171). A need for decisive actions in the region can probably be better facilitated the more autonomous the decision-making is. So, it can be concluded that international planners and politicians are an important but not sufficient element to regional development, while they appear inherently restricted in their ability to influence regional development.

I next turn to attitudes of business elites themselves. Characteristic of the perspective managers and Multinational Enterprises (MNLs) take towards an integrated market is the prevailing conviction that 'unifying the internal European market is a good idea' (Geroski, 1989). How good and how firms should respond to it is a matter open to debate. Quelch and Buzzell forecast homogeneity of consumer behaviour and call for single product campaigns and a pan-European strategy (Quelch, 1989). Gogel and Larreche however warn that 'it is important having a strategic perspective in order to avoid either immobilisation or overreaction' further suggesting that markets can be fragmented even after the mythical 1992 (Gogel, 1989). On the other extreme from Quelch and Buzzell is Geroski who predicts 'an increase in the diversity of goods and services offered to consumers' further arguing that 'the challenge comes from those willing to sacrifice diversity in pursuit of efficiency gains that are likely to prove modest in scale' (Geroski, 1989, p.75).

To make the issue slightly more intriguing all three above mentioned business articles are basing their predictions on the same report of the European Commission on 'The Economics of 1992'. The perspective of big corporations and managers suggests that they consider an internal market with uniform laws and similar consumer tastes as a prerequisite for the development of a Common Market. The importance of such a view is that they seem 'naturally' opposed to delegating power to regional authorities. If this is a correct assumption autonomy inspired regions will have to depend to a great extent on the small and medium-sized companies and the new entrepreneurs for business support of their aspirations to autonomy.[21]

Multinationals could be seen as lobbying for more legislative power of central authorities as expressed by Quelch and Buzzell (1989), who suggest a move of multinational enterprises head offices to the centre of Europe and increased lobbying in Brussels.

It appears therefore, that regional politicians can claim that they are better equipped to devise a regional development strategy, while big corporations and multinationals are averse to any moves towards regional autonomy in decision making, that could create aberrations to an integrated market. Support for regional autonomy is more likely to lie with SMEs whose proprietors/ managers are more likely to identify with a locality. I conclude with an examination of whether local entrepreneurs can be considered as an asset of a region, in the same way that we view natural endowments.

Regional Economic Space

On a qualitative evaluation of factors of growth it is tempting to regard natural endowments to have a diminishing role in the prosperity of a region. A commonplace example is the success of economies (in the course of the fourth Kondratieff cycle) with limited indigenous resources other than the human resources like Japan, Hong-Kong, Singapore or Taiwan.

Peter Robson (1984) argues that disparities between regions cannot be explained in terms of differences in initial natural resource endowments. When analysing regional dissequilibria it becomes apparent that unequal development is connected with industrial activity. Disadvantaged regions can be further identified as having lower productivity growth rates for a series of business cycles. These regional inequalities are likely to be aggravated in the medium-term within Europe if the often quoted statement by H. Girsch that 'the creation of a monetary union transforms balance of payment problems into regional problems' (1949, pp. 87–98) is proven to be still valid today.

Kenichi Ohmae (1995b) suggests that globalisation leads to the 'rise of regional economies'. His arguments, although topical to this discussion are however rather weak. His vision of regional agglomerations (Ohmae, 1995a) that transcend national frontiers conveniently ignores all political institutions that will be pegged against any such development. His prediction of the 'end of the nation state' seems at best premature. It is conceivable that the nation state will be challenged by stateless nations in Europe (Keating, 1996a) or that within the post-Westphalian state there will be 'a new balance between subnational and other identities' (Linklater, 1996, p.98). It is hard to conceive the dissolution of the nation state however, based on economic expediency alone.

To examine the basic tenets of regional economics it would be pertinent to start with Gunar Myrdal and his classic book *Economic Theory and Underdeveloped Regions* (1957) in which he stresses that labour and capital will move to regions already developed so that in the next economic cycle the deprived regions are likely to be in an even worse position. In Myrdal's 'Cumulative Causation Theory' lies the beginning of much research on agglomeration like those of Hirchman, Kaldor, Klaassen and others (Molle, 1988).

On the other hand it has been amply demonstrated (Commission, 1984) that peripherality can be a factor of regional development.[22] In effect location can be considered a natural endowment as 'it should also be mentioned that certain peripheral regions possess natural resources and advantages for the development of trade' (Commission, 1984, p.140). In other words, under certain conditions being in the periphery could be an advantage for certain regions.[23] Significantly it does not seem that research, can convincingly identify the reasons of regional economic marginalisation. Peripherality is a measurement of a static condition which evaluates the effect past policies or rounds of capitalist accumulation have had on the development of a region. It does not seem to be an effective tool in evaluating potential.[24]

But why are regional actors singularly important? Beyond questions of regional autonomy raised above, regional actor behaviour can diverge only to a limited extent from what national or international elites can do. After all regional actors belong to elite groups with similar goals and membership criteria for elites on a wider scale. The difference I see in the importance of regional actors has very much to do with what Hirschman has called 'a special kind of boldness' (Pinder, 1983). Both entrepreneurs and politicians need such a boldness to succeed in what continuously will be a 'competition between communities' for capital (Smith, 1988) while regional boundaries become less significant (Smith, 1988; Agnew, 1988). The local/regional context becomes more significant as the emergence of an identifiably regional behaviour takes place. Relevant to this debate is also the notion that the productive environment is determined by 'actions or behaviour' of economic actors in a locality. Baumol (1990) for instance argues that a legislative framework that promotes entrepreneurial incentives to innovate promotes 'productive entrepreneurship'. This can be the consequence of the reimagining of regional identity (Rosamond, 1995) and of the emergence of a 'multi-perspectival' polity (Ruggie, 1993) or of an 'invention of regions' (Keating, 1996a).

To turn back into regional economics it is relevant to note that with the phenomenon of fast and slow motions in urban and regional dynamics not fully chartered (Dendrinos, 1984) it is impossible to give relative weights to the importance of endowments vis-à-vis actors. It is obvious that both factors have to be present for economic development to occur but it is not easy to determine an optimal combination that could generate regional development. There is also difference of opinion on the development of regional dynamics. Some researchers believe that regional economic dynamics follow a cyclical pattern while others believe that a linear process is more typical of regional development. Prominent in the first group is Leo Klaassen who divides regions into four different categories according to their level of prosperity. He finds there is a pattern of prosperity-recession-depression-recovery, with approximately five-year periods for each position shift. In an application of his research design, regions either remain in the same position or move to the next with no region moving to a previous position (Klaassen, 1987). Similar views are expressed by Berg, Burns and Klaassen who claim regions follow the cycles of industries comprising their economy where 'vestiges of functional independence of regions appear to be rapidly disappearing as the world "shrinks" and spatial units become more and more integrated' (Berg et al., 1987).[25] An analysis that assumes linear regional development is the one by Krugman and Venables (1994) in which they theorise that globalisation of production unequivocally alters the economic relations between core and periphery.

So, what can be implied about the effect on regional growth of the behaviour of regional actors? A tenuous link can be made on the importance of regional actor behaviour as *one of* the endowments of a region. Surveying the literature can only suggest that this question has to be examined more closely.

Note should also be taken of apparent limitations to the present investigation. Important actors on a regional level may have very little to do with a region's prosperity to the extent that regional policy is directed from the centre. I must therefore point to the fact that national political actors can be considered for most European regions directly responsible, in policy terms, for a regions' level of development. This charge can also be made for the regions used in the present case studies. Analysing the role of local businessmen and politicians is based on the assumption that they are the most significant actors for regional growth at the regional level, this does not necessarily imply that they are the most powerful or influential ones overall.

Notes

1 Subsequent periodic reports such as the Fourth (Commission, 1991b) take a different angle from the first two, shifting the emphasis to specific regional problems rather than giving a general viewpoint of the regional situation. For that reason it can not be reasonably expected that they will dwell on such issues as the importance of regional elites.

2 Molle and Cappelin (Molle, 1988) also argue that long term economic cycle is 'responsible' for total production and unemployment; at this result they come using the FLEUR model (which explains changes in time, of the share of each region of EC in the total European employment by sector) in an effort to interpret differentials in unemployment levels.

3 An interesting point of view is expressed by French political economist Guy Sorman (1988), who suggests that Low Income Countries (LICs) experience adjustment problems to capitalist production because they try to duplicate Western models of development. Although he sees a direct connection of development with business and political ethics he does not codify his contentions nor does he identify a regional pattern.

4 The long term Schumpeterian economic cycle as a process by which innovation breeds innovation (Schumpeter, 1939) is considered relevant not only to entrepreneurship (Jensen-Butler, 1996) but is also a force that facilitates greater interaction between the private and public sector (Dunford and Bencko, 1995).

5 Pinder further suggests that 'repeated exposure [to] particular features of the objective environment will however, increase the probability of their inclusion in the behavioural environment ... [particularly] since people are most frequently exposed to those parts of the objective environment that are in the immediate vicinity' (Pinder, 1983). In other words entrepreneurs are influenced by what is closer to home than what is further away.

6 The concept of the 'entrepreneurial milieu' is comprehensively discussed by Jesper Rasmussen (1992) as it relates to entrepreneurs and their social networks in a locality. Camagni (1995) and Coffey and Bailly (1996) explore the concept of 'innovative milieu', while the relationship between entrepreneurship and regional development is examined by Sweeney (1987) and Bradley and Taylor (1995).

7 Whether the shift of power to the regions is feasible or even desirable, is a theoretical question. It has been suggested for instance that 'relations between the central government and autonomous communities remains a central issue facing Spain, although one with potentially beneficial implications' (Heywood, 1991, p.64). On the run-up to the ratification of the Treaty of the European Union certain governments were reported to be hostile to the institutionalisation of the Committee of the Regions, which they perceived as potentially enhancing regional autonomy (*The Economist*, 1992).

8 Christopoulos and Herbert (1996) and Herbert (2000, forthcoming) examine the importance of awareness among the regional elite of EU policy initiatives.

9 In this work it is suggested by Gary Marks et al. (1996), that 'an office in Brussels is a form of insurance against the hazards of a notoriously unpredictable policy environment' (p.58), furthermore irrespective of whether regions harbour a 'sense of distinctiveness [that] is party-political or cultural ... regional governments are driven to Brussels to secure

independent representation' (p.60). It is finally concluded that 'the only resource we find evidence for is that of associational culture, which presumably is linked to the entrepeneurialism of subnational decision-makers in pursuing opportunities for political communication and influence beyond their own region' (p.63).

10 For a discussion of the competition between European urban centres see Lever (1993).

11 In an article on the institutional reforms of the EC in The Federalist, Antonio Padoa-Schioppa, expresses these federalist ambitions for Europe when he calls for the endorsement of a statement, in the then pending Maastricht Treaty, of 'the constitutional principles of subsidiarity, popular sovereignty and the balancing of powers' (Padoa-Schioppa, 1991, p.72).

12 There have been suggestions that the policy of national governments, like the British one, have been consistent and that the control of European policy through the elimination of federalist overtones in European Treaties is a positive development (George, 1990).

13 It has been argued (Hadjimichalis, 1983) that there is a political and cultural subordination of the periphery within the countries of Southern Europe, that creates a core and periphery relationship similar to the North-South one within Europe. It is further argued that the developed agglomerations in the South derive their strength from the existence of such a periphery.

14 See Marks et al. (1996) for an account of the effectiveness of 'the mobilization of regions in the European Union'. It is further suggested that 'the association between regional political autonomy and representation in Brussels is clear for several countries' (1996, p.59).

15 In 'The Region Is Dead! Long Live The Region' Neil Smith (1988) argues convincingly that: a) internalisation of production; b) firm structure reorganisation; c) new labour practices that have increased productivity; and d) transport costs that have become of minimal concern, are leading effectively to a 'space of flows' to substitute a 'space of places'. Additionally, the tertiary sector, the fastest growing sector in the capitalist economies, has very limited transportation costs and low locational disadvantages (Illeris, 1989). Furthermore, as regional economics contends (Burns, 1987, p.18), bearing an acute crisis on the downturn of the business cycle, transportation costs are relatively declining through time.

16 For a (philosophical) definition of autonomy in its relation to politics see Castoriadis (1991).

17 Regional scientists however (Agnew, 1988) argue that there is no political core and periphery. It is also argued that economic regions no longer have 'life-cycles' with rising and declining economies of scale, while uneven development is not a pattern but a process. Effectively 'Regions are not actors with common experiences' (Agnew, 1988, p.131).

18 In a very important document (Commission, 1981b) in which the Commission gives the new dimensions of Regional Policy, exploitation of indigenous development potential is directed among others to 'dormant business capacity, which need support services in terms of information, research, technical assistance, market analysis etc.'.

19 Going back to the economic background of such an issue a quote from Verhoven and Klaassen I believe is enlightening to the trade-offs involved: 'The question can be raised whether South Wales has been better off with the combination of relatively high income for those employed, relatively heavy unemployment, and external aid, than it would have been if it could have devalued its "currency" dispensing with aid, reducing the real earnings of those in work, but also reducing unemployment and probably accelerating growth' (1987, p.241).

20 As argued on the report 'The Tourism Sector in the Community' (Commission, 1985) it is the approach peoples of different regions have towards tourism that make for the differences in growth of the sector. Italian tourism experienced a 'tired maturity' while Greek and British (and later Spanish) were experiencing a constant growth (Commission, 1985). This

report accounts for the situation in late 1970s and early 1980s. Obviously there is no account of the Greek 'maturity' of the late 1980s that followed or the blooming of the Spanish and later Turkish tourist markets in the Mediterranean basin.

21 This is evident in the warnings by the CBI to Scottish devolution or the latter day 'dealignment' of larger Quebecoise industries from the nationalist camp (Keating, 1996).

22 Lever (1992) gives an account of a successful local authority response in the West of Scotland, when the region met with the challenge of industrial decline.

23 An exhaustive analysis of European regional prospects completed by the European Economic Research and Advisory Consortium cited 'the strengthening of regional identities within Europe [as] one identifiable pan-European movement which is likely to have consequences for regional economic change' (ERECO, 1993, p.3).

24 The discussion on regional dynamics which follows is relevant to the questions of peripherality since it can be claimed that a regions' peripherality is temporal and that on the next business cycle it will be naturally led out of depression, a typical neoclassical economics argument.

25 An interesting evolution to this principle might be the idea that as an effect of 'shrinkage' and economic interdependence regions experiencing a cyclical development process are much more liable to affect the delicately balanced world economy today than they once were.

Chapter Three

Local Government in Strathclyde and Crete

The make-up of local and regional political institutions has an obvious and direct effect on the degree of 'autonomy' and 'emancipation' of political actors. That is the reason a brief overview of those institutions in 1991 is imperative in understanding the limitations and overall political context in which actors operated.

Scotland was selected as a typical example of a declining industrial region focusing on the Region of Strathclyde and in particular on the prominent city within that region, Glasgow.[1] The island of Crete (*Kriti*) appears to have the most appropriate cultural and historic background in Greece for the research questions explored here. A focus on the prefecture of Chania and city of Chania was deemed expedient. Crete was considered a least-favoured region by European Community standards (Padoa-Schioppa, 1987). I have thus focused on two urban centres and their surrounding region. If there were no regional historical or administrative regional boundaries, it could have been argued that the area of investigation pertains to Western Scotland and Western Crete.

So, this investigation is focused on one industrially declining and one underdeveloped region of the European Union. Both regions lie on the periphery. Scottish territory lies between the 30 per cent and 20 per cent peripherality contours (Commission of EC, 1984, p.136). This indicates a degree of peripherality similar to that of southwestern France and the Iberian peninsula, a position markedly more central from that of Greece and particularly of Crete which lies outwith the 10 per cent peripherality contour.[2] To understand the political context of the elites surveyed this section presents an overview of the structure of regional government in the regions investigated *at the time of this survey.*

In the Scottish system of local government, under legislation in force in 1991, there were two political tiers.[3] Immediately under the decentralised arm of the national bureaucracy (Scottish Office) were the Regional Councils, which contained a number of District Councils. There were nine Regional and 53 District Councils. Strathclyde Regional Council was by far the largest regional council in Scotland with 2.3 million people in its territory, while

Glasgow City Council was the biggest District Council in Strathclyde with 715,000 people within the City boundaries.

Councillors in both chambers were elected by majority vote in single member wards and served for four years. Local government in Scotland was financed by a Community Charge Tax, first introduced in 1989, which however was abandoned, as announced in March 1991, and replaced by a capital value property system introduced in 1993. Additionally, there was the Uniform Business Rate through which local business contributed to local government, while an amount of less than 40 per cent of local government expenditure was met by central government. The funding structure has drastically changed under the new single tier authorities (MacAteer, 1996) and is undergoing further change at present as local government is within the remit of the Scottish Parliament.

There have been numerous calls for reform of the local government system in Scotland and the UK. Overall, academic essays centred around the perceived failings of the existing system to provide efficient services (Gaster, 1991) or the fact that many local services were provided by non-elected bodies (Preston, 1992).[4] Strathclyde was considered by some as a successful authority, in spite of it's large size (Midwinter, 1985) or maybe because of it. The fear had also been expressed that such a large authority could not 'co-exist peacefully with the proposed Scottish Assembly (Midwinter, 1985, p 44), luckily for constitutional lawyers reorganisation in 1996 conveniently abolished the Region before the 1997 elections and subsequent referendum made possible the creation of a Scottish Parliament. According to commentators the City of Glasgow, which was the largest district within Strathclyde, was integrated well with the Region (Gordon, 1985) and did not consider the region to be an impediment in the services it provided.[5]

Relations with central government have been cited as one of the reasons that local authorities have been hindered in providing a high level of services. 'During the 1980s the relationships existing between central and local government in the UK have been characterised by much tension and at times open conflict' (Preston, 1992, p.120). This tension is easily identified on most articles on local government in the national press throughout the 1980s. Some consider it as part of a policy by the British government, during the 1980s, to centralise governmental functions, while it has been suggested that in the question of subsidiarity for European funding, government ministers 'would vehemently agree for it to be applied to Brussels, but emphatically disagree for it to be applied to Westminster' (*The Economist*, 1992). In order to understand the relationship between local government in Strathclyde and central government it would also be useful to draw a distinction between relations with the Scottish Office (which are comparatively amicable) and relations with Whitehall (characterised by mutual suspicion). It should also be noted that a degree of 'legislative devolution', by increasing the remit of the Scottish Office (Scottish Office, 1993) has not necessarily meant a decrease in the control of Whitehall on Scottish affairs. Westminster was, still determining Scottish policy priorities based on UK criteria. As a result local government relations with the Scottish Office, although vital, can not be considered as a direct substitute to relations with Westminster.

Both Strathclyde Regional Council and Glasgow City Council were Labour dominated in 1991. The Chairman and the Lord Provost were the figureheads, for the region and the city respectively, while the Leader of the Council and the Leader of the Majority were on top of the respective political party hierarchies and therefore responsible for decisions taken and policy made.[6]

The Greek system of local government had only one level, whose autonomy is embedded in the constitution. There had been attempts to create a second tier, notably law 1622/86 of 1986 which introduces a second tier of local government with regionally elected councils to undertake some of the responsibilities currently vested on prefects.[7] Prefectures (*Nome*) are the administrative arms of government locally and there are 54 prefectures of approximately similar size. There are thirteen regions (currently, since size and number of Greek administrative regions has varied with the introduction of new statistical methods by the European Commission and Eurostat) of merely statistical significance at the time of this survey.

At the time of the survey government appointed prefects were taking part in Regional Councils with consultative regional planning functions. These Regional Councils included some appointed political and business personalities of the region. The law on elected regional councils (1622/86) has been slow to enact for a number of reasons. One of these was a resistance from political parties to come to terms with the loss of power entailed in decentralisation (Verney, 1992).

The first (and only functioning at the time of the survey) tier of local government in Greece comprised of City and Local Councils (*Deme ke Kinotites*). There were 303 municipalities and 5,697 communes, while 83 per cent of the latter had less than 1,000 inhabitants. City councils (*Deme*) are those who had over 10,000 inhabitants or had city status historically or have been the seat of a prefecture. All other smaller communities had the status of a Local Council (*kinotita*). Their funding was done through taxes on property and land, a beer tax and local charges. Central government collected these taxes for the smaller of these communities. Additionally they received a percentage of inheritance tax, vehicle taxation and the duty on real property transfers. The government funded the local authorities through the prefecture as well, which in turn would oversee the legality of the actions of local authorities. Elections for local government are held every four years under the alternative vote system, which means that a ticket to be elected has to command an absolute majority. This one party ticket will have the majority of seats in the council but there is usually greater room for opposition councillors to be elected than in a single ward first past the post system. Most city councils in Crete were Socialist or Socialist/Left coalition dominated. This was the case for the City of Chania as well in 1991. The mayor, in the bigger city councils (*Deme*), is assisted by an executive committee of between three and six members. A mayors' role is executive, since the city council is responsible for making policy, fixing local taxes and so forth.

The contemporary picture of local and regional government structure is distinctively different from the early 1990s. In 1994 a number of Bills proclaimed the 'establishment of prefectural self-government' (Laws 2218/ 94 and 2240/94) and provided for the election of prefects (*nomarhes*) and prefecture councils. Elections to 50 Prefecture Councils were first held on 16 October 1994.[8] Significantly and perhaps dubiously the Law affirms prefectures 'do not have a superintendent role over local authorities' and that there is 'no hierarchical relationship between the two tiers' of local government and prefecture councils (Law 2218/94, section 1, p.1269). The state in other words retains the role of ultimate arbiter of both tiers of government for itself. At the same time the current administration wishes to be perceived as seriously dealing with the decentralisation agenda. A signal to that effect was the recent renaming of one of the main government departments to Ministry of Interior, Public Administration and Decentralisation.

Almost all commentators therefore agree that the national political elite is cautiously proceeding to a rationalisation of its administrative structures not as a result of pressure from below but rather in order to modernise and conform to European directives.[9] The latest attempt at this rationalisation process has been the successful introduction of the so called Kapodistrias Law (2539/97) of 1997, named after the first governor of the Republic, which reduced the 6,000-odd local authorities, most of which were small villages to just under 900 municipalities and local communities. This was done by forging neighbouring communities to consolidate their administrative structures. Interestingly, most resistance to this law came from the disruption of local clientelistic networks, while protests had a very small effect on eventual mergers.[10] The process of administrative transformation is also expected to eventually lead to an elected regional tier for the 13 regional cabinets and chairs (*periferiarhes*) who at the moment are still political appointees. We can only juxtapose on whether the new institutions will lead to an effectual 'emancipation' of regional units or will instead lead to fragmentation of local demands by tiering administrative structures between local, prefecture, regional and national.

The role of local government, being rather marginal to regional development, is further diminished by the party political platform which usually underpins local elections. Holding the mayor's office in the three biggest cities in Greece (and to a lesser extent in the next 10 biggest), is a political appointment, with national political appeal, which enhances influence within party structures and can lead to a seat in the national legislature.[11] This relates to the political elites perception that real political power exists only at the national parliament. The aspirations of influential local politicians are therefore directed towards the national parliament, which is one of the reasons why they failed to lobby effectively for the creation of a second tier of regional government.[12]

To establish the degree of comparability for the two different systems of regional government a useful aid will be the comparison of the competencies of local government under the two systems. In Table 3.1 a list of functions is matched to the degree possible. There are a number of differences in the mandate of local authorities in the two countries that make direct comparisons at times tenuous. It is also the case that some of the alleged local authority functions are misleading. When 'economic development' responsibilities are 'transferred' to a Greek local authority, their remit does not by any stretch of the imagination encroach upon the national ministries' work and would at best indicate a marginal role in regional or urban economic regeneration. Comparison of functions in Table 3.1 suggests a good degree of correspondence in competence between local authorities in the two regions. It must be stressed however, that Greek local authorities exhibit much less autonomy in decision-making from what their 'formal competence' might indicate.

The Greek system of prefectures having been modelled after the French centralised system of government, appears comparatively monolithic in its centralisation. The main consideration however, when this system was introduced, was to keep a very divergent country under a central authority and most importantly to cultivate allegiance to that centre.[13] The population of Greece was too small, it was feared, for allowing for the existence of autonomous entities that might eventually create centrifugal forces to the

Table 3.1   Local authorities' functions and responsibilities

Greek City and Community Councils	Scottish Regional Councils
• Water supply	• Social services
• Roads	• Highways
• Sewerage	• Personal social services
• Waste collection and disposal	• Education
• Lighting	• Policing
• Transport	• Fire Brigade
• Markets	• Libraries
• Cemeteries	• Strategic planning
• Parks and recreation	• Transport (Strathclyde)

Some Local Authorities are also in charge of	District Councils
• Preschool education	• Recreation
• Economic development	• Housing
• Planning	• Local planning
• Environmental protection	• Environmental health
• Libraries and museums	• Libraries
• Tourism	• Cemeteries/crematoria

Source: European Municipal Directory, 1991.

country's unity. Furthermore Greece's centralisation drive has been re-enforced by the country's nation building experience which involved a consolidation towards an outside threat (the Ottomans) and a subjugation of the many regional (and perceived parochial) identities to the one national (modernising) identity. It has been, the almost unanimous view of all officials I interviewed, both in the survey and the pilot interviews that assisted in planning the survey, that the time is ripe and the need urgent for the introduction of greater autonomy at least in the design and implementation of policy making.[14] The question naturally arises for the political scientist, whether that is a call for decentralisation or devolution and whether this can be associated with a re-enforcement (or reawakening) of regional identity.

Crete and Scotland in a Comparative Perspective

Selection of the particular regions must be attributed, up to a point, to the availability of regional statistics. The European Commission has developed a system called NUTS (Nomenclature of Territorial Units for Statistics) which effectively determines the way statistical information is gathered and processed. Scotland is a level I region (NUTS I) with Crete included in Eastern and Southern islands NUTS I (*Anatolika ke Notia Nisia*). Obviously to move to level II in order to work with Crete we have to compare it with an equal level region in Scotland, in this case Dumfries-Galloway, Strathclyde. To further narrow the scope to NUTS III when possible, analysis is supplemented with data on Nomos Chanion and Strathclyde Region. From the official publications of the EC readily available there is very little comparable evidence available prior to 1983 for level II regions.

As expected, Crete is found on the bottom of the ladder regarding gross domestic product (GDP), with 34 per cent of Community average in ECUs in 1981. The picture looks slightly better if converted to purchasing power standard (PPS) units, where Crete attains 45 per cent for the same year. What is remarkable, is that by 1984 Crete has moved to 43 per cent of ECUs and 54 per cent PPSs – an increase of more than one-quarter in ECUs and one-fifth in PPSs in just three years! Although between 1983 and 1984 there is almost no growth from 1985 onwards GDP was expected to increase as a result of the implementation of the Integrated Mediterranean Program for the region.

Another very interesting feature is that between 1983 and 1984 Crete has altered its gross value added (GVA) composition by moving away from industry and services and into agriculture. This has been an effect of out of season covered and greenhouse crops that were particularly favoured with accession to the Common Market (Commission, 1983). So between 1983 and 1984 agriculture increased from contributing 32.1 per cent to 39.1 per cent of regional value added, industry declined from 19.8 per cent to 18.1 per cent while services fell from 48.4 per cent to 42.8 per cent.

Statistics for Strathclyde (including Dumfries-Galloway) are rather fragmented. There is no specific data for Strathclyde on GVA in the European Community publications and I therefore use statistical figures provided for Scotland, while on GDP data exist only after 1983.[15] Between 1983 and 1984 GDP in ECUs fell from 94 per cent to 88 per cent of Community average while in PPS from 95 per cent to 91 per cent. In the Scottish economy as a whole there is a move from industry to services. In 1981 industry accounted for 40.5 per cent while services for 56.6 per cent of GVA while in 1984 for 37 per cent and 60.2 per cent respectively.

Between 1986 and 1987 Crete had a fall in unemployment from 4 per cent to 2.7 per cent,[16] while Strathclyde had a minor increase from 16.7 per cent to 17 per cent. Both unemployment and GDP figures improved significantly for Strathclyde through the 1990s.

So, as the relevant statistics indicate I have used two distinctly different regions, in terms of composition of output, employment level and market orientation towards the future. Their common elements are their below EC average GDP and, as already mentioned, their peripherality and particular sense of regional identity (a theme upon which I will expound further on). The fact that there is a regional identity that separates these regions from their respective national entities makes their study easier and at the same time more complicated. People in Scotland and to a lesser extent Crete see themselves as the inheritors of a distinct ethnic identity.[17]

This research could be relevant to the examination of actions of regional units, (assuming they will exhibit independent, consistent and coherent patterns of conduct) as subnational actors in a supranational arena. The choice of regions here targets assumed differences in 'mentality' (and therefore possibly value systems and attitudes) between the two regions. Scotland has an industrial past and Scottish see themselves as northern Europeans with a Celtic and Nordic inheritance, distinctly different from the rest of the British. Cretans perceive themselves as a gifted ethnic group, different from the rest of Greece and in the process of transformation from a backward agricultural region, to a model developing region. Their centuries old pride in their ethnic identity is reinforced by this success.[18]

Scotland and Crete have an autonomous past and are located on the periphery of Europe in geographical terms. This similarity is one of the reasons they constitute a valid pair for a comparative study. Their divergent industrialisation and development experience, together with their different level of development is not just a limitation on validity. Their difference enhances the comparative character of this work and allows for a greater degree of universality from conclusions. In many respects this is a 'most different systems design' approach as far as political culture, position in the industrialisation cycle and institutional structures are concerned. Similarities in a number of other variables as mentioned here make this a particularly interesting comparison.

In this context a further difficulty has to do with the artificial division of territorial units into regions by government bodies for political reasons, which is why I have focused this study on the West of Scotland and West of Crete.[19] I have thus tried to take account of boundaries of identity (a sense of belonging to a region) rather than administrative boundaries. That has not meant that the administrative boundaries have been transcended when seeking interviews, but rather acknowledging that these administrative boundaries do not necessarily contain all those identified with the respective regions.

Finally, in order to proceed with an examination of the economic conditions in the two regions it has to be noted that, to the extent that this is a study of integration of regional units, 'any analysis of the integration of regions risks being tautological for in a sense a region is defined by the extend of its integration' (Bernstein, 1970).

Issues Raised: A Critical Appraisal

The preceding chapters of this volume have offered an overview of the literature published by the European Commission in conjunction with opinions held by academics on the importance placed on the behaviour of regional actors and the relevance it may have to regional economic development. It is obvious that in most sources discussed there is a connection between a positive business climate with economic development, yet a great number of authors fail to identify the importance of regional political and business actors. Most also shy away from connecting the local businessman/woman with the local politician as a factor of development of a region. This is understandable since regions in the EU were not considered to possess significant political clout (compared with nation states), which appears to be the case even in relatively autonomous and distinctly independent regions such as Bavaria or Cataluña.[20]

From the US, the EU is perceived as having the characteristics of a regional federal state (Sandholtz, 1989) but this perspective 'demotes' national units which acquire the characteristics of these 'new regions' of the EU. So, political actor importance will be assumed to exist only in national parliaments or European institutions. This view fails to identify existing diversity, even among comparatively homogeneous nations such as Greece.[21] My belief in the importance of hitherto comparatively marginalised actors comes from my judgement that further consolidation of power to the EU centre will inevitably free autonomous aspirations in the regions. A natural balance, to an empowered European centre, could be created by segmenting the competencies of national units along the principles of subsidiarity.[22]

In the previous chapters there has been an attempt to determine whether regional actors can be considered relevant in affecting local economic development. It appears that academic literature has not sufficiently explored that issue yet. Restrictions arising from the 'relative political weight' and 'credibility' of regional political actors are considered relevant to the limited attention local actors receive. A synergistic (if not local corporatist) relationship between business and policy planners can be perceived as one of the most promising development prospects for European regions.

Overall, in the academic discourse it has not been conclusively established whether regional autonomy favours regional development or hinders it, although there are indications that there is a relationship between the two. Neoclassic economic theory would suggest that market segmentation leads to an increase in costs but local autonomy in regional development planning can conceivably lead to efficiency gains as well.

In the penultimate part of this analysis the question of endowments was considered in brief since the basic economic arguments about the relative importance of endowments is not a contested issue among the academic community. A discussion on how a region becomes peripheral and the possible hypothesis of whether regional actors can be a force in that process ties in with the rest of the theoretical considerations expressed here. The discussion on regional dynamics and patterns of regional development was intended to demonstrate the importance of national (or regional) state intervention to ameliorate the effects of growth cycles. Consequently, the significance of implementing state intervention tools at the regional level (whether on a deconcentration, decentralisation or devolution principle) should be apparent.

A number of research questions have been examined in this project. Primarily I set out to determine whether business and political elites are different and whether that difference relates to their regional identity. Then attitudes on regional devolution are correlated to perceived business prospects for a region, while attitudinal concordance is correlated with the economic performance of the regions examined.

This investigation focuses on elite attitudes, assuming elite behaviour to be congruent with those attitudes, while using both quantitative and qualitative techniques in the survey tools employed. It has to be stressed that although the main research design is based on exploring certain hypotheses (suggesting hypotheses testing would imply certain qualities not present in the sample) it is extensively supplemented from literature and observations that are predominantly based on an *ex post facto* analysis.

In the concluding chapter of this work questions explored in this primary literature survey are revisited with concepts that are validated from exploring these initial hypotheses. Findings from examining these questions are compared with propositions in the literature to provide an ultimate measure of construct validity on the points argued.

Notes

1   In this work I accept the definition of a declining industrial region given by Padoa-Schioppa (1987, pp.162–4), Scotland in this sense is considered a region, although it has been effectively argued that it has a distinct national identity (Kellas, 1989; Midwinter et al., 1991).

2   The particular study cited here (Commission, 1984) estimates accessibility in 1979, while a big effort has been made since, in improving infrastructure and communications to ameliorate the situation.

3   For the change of local authorities legislation and the political debate on the enactment of a single tier local authority system see the relevant documents by the Scottish Office (1991, 1992) and the Strathclyde Regional Council (1993). For the relevant debate on the introduction of a single tier local government in Scotland see Padison (1995) and MacAteer (1996).

4   A comprehensive account of the theoretical debates in contemporary British local democracy is presented in an edited volume by King and Stoker (1996).

5   Both the Leaders of the City Council and the Regional Council when interviewed, supported the idea that relationships between the two Councils are at a very good level and not at all competitive. Keating however, has argued that 'it would not be true to say that the relationship between the tiers [of City and Region] are characterised by harmony and collaboration' (Keating, 1988, p.73). Tensions, among other sectors, are reported on the development of the highway network. Distrust and internecine conflict between Strathclyde and the district councils is reported in the Stodart Report (1981).

6   A major role in the development of the regions and districts is played by the respective local government bureaucracy the head of which is the Chief Executive, a non-political post. The importance they have in both implementing, but also advising on policy, gives them particular political significance.

7   An account of the recent history of decentralisation and relevant legislation in Greece is provided by Verney and Papageorgiou (Verney, 1992). Laws 1622/86, 2218/94, 2240/94 and 2307/95 have introduced elected prefecture Councils, Regional Councils and Regional Development Funds for each Region. The changes where brought about by the requirement of the European Union for local management of financing, together with the perceived need for decentralisation of the Greek state. The first prefecture/regional elections took place on 16 October 1994. For an update on the pressures on the Greek state to decentralise see Christopoulos (2000).

8   Manolopoulos and Loulis (1999) examine electoral variation between the first and second prefectural elections in 1998. They remark on the loss by the socialists (PASOK) of overall majority in the number of councils they control (22) as compared with the conservatives (Nea Democratia) that have gained control in 24 prefectures. This according to the authors signifies an increased politicisation of the elections. The 50 electoral districts include three super prefectures of agglomerated districts. The total number of administrative prefectures is 54.

9   Among the critics of the Greek administration are Andrikopoulou (1992) who talks of a failure to effectively utilise regional elites by giving them power for local development planing and Ioakimidis (1996) who argues that the state continues to be centrist. Theodorou (1995) gives a comprehensive account of the history of local government institutions in modern Greece, while Kostopoulos (1996) discusses the possibility that in Greece we witness a case of 'decentralised centralisation'.

10 It has also been argued that localism is a facet of Greek political culture inextricably linked with the birth of the modern Greek state (Diamandouros, 1983; Clogg, 1983; Demertzis, 1997).

11 Holding an elected position in national and local government is incompatible under Greek law. The impossibility of a 'cumule de mandats' probably diminishes the influence of local government in the national legislature but could also be considered to increase its independence.

12 Attempts at decentralisation in the contemporary Greek state commenced with law 3200/55 of 1955 which introduced advisory prefecture councils but was thwarted by the centralisation imposed by the 1967–74 dictatorship. An attempt at reform was introduced by law 1235/82 shortly after accession to the EEC and with the Socialist government of the day having a decentralisation platform which extended the role of prefecture councils but maintained their non-elected advisory capacity.

13 Diamandouros notes that after Greek independence 'an ethos of pronounced localism and parochialism ... [impeded] national integration by placing a premium on primordial sentiments, and by producing fierce and lasting local and regional attachments' (Diamandouros, 1983, p.46).

14 The former Greek MEP Phillipos Pierros has remarked that 'the basic problem lies in the fact that other authorities have the implementation competence and others the supervision. To face the problem there must be a conjunction of the two competencies ... [and] ... a transfer of competencies to the periphery ...' (liberal translation from the Greek prototype) (Pierros, 15 August 1991, p.55). This criticism refers particularly to problems in the implementation of Regional Development and Integrated Mediterranean Programs.

15 There are extensive regional statistics provided by the Bureau of Statistics in the UK and the Strathclyde Regional Council. For reasons of comparability I try to arrive to most comparisons from Eurostat statistics supplementing with national one's only if necessary.

16 In a report prepared by the prefecture of Chania it transpires that during the winter months Nomos Chanion and Crete as a whole suffer from chronic winter labour shortages (Protopapadakis, 1987, p.69), while the year round unemployment figure they estimated at 3.3 per cent

17 This trend however, as Juliet Lodge asserts, should be seen in the perspective of an emerging new 'European Order' where an increasing 'Europeanisation of domestic issues' is the natural course of events (Lodge, 1989), this trend may be applied to regional actions as well but its universality remains to be proven.

18 The social situation in Crete after WW II is analysed in socioeconomic research by Allbaugh (1953), while a more contemporary anecdotal account is given by Hopkins (1977) and an anthropological account by Herzfeld (1985).

19 In the case of Scottish regional boundaries, the accusation has often been made, that regional or district borders are redefined with a view to gerrymandering from the national government. A factor that has been coming to the fore in latter years, is the extent to which regional borders permit different localities to qualify for different types of regional aid, as in objective 5b (rural areas) or 2 (industrial decline) regions.

20 Evidence for a 'Europe of the Regions' is at best weak. Academics have rarely found any real evidence for a shift in power in European institutional structures in favour of the regions (Jones, 1995). A number of times as a result of regional tensions within member states a shift of power to the regions is evident. This at times gets blown out of proportion by journalists who declare the emergence of the 'age of the regions' (Klau, 1996).

21 There are many ways in which regional diversity in Greece can be demonstrated but I need only refer to the completely different social, political and economic background, between regions like Thrace in the North and Crete in the South of the country.
22 Taking account of the vagueness of the meaning of subsidiarity as suggested by Peterson (1994).

Chapter Four

Scottish Regional Elites: The Challenge of Post-Industrial Regeneration

The Strathclyde Economy and Glasgow City in the Early 1990s

In the present chapter I attempt both an analysis of the economic geography of the region and an account of the development prospects and expectations in Strathclyde at the time of survey. Scotland extends to an area of 77,080 sq. km, of which 73 per cent is utilised for agriculture. There were 4.957 million people living in Scotland in 1991 according to that year's census. There were 14.9 students for each teacher in secondary public education (UK level data), while there were 281 cars per thousand people in Scotland (CSO, 1992).

In 1991 5.1 million people were recorded resident (note the difference between being resident and being recorded in the census) in Scotland of which 2.25 million were resident in Strathclyde. In the same year 1,973 thousand people were employed in Scotland of which 30,000 were employed in the primary, 591 thousand were employed in the secondary and 1,353 thousand in the tertiary sector.

Unemployment as a percentage of the work-force was at 9.9 per cent (1990) in Strathclyde and 7.8 per cent for the whole of Scotland. Overall, there seems to be a consistent 1–2 per cent gap in the unemployment rate between Great Britain, Scotland and Strathclyde from 1977 to 1991, as Strathclyde maintained a persistently higher unemployment rate.[1]

Scottish Gross Domestic Product (GDP) at current prices was £5.756 per capita in 1987 which represented 94 per cent of the UK average. Gross Regional Product (GRP) for Strathclyde stood at £5,419 per capita at current prices up from 3,281 in 1981.[2]

In 1990 there were 59,054 companies registered in Scotland up from 32,978 in 1978. In 1979 domestic consumption of energy accounted for 1,389 million therms while industrial, transport and other consumers for 4,314 therms. By 1989 consumption of energy had dropped to 1,326 from households and to 4,011 million therms from industrial, transport and other users. Energy consumption has maintained a 1:3 ratio between domestic and productive uses throughout this period.[3]

Table 4.1   Household economic situation in Strathclyde and Glasgow in 1991

	Strathclyde	Glasgow
No. of households	903,339	289,855
% privately owned	47.1	37.2
% central heating	76.4	62.7
% without car	49.2	65.5

Source: General Register Office for Scotland, HMSO, 1993.

Table 4.2   Population and employment by sector according to the 1991 Census for Strathclyde and Glasgow City, primary and secondary sector

In thousands	Strathclyde		Glasgow	
Resident population	2,249		663.0	
Total Employed	862		222.0	
Agric./fishing	11	1.3%	0.3	0.1%
Mining	19	2.2%	2.3	1.0%
Manufacture	155	18.0%	35.0	16.0%
Construction	73	8.5%	19.0	8.5%

Source: General Register Office for Scotland, HMSO, 1993.

One interesting indicator for understanding the degree of entrepreneurial vitality in Scotland is the percentage of self employed in the work-force. Data for 1990 reveal this figure to be little over 10 per cent for Scotland compared with the UK average which was 12.5 per cent.[4]

Beyond a picture of 'hard facts' on the situation as it was it is reasonable to assume that elite attitudes would also be influenced by future business prospects and in particular with comparisons of the Scottish versus the UK economy. The Scottish economy outperformed the UK economy achieving a 2 per cent growth in 1990 compared with a UK average of 0.7 per cent. The figures for the previous year are even more impressive as Scotland achieved a 3.5 per cent growth compared to 1.9 per cent in the UK. Similarly, unemployment change which is another indicator of the force of the recession across regions, showed a less marked increase in Scotland of 11 per cent while in UK the change was 42 per cent and in the southeast unemployment grew by 80 per cent. These figures agree with a number of surveys conducted during 1991. The CBI for instance indicates that the Scottish recession 'has been both shorter and shallower than in the UK as a whole' (*Scottish Economic Bulletin*, No. 43, pp.9–10). A forecast by Cambridge Econometrics was predicting a fall of 5.7 per cent in manufacturing output in 1991 to be followed by 0.8 per cent fall in 1992, which would induce a fall of employment in the sector. An export led recovery was predicted to follow in the latter part of 1992. The service industry was expected to fare better with output growth of 0.9 per cent and 1.8 per cent in 1991 and 1992 respectively. Tourism and leisure were expected to lead this revival although employment was expected to decline overall.[5]

The most important factors that were likely to affect growth in the short term, according to the Scottish Office, were the lag in international trade growth, to be further aggravated by problems in the Uruguay Round of the GATT negotiations, as well as the US budget deficit and German costs of unification. Prospects for Scotland were considered uncertain in the medium term particularly because of higher inflation and unit costs of labour than its international and particularly its EC/EU competitors.[6]

The overall performance of the Scottish economy was naturally linked to the performance of the British economy as a whole. Furthermore, the relevant position of the UK economy within the European integrated market was considered of paramount importance. Problems that might evolve from a 'traditional' British reticence to further integration could hit the regions hardest. Some analysts believed that Britain has overall received a negative economic impact from accession to the Community (Bulmer, 1992). Others believed that Britain had failed to make the best of opportunities, particularly in the regional development level, where the British government refused to accept the additionality principle in regional aid.[7]

The Scottish Business Elite

In attempting an insightful look in the principal actors responsible for the economic performance of Strathclyde I sought out those people most likely to be responsible for taking those decisions that would make a difference. Since I have never been convinced by those leadership theorists that seek out the 'lone individual' as an 'engineer of change' I attribute important decisions collectively to a greater class of actors. In Weberian fashion I call these collectively the Scottish business elite. Interviews were conducted with those business executives/proprietors that responded to an initial mailing randomly selected from a pool of approximately 2500 businesses. My interest was with the 'belief structure of their class' as they can be determined by a small sample.

Most of interviewees (21 out of 24) were managing directors, chairmen or board directors of their respective companies. The three junior managers I interviewed were a company accountant, a sales manager and a personnel manager. Their junior status within their respective companies does not disqualify them from being considered as part of the elite group, since to a great extent they all had direct access to their companies' managing directors, while their position within the hierarchy was more relevant to their young age.[8]

Their respective company profiles reveals most companies to be in the medium to large category with 46 per cent having more than £20 million annual turnover and 71 per cent having more than one hundred employees (Table 4.3). This apparent bias towards larger companies is considered more extensively in the discussion of response rates in the methodological appendix.

Concurrently with issues of representativeness of the sample, consideration has to be given to the level of interaction between business and political elites. This must be influenced by the size of the local economy and respective average company size. I assume that where the average enterprise is larger, business elites will usually come from these larger enterprises. In this respect I trust that, the Strathclyde businessmen interviewed comprise a representative sample of the local business elite.

Table 4.3   Size of Scottish business surveyed by annual turnover and numbers of employees

	<£5 m	£5–20 m	>£20 m	Total %
21–100 employees	4	3	–	29.2
Over 100 employees	–	6	11	70.8
Total %	16.7	37.5	45.8	100.0

Intuitively I can point to the fact that small and medium enterprises (SMEs) in the United Kingdom account for 46.8 per cent of employment while large companies account for 30 per cent and that comparatively '... more employment is provided by SMEs and large firms in the UK than in the Community' (Commission of the EC, 1990, p.6.8). Previous research on economic elites has employed similar methods for identifying company directors from companies with a large turnover.[9]

A noteworthy aspect of this sample is that 21 per cent declared that they consider themselves entrepreneurs, while the rest said they consider themselves to be executives. On occasion a chairman or managing director seemed hesitant deciding between entrepreneur and executive status. A good number were holders of a large part of equity in their respective companies and had been personally responsible for their company's growth. Without fail all those who were indecisive ended-up opting for the executive status answer. A number of possible explanations can be offered for this attitude. One could be that entrepreneurship is associated with creativity and in that sense it would be like bestowing themselves with a compliment; alternatively, for some an entrepreneur may not command a very high status in society. Since this survey had to be limited to particular hypotheses on the political economy of the regions, etymological and conceptual fine points were deemed beyond the present attempt.[10]

Another noteworthy distinction between entrepreneurs and executives seems to be the former's support for a federal Europe and international control of macroeconomic aspects of the economy. Executives seem to overwhelmingly support national macroeconomic control while at the same time supporting a federal structure for Europe. This marks an oddity which if not relevant to sample restrictions, must point to entrepreneurs having a more internationalist attitude than executives. Sixty per cent of entrepreneurs, but none of the executives, expressed support for international macroeconomic control in their region.

Another unexpected result relates to the apparent contradiction between Federalist and Nationalist views of the executive sample.[11] Sixty per cent of respondents that think a federal Europe is viable do not believe that nationalist movements are good, while of those that believe nationalist movements are good 55 per cent believe a Federal Europe not to be viable. I have to assume that nationalism and federalism are incompatible values for this sample. Obviously an understandable confusion could exist between nationalism as a notion and the SNP as a political party.

A high percentage of the companies in this survey were private, with their shareholders primarily Scottish (Table 4.4). This category accounted for 67 per cent of the sample. Another 25 per cent were public companies, primarily of UK origin outside Scotland while 8 per cent were companies with an international parent. Again note should be made of the bias which exists by approaching companies registered in Glasgow, since some – particularly large UK companies – might be operating in the area without necessarily being registered here. I expect this bias to be limited however, as executives based in Glasgow working for non-Glasgow registered companies are unlikely to be senior within their company and therefore less likely to be part of the local business elite. It is also the case that defining the elite as the influential in the local setting I was less interested in those that were not directly involved with the locality.

Table 4.4   Ownership of companies surveyed in Scotland and Greece

	Regional privately	Regional publicly	National publicly	International
Scottish companies	16	1	5	2
	66.7%	4.2%	20.8%	8.3%
Cretan companies	16	1	3	1
	76.2%	4.8%	14.3%	4.8%

Note: Region here refers to Scotland and Crete respectively, while nation refers to UK and Greece.

Half of this sample consists of companies exporting to more than two countries, reinforcing the probability that there is a bias of representation towards more successful companies (Table 4.5). Thirty-three per cent operated on a local-regional basis only, while 17 per cent operated on a national basis exclusively.

From the business interviewees, 88 per cent considered their ethnic origin to be Scottish which is slightly higher a percentage than the total sample average.

I proceed to present an overview of interviewees attitudes towards nationalism and devolution, local government and local entrepreneurs as well as European integration. Asked whether they think Strathclyde will benefit from an increase in the powers of the Strathclyde Regional Council (SRC) 54 per cent answered negatively while 42 per cent answered positively.[12] Subsequently, when asked if business would perceive autonomy favourably 58 per cent answer negatively. Interestingly, from those that viewed an increase in regional powers positively 30 per cent view autonomy negatively. A relation seems to exist between a favourable opinion for Strathclyde's increase in regional power and a perception of constructive role for nationalist movements like the SNP. This was expressed as a majority of those favourable to nationalist movements supporting an increase in SRC powers (55 per cent) and conversely those not supporting nationalist movements not supporting an increase in SRC powers (69 per cent). This correlation becomes more pronounced when the question becomes one of their own business benefiting from an increase in the powers of the SRC.[13] There also exists a strong link between those who responded positively on whether the region will benefit from an increase in the powers of the SRC and those who believe their business would benefit from such a shift as well.[14]

Table 4.5   Area of operations of interviewees firm

	Local	Regional	National	Exports up to two countries	Exports to more than two countries
Strathclyde business	1	7	4	–	12
	4.2%	9.2%	16.7%	–	50%
Cretan business	8	5	5	2	1
	8.1%	3.8%	23.8%	9.5%	4.8%

The number of those having ethnic Scottish roots (Q4) that did not think an increase in the powers to the SRC will be good for the region was twelve, against nine who viewed such a development favourably.[15] This is in accord with the predominantly negative attitude towards an increase in SRC power but offers no support to one of my assumptions that a 'strong ethnic identification with the region will associate with a positive view of enhancing regional political autonomy'.

For those of the respondents who find there are great differences between people in Strathclyde and the rest of Scotland, 40 per cent are negative about the benefits to the region from an increase in the powers of the regional authority while at the same time negative about nationalist movements in regional politics. So, those who find differences among their region and the rest of Scotland do not support nationalism and believe an increase in the powers of the SRC will be detrimental to their business. For those who do not distinguish between people in their region and the rest of Scotland there is a clear distinction towards either being positive on nationalist movements and at the same time being positive towards SRC powers or being negative towards both.

There are three major attitudinal patterns that can be identified in regard to this sample:

a) the Scots are different from other Britons, nationalism is bad, an increase
   in the powers of the SRC is bad;
b) the Scots are similar to other Britons, nationalism is good, an increase in
   the powers of the SRC is good;
c) the Scots are similar to other Britons, nationalism is bad, an increase in the
   powers of the SRC is bad.

Together these three categories account for 57 per cent of cases. They
point to a trend since for those who see nationalism as bad (a) and c)) so is an
increase to SRC powers, while for those in the first group (a) Scots are different
from other Britons and those in the third group (c) Scots are similar to other
Britons. For those who see nationalism as good, so is an increase in the powers
of the SRC while Scots are all similar (b). This may point to a relationship
between support for local government and nationalism.[16]

Comparing the replies of those who consider their region to be in a worse
or better position than the nation with replies on whether Europe represents
more opportunities or risks I can identify two concentration of replies. There
is a high degree of confidence in Strathclyde and its European future,
particularly the latter, since the concentration around more opportunities is
the strongest. A number of respondents (13 per cent) see more risks in Europe,
while at the same time they believe their region to be worse off than the
nation. The size of the sample does not permit investigating the hypothesis of
whether Scottish 'euro-sceptics' at the same time feel their region to be
underprivileged within the UK. A possible discussion on 'euro-scepticism'
should not fail to take account of the fact that all respondents affirmed that
Europe does represent a challenge for their region. In this light, even those
who view their region's future in Europe negatively claimed that Europe
represents a challenge.

Most respondents seemed pessimistic about the economy's preparedness,
which was anticipated, given that interviews were conducted in the middle of
a British and world recession. Sixteen of the respondents answered that the
economy was not prepared at all or plainly unprepared, seven thought it was
just prepared and only one took the view it was well prepared.

Little inference can be drawn from the primary analysis of the group of
questions pertaining to how well businessmen know their political
representatives. The two largest groups of a quarter of the sample each are
those who either know all of their local political representatives, Councillors,
MPs and MEPs or none.[17] In order of 'obscurity' 15 did not know their City
or Regional Councillor, 13 did not know their MEP and nine did not know

their MP. Eight out of nine businessmen that did not know their MP did not know their Councillor, while six did not know their MEP either. This points to a possible polarisation at the one end of which we have 'politically informed' and at the other 'politically uninformed' businessmen, which could be taken one step further in stating an obvious condition. Only some elite businessmen are politically active while at least a quarter appear politically indifferent or inactive.

Cross-tabulating data referring to questions on whether local representatives are better at promoting the economic interests of the region and more receptive to businessmen compared with MPs, with the degree of respondents acquaintance with office bearers, I find great similarities in the distribution of replies to these questions. Their answers show that 12 and 13 cases respectively support the statement that Councillors are much more or slightly more fervent and much more or slightly more effective than MPs. This is in spite the fact most do not know their local or regional Councillors. To illustrate, five out of seven businessmen who said Councillors are much more fervent than MPs did not know their local Councillor while, of the same group, five knew their local MP. I can make the assumption that they are plainly dissatisfied with the performance of their local MPs rather than happy with the effectiveness or fervour of their local Councillors.

Cross-tabulating questions on how fervent with how effective this sample finds Councillors compared to MPs I see the emergence of a clear division between those that find Councillors much less fervent and much less effective and those that find Councillors much more fervent and effective.[18]

Another noteworthy observation is that those that had chosen the options of equally fervent, effective or receptive – for Councillors' and MPs' performance – belong to either of the two groups of respondents who either know both or neither of their respective MPs and Councillors. Also in the case of a question inquiring on how receptive political representatives are – which is based on the assumption that councillors are more accessible and therefore, businessmen probably feel them to be more receptive than MPs – I found a fairly balanced response with five of the respondents believing Councillors much less or slightly less receptive, 10 finding them equally receptive, and seven finding them slightly more or much more receptive. Overall response patterns to this group of questions were rather unexpected and against some of my initial assumptions of businessmen's perception of Councillors and MPs.

There are two possible interpretations for this discrepancy. The first interpretation is that respondents are not giving an evaluation of the respective

Councillors and MPs individually but of the institutions they represent. So, fervour and effectiveness were related to the Glasgow City Council and the Strathclyde Regional Council respectively. This view is supported by the qualifications to responses I received which express a wide support, of the Regional Council particularly, among the business community. The second possible reason for these responses could be the disaffection of the Scottish business elite with existing institutional structures. This view, although not expressed as strong support for nationalism, can never the less be perceived as strong support for federalism.

In respondents' expressed high locational mobility – a measure of their ties to the region – consideration must be given to the fact that the majority are executives and that only five are over 56 years of age. Of those who said they were prepared to do the same job in another region of UK, 57 per cent said they were prepared to do the same job in another region of the European Communities as well. Ten in total were not prepared to move at all.[19] These results seem consistent with expected relocational patterns of executives, since those that are prepared to move are maybe not prepared to move to Europe but those that are not prepared to move to another UK region are more unlikely to want to move to another European region. There seems to be no pattern in the distribution of replies pertaining to the willingness to work elsewhere in Great Britain and their perception of difference between Scottish and British people.[20]

Respondents were unanimous in their confidence that local entrepreneurs could function in a different UK region than their own, while they were almost unanimous in claiming that they could function in a different European region outside UK. There was some dissent, however, on whether multinationals are detrimental to the performance of local entrepreneurs, with a quarter claiming they would perform worse and two-thirds that they would perform better in the presence of multinationals.[21] Whether respondents see themselves as entrepreneurs or executives seems to mildly affect their views on SMEs growth. All of those declaring themselves to be entrepreneurs also believe there will be a growth in small and medium-sized enterprises. Of those who see themselves as executives most but not all believe that there will be a growth in SMEs.

In conclusion, attitudes of Scottish businessmen in this sample, associate an increase in the powers of the Strathclyde Regional Council with support for nationalist movements, while there is a negative correlation of nationalism with federalism. They are pessimistic about the regional economy's prospects and are more likely to know their local MP than their local Councillor.

Political Actors in Strathclyde

In the sample of political actors interviewed there was no attempt made at achieving some form of proportionality between the different levels of elected representation. Of those interviewed three were City Councillors, six were Regional Councillors, three were Members of Parliament at Westminster and two were Members of the European Parliament. Three of the respondents were not elected members of political bodies. One was a senior administrator, in charge of economic policy for one of the Councils, considered by all Councillors interviewed to be directly related, if not responsible for many of the Council's policy initiatives and naturally directly involved in the Council's budget (a classic case of a policy entrepreneur). One of the respondents was a candidate at the forthcoming parliamentary elections and one was a candidate in the last Regional Council elections. Both candidates were considered very close to the top of their respective party structures, were in their mid-30s and although not directly involved in policy decisions, one as Parliamentary Assistant and both as activists were very influential and rather close to the decision-making elite. They would easily fit to classic definitions of an 'elite in waiting' according to regular assumptions on elite recruitment.

In this section of the sample I encountered the only two females of the Scottish section of this survey. One was an MP and the other an MEP. Their uniqueness within the sample makes it impossible to treat them as a subgroup with any significance in statistical tests. I therefore, incorporate the female cases with their male counterparts in statistical analysis and will only refer to their identity when that can make a significant contribution in the qualitative analysis.

The respondents age group structure is a normally distributed bell shaped curve, centred around the 46 to 55 years age group. Respondents were predominantly Labour (13 out of 17), Liberal Democrats (three out of 17) and Scottish National Party (one out of 17). There were no Conservative or minority party representatives. The strong dominance of Labour is normal, since sampling was centred in the Glasgow area.[22]

Of the political respondents, 70 per cent have their ethnic roots in Scotland, a figure noticeably lower than the business average for Scotland of 87.5 per cent (Table 4.6). Much more unanimous than their business counterparts, 82.4 per cent of the political sample believe that nationalist movements are 'definitely' not constructive in regional politics. This is an anticipated result. The confrontation between Scottish Nationalists and the Labour Party has been severe as they both vie for voters in the same section of the political

Table 4.6   Respondents' identification with their region

	Roots in region	Roots outside region
Scottish politicians	12	5
	70.6%	29.4%
Scottish businessmen	21	3
	87.5%	12.5%

Note: Question Q4: 'Are your family/ethnic roots in Scotland?'

spectrum. While Scottish businessmen favoured an economy controlled at the national centre, politicians favoured more regional rather than national control. The Regional Council was favoured by 47 per cent, while 40 per cent favoured the national institutions in macroeconomic decision making.

Essential in understanding the potential and patterns of interaction between the business and political elites are opinions they hold about each other. To have a more complete picture of their overall belief structure I proceed here with a presentation of their attitudes towards local entrepreneurs, local and multinational business as well as the state of the regional economy.

A general observation is that regional political actors did not think themselves as significant players in the 'political game'. So where does power lie? Nine out of 17 politicians believed that MPs receive most lobbying even for issues of regional significance, 56 per cent of them however suggested that macroeconomics should be controlled at the regional level.[23] Replies to questions comparing trust in local entrepreneurs and respondents ethnic origin are particularly interesting since 80 per cent of those not born in Scotland believed that prosperity depended on local entrepreneurs while reversely, 60 per cent of those with their roots in Scotland perceived multinationals to be more important.

A majority of two out of three of those that expressed a preference believed business would perceive autonomy positively, which points to a serious difference in attitude from Scottish businessmen, since 61 per cent of those expressing an opinion did not see the prospect of autonomy as a positive development. A cross-tabulation between their perception of business being positive to autonomy with politician's trust of local entrepreneurs or multi-nationals, reveals 35 per cent of respondents to believe in local entrepreneurs and at the same time to find that business see autonomy positively.[24] There appears to be a notion that an economic future underpinned by the support of multinationals is compatible with business being positive on autonomy.

Politicians expect that 82 per cent of small and medium-sized sized enterprises (SMEs) will maintain operations in the region in spite of a recession, while on the other hand 59 per cent of multinationals would shift operations to another region.[25] Fifty-eight per cent of those expressing an opinion said the economic future of the region depends on out of region capital investment, while 29 per cent of this sample had no view on whether the region will depend on indigenous or exogenous investment.

The image of MEPs appears very positive, 41 per cent of respondents finding they have the longest term perspective among elected representatives. Councillors came second in preference with, 24 per cent of the sample believing them to be economically farsighted, while only one respondent supported the premise for MPs. The large majority of respondents (71 per cent) believe that MPs are not held accountable for decisions taken by regional authorities, at the same time the majority (53 per cent) believed that MPs are accountable for regional development.[26]

A possible inconsistency exists between answers to questions of whether future economic growth depends on local entrepreneurs, and whether the regions prosperity depends on local entrepreneurs.[27] Only 54 per cent of those that believed in local entrepreneurs answered similarly on whether regional prosperity depended on local entrepreneurs. Although remarkable as an inconsistency it could be possibly explained by the time reference in each question. The first one is inquiring about the future, so replies can be more 'optimistic', while the second one is asking respondents about the present situation.

On the issue of whether MPs are receiving most of the lobbying for issues of mainly regional importance, the predominant attitude was that this was the case. A similar majority said that they have been on the receiving end of lobbying efforts.[28] A total of 56 per cent of lobbied respondents also believe MPs are lobbied for issues of regional importance. As apparent from the correlation coefficients however, these attitudes cannot be associated.

A correlation also exists between respondents impression of the Regional Council and their identification of Councillors as possessing a more accurate mental map than MPs.[29] Those that found Councillors possessing a more accurate mental map tended to find the Council more dynamic compared to those that did not think Councillors had a more accurate mental map. Most of those who had a negative view on Councillors mental map tended to view the Regional Council as simply active.

Overall, in the whole Scottish political sample only 17.6 per cent had a negative view of the Regional Council. The existing correlation points to a positive view of the Regional Council being linked with a positive view of Councillors. There is also a relationship between Councillors' assumed accuracy of their own 'mental map' with their perceived receptiveness to businessmen.[30] From those that find Councillors possessing a more accurate mental map 60 per cent also find Councillors more receptive than MPs. From those that do not find Councillors having a more accurate mental map than MPs 67 per cent do not believe that they are more receptive than MPs. Overall consistency of responses suggest the existence of two groups. One which strongly believes in Councillors ability and fervour and one which strongly believes that Councillors have limited utility. Overall results on question on Councillors receptiveness are rather negative with 47.1 per cent of the sample taking a negative view. Since most of this sample were themselves Councillors this indicates a widespread low esteem for the job.

In replies to questions on whether the British and Scottish economy are ready for 1992, I find a remarkable consistency in replies which tended to coincide between their answers for Scotland and Britain with very small variations.[31] So, if respondents found the British economy ready for European competition, they thought the same for the Scottish economy and vice versa. This signifies an identification of the region with the economic fortunes of the nation that can be considered relevant to the position this subgroup takes towards nationalism and devolution.

When however they were asked whether Scotland is in a worse position than the rest of UK the distribution of their replies is balanced between those that find Scotland slightly worse off with those that find it slightly better off than the rest of the UK. This suggests a diversity of opinion that only becomes apparent when this particular issue of the region vs the nation becomes explicit. In replying to questions on the preparedness towards 1992 they were not requested to draw a comparison between their region and the rest of Britain. When this is done, I assume that their replies become influenced by their political beliefs and ethnic background in showing a divergence from their initial response.

In an effort to further identify bias, if and when it exists, I cross-reference questions of those that find there is a difference between the people in their region and the rest of Scotland or between their region and Britain, with the question that asks whether they believe the region's prosperity depends more on local entrepreneurs or multinationals. I find that 67 per cent of those who believe there are great differences between people from Strathclyde and the rest of Britain also believed their region's prosperity to depend on local entrepreneurs. The only respondents who did not believe there are great differences between people from Strathclyde and other Britons, where found in the group that had answered in favour of multinationals on the regional prosperity question. So those that believe local entrepreneurs to be closely associated with the region's future also find the Scots to be different from the British, while a great number of the sample of Strathclyde politicians who find multinationals to hold more promise for the region's future also find the Scots and the British to be alike. There emerges a pattern, according to which, those that think there is no difference among the Scottish and British tend to believe in the importance of multinational enterprises, while those finding a difference among the Scottish and British tend to believe in the importance of local entrepreneurs for regional development.

I finally investigate the distribution of replies among those that believed autonomy will be perceived positively by business, 60 per cent of which believed future prosperity lies with local entrepreneurs.[32] Similarly 60 per cent of those that gave an answer, believing autonomy will be perceived negatively by business thought that the future of the region lies with multinationals. The two groupings seem consistent with the assumption that supporters of local entrepreneurs will support autonomy as well, while supporters of multinationals will view autonomy negatively.

Overall, Strathclyde politicians believe that business perceive autonomy positively, MEPs have the longest term perspective and the Regional Council is a dynamic institution. There is also a link between a perception of difference of the Scottish people from the rest of the British, a positive view of entrepreneurs and a positive view of autonomy.

Notes

1   This is readily apparent in statistical analysis and graphical representations of unemployment trends for Strathclyde, in *Strathclyde Economic Trends* (No. 32, October 1991, p.18).
2   Comprehensive economic statistics for Scotland and its regions can be found in the *Scottish Economic Bulletin* (1991), No. 43, June, HMSO, pp. 59–72 is referred to here.
3   Ibid., pp.76–80.
4   Ibid., p.52. Entrepreneurial vitality can be also related to growth of the number of SMEs or rate of business failures or by evaluating the 'entrepreneurial milieu' in a region.
5   *Scottish Economic Bulletin* (1991), op cit., p.11.
6   Ibid., pp. 11–12.
7   A good analysis of the impact – or the lack of it – of European Regional Policy in British regions is given by Richard Harrington, who describes ERDF transfers as a 'disguised rebate to the UK government' (Harrington, 1992, p.64).
8   All three were in their mid-30s, one put himself in the less than 35 years old group and the other two in the 35–45 years old group.

9   Reference here is made to research conducted by R.E. Pahl and J.T. Winkler (Pahl, 1974). The researchers studied companies whose turnover was £250,000 or greater. Indexing between 1974 and 1991 will produce a minimum turnover value close to the one I applied. Considerations of systematic bias were made in that survey as well, particularly to the degree that successful companies were more prone to participating. My discussion on validity in the relevant appendix entails these considerations.

10 Respondents conceptual perception of entrepreneurship may effect their relevant responses to the questionnaire. This limitation, could be particularly relevant for comparisons between the two different national groups. A context of different understandings of entrepreneurship is often encountered in the book edited by Goffee and Scase (1987) on 'Entrepreneurship in Europe'.

11 Spearman correlation coefficients for both groups are negative. More so for the executives with a value of -0.368 (sig. 0.121) than for the entrepreneurs with a value of -0.167 (sig. 0.789).

12 Discrepancies in percentage totals stem either from rounding or from respondents declining to express an opinion or expressing an individual opinion outside the options given. When answers diverged from the set options in significant numbers these new categories were also tabulated.

13 Spearman correlation coefficients (questions Q3 and QB1) were 0.296 (sig. 0.160) while for questions Q3 with QB2 took a value of 0.497 (sig 0.014).

14 The Spearman correlation coefficient (question QB1 with QB2) is 0.461 (sig 0.024) pointing to the strong relationship of the two variables.

15 The Spearman correlation coefficient (questions Q4 and QB1) is -0.062 (sig. 0.773) which points to the limited association of the two variables.

16 As mentioned earlier, this survey was conducted long before the Scottish Constitutional Convention had presented any concrete plans for devolution from Westminster. Questions on nationalism and Scottish nationalism can be associated with sympathy for the SNP, while questions inquiring on an increase in power for the now defunct Strathclyde Regional Council, with support for devolution.

17 Spearman correlation coefficients (questions QB6 and QB7) of 0.422 (sig 0.040) point to a strong correlation between businessmen knowing their Councillor and MP. A high coefficient value (questions QB6 and QB8) of 0.497 (sig 0.014) points to a strong correlation between businessmen knowing their Councillor and MEP. A weak correlation (questions QB7 and QB8) at 0.194 (sig 0.363) points to a low association between businessmen's knowledge of their MP and MEP.

18 A Spearman correlation coefficient (questions QB11 and QB12) of 0.666 (sig 0.001) points to the very strong correlation between the two concepts.

19 There is a very strong correlation between respondents replies to these questions (QB14 and QB15) as a Spearman correlation coefficient of 0.598 (sig. 0.002) reveals.

20 The Spearman correlation coefficient (questions QB14 and QD9) is 0.070 (sig 0.747) pointing to no association between the two variables. This runs contrary to the assumption that if respondents believed there were great differences among the Scottish (QD9: positive) they would not be prepared to work elsewhere in the UK (QB14: negative). I assumed that this could be an indication of prejudice towards the English.

21 The weak association is also apparent in the relevant Spearman correlation coefficient (questions QB17 and QB18) of 0.049 (sig 0.825).

22 Labour history and effective dominance in Glasgow is covered by Keating (1988, chs 2–3), while political life in Scotland is covered in Midwinter et al. (1991, chs 1–3).

23 A Spearman correlation coefficient (questions Q1 and QC1) of 0.296 (sig. 0.266) indicates a moderate association between their views on macroeconomic control and lobbying of MPs.

24 A Spearman correlation coefficient (questions QD1 and QC4) of 0.402 (sig. 0.109) points a high degree of association between the two variables.

25 The Spearman correlation coefficient (questions QC5 and QC7) is 0.571 (sig. 0.021) which points to a high level of association between the two variables. If respondents thought SMEs will maintain operations were very likely to think MNLs will maintain operations and vice versa.

26 A Spearman correlation coefficient of -0.085 (sig. 0.746) points to no association in respondents replies between the two questions.

27 A Spearman correlation coefficient of 0.336 (sig. 0.163) points to a relatively high degree of association between the two variables however.

28 Respondents exhibit no consistency in their replies however, as a Spearman correlation (questions QC1 and QC13) of 0.054 (sig. 0.838) signifies.

29 The overall Spearman coefficient is modest however, at 0.159 (sig. 0.588).

30 There is a considerable correlation in respondents replies to the two questions with a Spearman coefficient of 0.463 (sig. 0.071)

31 A very high correlation coefficient of 0.817 (sig. 0.000) signifies a very strong association between the two questions.

32 The high Spearman correlation value of 0.402 (sig. 0.109) points to a strong association between the two questions.

Chapter Five

Cretan Local Elites: A Struggle Against Centralisation and Clientelism

The Prefecture of Chania within the Cretan Economy

The region of Crete is one of 13 regions that the National Statistical Office subdivides Greece. The number of inhabitants according to the 1981 census were 502,000; 188,560 of them declared being employed while 4,614 unemployed. The unemployment figure reached 10,942 by 1988. The disposable per capita income was 163,296 drachmae in 1981. During the 1980s agricultural land use had slightly declined from 3,223 thousand *stremmata* to 3,177 thousand; in the rest of Greece this decline is more pronounced. The average agricultural property is 30 *stremmata* in size (30,000 sq. m) and segregated in eight lots. The average yearly temperature is 18.3 degrees Celsius and the average rainfall is 800 mm per year.[1] Industry and handicraft operations represent roughly 5 per cent of the national total at 7,349 operating units (1984). Use of units of electricity where the national ratio is 2:3 between domestic to industrial, is reversed in Crete to 7:2, obviously indicating small industrial units with limited use of industrial machinery (1988).

Other basic economic indicators (1988–89) show two telephones for every five people, one doctor for every 48 people, one teacher for every 12 pupils in high school, while the public finance indicators show declared income which is 75 per cent of the national average per capita. All of the above figures are below the national average figures from between 10 to 35 per cent.

Tourism is very important for the island with 71,634 beds and 7,929,097 overnight stays from foreigners in 1989. This represents almost a quarter of the national average. There are an estimated further 45,000 seasonal tourist beds available in the black economy for which there can only be assumptions on the overnight stays they provide. It is also estimated that approximately 30,000 people or 19 per cent of the work-force are employed in tourism.

The high peripherality of the island placed as it is on the eastern Mediterranean and the southernmost tip of Europe, creates problems of accessibility that are aggravated by poor communication links. This is made worse by limited and at times poorly maintained infrastructure on the island

Table 5.1   Cretan land morphology

	Chania	Crete	Greece
Plains	18.7%	23.4%	30.3%
Semi-mountainous	19.1%	26.7%	27.1%
Mountainous	62.2%	49.9%	42.6%

Source: Protopapadakis, 1987.

itself. At the time of survey there was no paved road traversing the southern part of the island on an east to west axis. A very limited length of existing roads qualify for the term carriageways and the plans for extending or upgrading the network are not conforming to a comprehensive feasibility; subsequently public works projects have a difficulty qualifying for EC grants.[2]

The prefecture of Chania comprises the westernmost part of Crete and it is one of four administrative sub-regions the island is divided into, with an area of 2,379,000 *stremmata*.

Crete has a density of 53 inhabitants per sq. km compared with the national average of 75 and the EC average of 164 (Eurostat, Statistical Office of the European Communities, 1987). Employment figures show Agriculture to have the largest share with 42.82 per cent, but only supplying 28.5 per cent of the income (see Table 5.2), employment in the primary sector shows a drastic decline from the 1971 figure of 70.9 per cent but it should be noted that people employed in the secondary and tertiary sectors are also occasionally employed in the primary. Although unemployment levels are negligible there is still a serious problem of underemployment (Protopapadakis, 1987).

Table 5.2   Employment by sector in Chania, Greece and the EC

	Chania (1981)		Greece (1985)	EC (1985)
	Employment	Income generated	Employment	Employment
Primary	42.8%	28.5%	28.9%	8.6%
Secondary	19.1%	22.0%	27.4%	33.8%
Tertiary	38.1%	49.5%	43.7%	57.6%

Source: Eurostat for Greece and EEC; Protopapadakis, 1987, for Chania.

In 1991 there was one industrial park in existence that had proven quite inadequate, there were three more parks under construction and one at the planning stage. To the degree that these parks conform to national trends their operation would not necessarily indicate industrialisation as most enterprises would be small and geared towards handicraft. In total 51.7 per cent of sold lots in industrial parks in Greece were for lots of between 2,000 to 5,000 sq. m which indicates a strong orientation towards small and medium-sized units; 88 per cent of the sales were for lots of 15,000 sq. m or less.[3] Invariably established industries were related to agricultural production, which suggests it is less likely for new industries to proceed in novel industrial fields or production patterns. The list of existing industries in Crete according to Protopapadakis (1987) includes:

a) olive oil products;
b) wine and spirits;
c) raisins;
d) concentrated juices;
e) processing of sugarcane;
f) milk, cheese, ice-cream;
g) processing of leather;
h) canning of agricultural products;
i) silk weaving;
j) textiles.

The prefecture had set out a list of proposed industries' with the scope of inducing industrial development in Crete (Protopapadakis 1987). This list included among others:

a) petrochemicals;
b) cement and building materials;
c) gypsum production;
d) shipyards;
e) construction of earth moving equipment;
f) air-conditioning and solar power systems;
g) fertilisers;
h) electronics;
i) textiles;
j) tourist and silverware artefacts;
k) irrigation and greenhouse equipment.

As is evident, proposed industries attempted to induce industrialisation while at the same time increase the region's autonomy from outside suppliers. However haphazard planning and limited environmental impact feasibility studies created concerns on the introduction of such industries on the local economy. Furthermore, although there seems to be a market for each of these products within Crete, proposed industries did not seem to be export oriented (Mavromatis, 1989).

All major urban centres are on the north side of the island where most of the cultivated lands exist as well. There are three major ports on the north side while there are no substantial port facilities on the south side. This uneven orientation is reflected in the development of the island as an appendix of the Greek production system.

Future economic trends point to the need of 'autonomous' regional development and reorientation of the island's economy to take advantage of its geographical position and production strengths. This realisation was manifest in local authority plans to establish a regional airline company to transfer tourists and agricultural produce directly to the European markets. Furthermore, the three major companies conducting the sea transportation to the island were about to merge, to become the biggest such carrier in Europe, with plans to expand their network to other direct destinations in Europe and eventually the Middle East.[4]

Cretan businessmen seemed to aspire to the development achieved since the mid-1970s by Cyprus an island of similar size, population and location. They understood that they could not depend on industry for their development, and seemed to concentrate their efforts on agriculture and services. Notably they had managed to increase both the quality of agricultural products and the productivity of land with covered or greenhouse cultivation, while between 1981 and 1990 they had almost doubled their capacity in tourist beds. Cretans believed in achieving self sufficiency, as 'Crete makes an integrated economic unit, probably the most integrated in the country', a phrase coined by Manolikakis (1963) and one frequently quoted in academic research on Crete.

Crete had something to show for the attention it received in planning departments of the Greek ministries. Between 1970 and 1981 GNP for Greece rose in fixed 1970 prices from 100 to 161, Cretan GRP by comparison rose to 178 (Voloudakis, 1984).

The prefecture enjoyed many benefits from Greek accession to the EEC. There were also a number of problems, relating to its peripheral nature and the problems of Greek economic integration to the Community. Regional development grants, aimed at agriculture and infrastructure and the Integrated

Mediterranean Programmes (IMPs), had a positive effect on the income, productivity and standards of living particularly of the agricultural community (Protopapadakis, 1987). Negative effects included primarily those of the integration itself, which brought stagnation and high inflation to the Greek economy, while agricultural production had to face steep competition from similar products from the rest of southern Europe. Additionally, the lack of a developed administrative mechanism to support agricultural production and the lack of complete information for taking advantage of Community programs, added to the disadvantages the region experienced compared with a number of other regions in southern Europe. It should be noted finally, that the economic condition and development of Crete is closely linked with that of mainland Greece. The main concern during the early 1980s was that the Greek economy could not undergo the structural adjustments necessary to successfully integrate in Europe.

The position of the Greek economy in the European integrated market is directly relevant to the ability of the Greek regions (particularly the more remote ones) to attain sufficiently high levels of growth to attain convergence with the rest of Europe.[5] Research evidence indicated that Greece had remained in the periphery of European growth during the 1980s and was under danger of being marginalised economically within the European Community (Commission, 1991).

The Cretan Business Elite

The age structure of respondents in this sub-sample shows 52 per cent to be 45 years old or younger, while only 14 per cent of them were older than 56 years. The character and average size of business in Crete precluded the possibility of many members of the business elite being executives. This is not only due to the comparatively small size of incorporated companies, but also due to the predominance of family controlled business, which still comprise the backbone of Greek business. This picture was confirmed in their responses in the survey as 64 per cent of them declared being entrepreneurs and only 32 per cent declared being executives.

In my definition of eligible elites for this survey, 'eliteness' is not limited to the relative position a businessman has within a regional economy (positional eliteness) but also relates to the degree to which he is influential in the local community (functional eliteness).[6] For this reason, certain interviewees, although controlling comparatively small companies, were interviewed, as they appeared to be held in high esteem by officials in their local trade organisation. Furthermore as mentioned earlier in this chapter, interlockingness between the local political and business elite is assumed to be related to the size of the local economy. The small size, in this case, of the Cretan economy makes the holding of a position in both elite groups a more frequent occurrence than witnessed in the Strathclyde sample. Two cases interviewed had an important role in both elite groups. One of them a managing director of the biggest company in the prefecture was eliminated from the political sample (as a local councillor) and was only included in the business one. Similarly an editor/proprietor of one of the local papers was eliminated from the business sample and his responses are included in the political one.

Some basic aspects of their attitudinal profile are revealed in answers to the question inquiring whether respondents believe a federal structure for Europe is viable, were an overwhelming majority of 86 per cent said they believed this to be the case. Half of those also argued that macroeconomics should be controlled at the international level. It is noteworthy that only 19 per cent of the sample supported the proposition that macroeconomics should be controlled at the regional level, while another 19 per cent supported the proposition that it should be controlled at the national level.

So Cretan businessmen show themselves to be much more internationalist than their Scottish counterparts (75 per cent of whom supported national control of macroeconomic policies). An apparent explanation of this, as of responses to many other questions, is that businessmen from the prefecture find the national administration inefficient and trust the European Commission as a comparatively uncorrupted bureaucracy. The efficiency and higher level of development of European business also make them a model which Cretan businessmen aspire to. By comparison Scottish businessmen may perceive Brussels as a bureaucratic organisation which competes with their national government for imposition of taxes, standardisation of production and the establishment of a Social Charter. The European Commission may be perceived thus, as an impediment to business by Scottish businessmen.

A total of 76 per cent of the sample perceive nationalist movements negatively which is a similar figure with the Cretan political elite response, but is far higher than the Strathclyde business figure of 54 per cent of respondents being negative on nationalist movements.

Another interesting distinction in responses of entrepreneurs and executives' is that 31 per cent of entrepreneurs could not decide whether nationalism was bad, while at the same time all executives had a clearly positive or negative position. Divergence in their views on nationalism, cannot be ascribed to their declared ethnic roots either. Most respondents replied that their roots are Cretan, a 19 per cent minority in this sample consider their roots to be outside Crete. This fact in itself is significant, to the degree that it points to, the business elite not being as homogeneous in its background, as the respective political elite.

Trying to determine whether there are variations on the approach to nationalism and international economic control which depend on the status of respondents, I divide respondent replies on whether they perceive themselves as entrepreneurs or executives. A noteworthy concentration of replies consist of those who identified the region or the nation as most appropriate to exercise macroeconomic control. Only 13 per cent of executives support the nation as most appropriate level of management of the macroeconomic policies of the region.

I proceed by giving an account of interviewees attitudes towards devolution, local business, local politicians and European integration. Remarkably, an overwhelming majority of 95 per cent of respondents believed that the region will benefit by an increase in the powers of the prefecture. While 90 per cent believed their business will benefit from such an increase in regional powers as well.[7] A negative perception of nationalism does not preclude an almost unanimous support of an increase in the powers of the regional administration. This strong support for devolution from a rather demoralised and centrally dependent regional bureaucracy, points to the distress that the workings of the existing structures bring to businessmen in the region.[8]

Although 95 per cent of respondents believe their prefecture will benefit from devolution from the bureaucracy in Athens, only 29 per cent find that business will see autonomy positively while a majority of 62 per cent think that although the prefecture will benefit from devolution, business will not like autonomy. This reply is particularly intriguing if one considers that this group of respondents are businessmen. From relevant qualifications, respondents gave to their replies, the most apparent interpretation to this 'contradiction' is that, Cretan businessmen can see the benefits of devolution in the administration but would view with unease the possibility of severing their ties with the Greek business community. It seems also to be less the case of resource dependency of the Cretan economy to the mainland for imports, than dependence on the Greek market as an outlay for their products and services.

A high correlation exists on whether they foresee more SMEs and whether this is beneficial to their own firm that is dependent on whether they have declared themselves to be entrepreneurs or executives.[9] This association is directly relevant to the perceived role of respondents in the business community. I can assume that entrepreneurs view SMEs as competition, while executives view them as a wider market for their products.

From those who responded that more SMEs will create a more devolved economy, 77 per cent have also found business holding a negative view of the possibility of autonomy.[10] Those that answered that the economy would become more dependent, were equally split, 50 per cent of them believed business to be positive and 50 per cent to be negative to autonomy. An overall majority of those who perceive SMEs to create a more devolved regional economy perceive business to be negative to autonomy.

Those who believe people from Chania to be different from other people in the region (Crete) or the nation represent 48 per cent of the sample; those who believe neither people from the region nor people from the nation to be different from people in Chania represent 24 per cent; finally, those who find there are great differences between people in Chania and the rest of Greece, but no differences between people from Chania and the rest of the region represent 19 per cent of respondents. So, as with the Cretan political personalities I can distinguish three major groups of respondents.

A relationship between their ethnic roots and a perception of difference of the regional people can be demonstrated by the fact that 59 per cent of those who declared their ethnic roots to be Cretan believed there are great differences between people in their prefecture and the rest of Crete.[11] The inverse is true for those who do not have their roots in Crete, 75 per cent of which believe there are no great differences among the prefecture and the rest of Crete.

From those that would be prepared to work elsewhere in Greece, 63 per cent perceived no great differences of people within Crete. From those that would not be prepared to work elsewhere in Greece, 67 per cent found there are great differences between the people in their prefecture and those in the rest of Crete. This attitude is consistent with assuming that those who find great differences within their region are not prepared to emigrate and *vice versa*. Further evidence from their qualitative replies identifies this group as the potential 'hard-line' (substate) nationalists in the region.

There is an interesting inversion from replies in the Scottish sample here. When asked if they would be prepared to do the same job they perform here in another part of Greece 57 per cent replied they were not prepared to move, this reply was partly anticipated since this sample consists mostly of entrepreneurs with comparatively small operations, who believe their region to be better off than the nation. When replying if they would be prepared to do the same job in Europe, 52 per cent reply in the affirmative. The inference from the Scottish investigation of replies, was that if someone was not prepared to work outside Scotland in the United Kingdom he was less likely to be prepared to do so in Europe. Many assumptions can be made why Cretan businessmen would be more willing to work in Europe than they would be to work elsewhere in Greece. Most apparent is the presumption of a better organised state infrastructure and better returns for their efforts in most of western Europe. I must not fail to identify their entrepreneurship and keen sense of adventure, neither the long history of emigration and immigration (particularly acute in the 1950s and 1960s) from the region and Greece as a whole.

Respondents knowledge of their elected representatives is very high. All respondents knew who their elected representative was, in both the city or town Council and national legislature. A total of 57 per cent also knew a Cretan MEP.[12] The presumably high degree of interlockingness of the two elite groups, the comparative small size of the prefecture and above all the importance of political patronage in the economic life of Greece comprise the background for a high level of interaction between the two elite groups. This fact poses certain problems in dividing the two groups and identifying which is the dominant function of individual cases in the Cretan sample. It is partly because of the nature of Greek political reality in the regions but also because of an implicit 'forced participation' in political life that there exists such a high awareness and involvement with politics.[13]

In assessing effectiveness, receptiveness and fervour of their local Councillors compared with their local MPs, distribution of replies follows a pattern remarkably different from the Scottish one. An equal percentage (44 per cent) of those respondents who expressed an opinion found their local Councillors less or much less fervent from local MPs with those that found them more or much more fervent. A majority of 63 per cent of those who expressed an opinion believed that local Councillors are less or much less effective, compared with 25 per cent who found them more or much more effective. On being questioned on the receptiveness and accessibility to local Councillors 48 per cent found them more or much more receptive, compared with 24 per cent who found them less receptive.[14] In cross-tabulating the three questions there was negligible correlation between replies to questions, while their distributions showed no direct patterns and replies to one did not seem to preclude replies to the other, save for an association between receptiveness and fervour. Most importantly their appreciation of the local political elite's effectiveness is small and its correlation with Councillors fervour and receptiveness not extremely impressive. This leads me to assume that although the relation of the local business elite with the local political one is direct, (as it has been demonstrated in their replies to earlier questions), their appreciation, of the local Councillors' and Mayors' ability to be instrumental, in promoting the region's or their individual interests, is obviously limited.

Perceived receptiveness of Councillors seems also linked to respondents position towards the respective local authority. A majority of 57 per cent of those that found their local authority to be 'dynamic', also found the local Councillors to be more receptive.[15] Similarly, from those that found their local authority to be 'active' or of 'minor importance', 80 per cent believed their local Councillors to be equally or less receptive than MPs. It seems thus that a positive impression of Councillors receptiveness and accessibility is linked with a dynamic image of the local authority and vice versa.

As anticipated, all of those that believe their region's economy is prepared for European integration belong to the group of those that believe their prefecture to be in a better position than the nation.[16] Replies to the question, on the competitiveness of the Greek economy, showed no correlation with those that found the prefecture in the same or worse position than the nation. Since their replies on the position of the prefecture towards the nation does not seem to correlate to their replies on the state of the national economy, I assume this subgroup does not make that attitudinal connection.

In conclusion, Cretan businessmen supported devolution, were mostly apprehensive of the prospect of more SMEs and were prepared to work elsewhere in Europe. They tended to know all their elected representatives and believed Crete and Greece to be unprepared for the Single Market.

The Cretan Political Elite

Fourteen interviews are included in the analysis representing a number of political bodies. Most interviewees were aligned on the 'left' of the political spectrum representing either the Socialist (six cases) the Communists (one case) or a Socialist-Left coalition (one case). Three of the respondents declared belonging to the Centre of the political spectrum although two were elected with the Socialists and one with the Conservatives. Another two respondents were right-wing conservatives. Remarkable is the case of the respondent who declared allegiance to a political party which, for all practical purposes, was at the time defunct (*Enosis Kentrou*). It is possible that the party dealignment evident in the willingness of respondents to give and receive support from the two major political parties in contemporary Greek politics (*Nea Democratia* and *PASOK*) has to do with the character of politics in Greece. The clientelistic and leader-worship political culture makes ideology almost irrelevant to political alignment and support of a party. Hence, the often opportunistic realignments and coalitions based on shifting patronage relationships.

Table 5.3   Declared political affiliation of Cretan political interviews

Party affiliation	Cases	%
Communist Left (Synaspismos – Aristera)	1	7%
Socialist Left (Left-PASOK)	1	7%
Socialists (PASOK)	6	42%
Centre Socialists (Centre-PASOK)	2	14%
Centre (Enosis Kentrou)	1	7%
Conservative (Centre)	1	7%
Conservatives (Nea Demokratia)	2	14%

The predominance of Socialist representatives in this sample is an accurate reflection of the political map of local government in Chania at the time. A strong sense of a democratic tradition, which people in Chania feel links them to the days of Eleftherios Venizelos, is probably indicative of the prevailing feeling in the political community at large. This attitude is important for the analysis, since it points to a tendency for consensus politics that may be uncharacteristic of other regions in Greece.[17]

Of the non-elected interviewees one was a senior influential figure in the local political scene, a labour leader or '*ergatopateras*' (literally: 'father of workers'), he was also the editor of one of the local union publications and a person directly involved with the party political machine being very influential in the local political party scene. The other one was the publisher and editor of one of the most important local papers, he was affiliated with the Socialist party and was directly involved in the political power struggles of local politics. Both cases have an intense and direct involvement to the local political scene and I believe easily qualify as members of the local political elite. One of the interviewees was a female, in this case similar to the Scottish sample, her uniqueness disallows any further testing relating to her gender.

The age group structure reveals a comparatively youthful sample with only 21 per cent of the respondents on the 'over 56 years of age' category. Forty-three per cent of the Cretan compared with 29 per cent of the Scottish politicians were younger than 45 years of age.

Representation of certain political institutions – like the Greek Parliament or the European Parliament – could not be achieved as political actors if those bodies refused to participate. I feel however that loss of the respective individuals from the sample, only limits the investigative search in as much as it eliminates certain hypotheses that can be relevant to the respective political institutions and does not reduce the value of the results in any other way.

All of the respondents in this sub-sample declared their roots to be Cretan which makes a contrast with all other subgroups of this survey. I believe this to be the case for all local MPs in the national parliament as well. This fact if indicative of a larger national or regional trend in Greece could be relevant to a possible direction regional politics might take in the future. Since relevant statistics are unavailable for other regions in Greece however I cannot dwell on this topic further.

Respondents in this part of the sample found that macroeconomic policies should be controlled at the regional level by 58 per cent compared with the Scottish political sample where 47 per cent of respondents held the same view. A big majority of 71 per cent also believed that a federal structure for Europe can be viable. It did not come as a surprise that 85 per cent of respondents found nationalist movements not to be constructive in regional politics. As explained concurrently with the testing of the hypotheses Cretans are particularly weary of any talk of secession from the mainland. The threat of Turkey is considered very real while for many Cretan respondents nationalism has an inherently negative meaning.[18]

I find however a noteworthy comparison between their responses to the first group of questions in the questionnaire. By a great margin they seem to think macroeconomics should be controlled at the region, while federalism is viable at a European level. Furthermore, they do not find nationalist movements constructive. It could be that existing nationalist movements or parties do not have the confidence of the elite. It is the case as well, that the semantic meaning of the equivalent Greek word for nationalism, '*ethnikismos*', has inherently negative connotations. An alternative definition that would use the word '*patriotismos*' would have a distorting effect in that it would best be associated with 'the love of ones country' and has not been employed in the questionnaire analysed here.

It is possible, however, that if this is indeed a contradiction not related to the measures employed, that Cretans could make the 'logical leap' of supporting a federal structure for their region.[19] Obviously, I am not suggesting that nationalism is positively related to federalism.[20] Interestingly in the many orientation interviews with officials from the planning agency of the prefecture and the local chamber of commerce (not constituting part of the questionnaire), it was relayed, that the local administrative elite was frustrated with the existing decision-making structures and would hope and lobby for a regionally autonomous administration.[21]

I proceed by analysing Cretan politicians attitudes on nationalist movements, local entrepreneurs and multinationals, the regional economy and national parliamentarians, as well as, the European Community. A common opinion expressed, was that the Cretan economy is able to outperform the rest of Greece and would be probably better off without the burden of central Greek administration and taxes.[22] So not only there is evidence of discontent but also strong confidence in their own ability to do better. Significantly, all those who found nationalist movements constructive claimed also that national policies for the region have failed.[23] Those that found nationalist movements not to be constructive were almost evenly split between those that thought nationalist policies have failed and those that did not think that to be the case.

Eighty-six per cent of interviewees said MPs receive most of the lobbying, while 58 per cent of them said that macroeconomics should be controlled at the regional level.[24] In a country where political patronage is a facet of the state machine, it is considered natural to lobby at the state legislature, which is the highest decision making body. The dependence of local authorities on the central administration further explains this pattern. Of those who believed macroeconomics should be controlled at the national level came the only two respondents to support the proposition that MPs do not receive most of the lobbying for issues with regional impact. If they represented a more significant part of this sample, I could deduce that such a group sees the national administration as the most competent agent for dealing with the regional economy and at the same time feel there exists a balance by lobbying for regional issues at the competent authorities for the region; such a group would obviously favour the status quo of affairs for the region.

In terms of trust of the local entrepreneurial skills, 64 per cent of respondents believe their region's prosperity depends on local entrepreneurs, while 71 per cent believe future economic growth will depend mainly on local entrepreneurial skill.[25] A group of respondents representing 29 per cent of the sample believed the economic future of the region lies in out of region capital while at the same time regional prosperity depends on companies with headquarters outside the region; this same group also believes future growth will depend on out of region entrepreneurial skill or have no opinion on the issue.[26] On the question of whether the capital resources for future growth will come from within or outside the region a total of 43 per cent of the sample, expect capital to come from outside the region.

The strong trust on local entrepreneurial skill is mirrored in replies of the business part of the Cretan sample. I find it indicative of the natural pride on their own ethnic identity. The big proportion of those that expect capital resources for their region's growth to come from outside the region shows, to some extent, the degree of their perceived dependence on such sources for growth.

A concentration of replies exists between those that perceive the future of the region to depend on local capital and at the same time expecting SMEs to stay in the region.[27] Overall 93 per cent of respondents expected SMEs to stay in the region in the case of a recession, while only 50 per cent of respondents expected multinationals to stay in the region in a similar case.

In their views about multinational's commitment in the region, compared with their views on local or international resources for their growth, I find two significant concentrations of replies. One was of those who believed the future of the region lies in out of region capital, 67 per cent of which believed multinationals will stay in the case of a recession; while the second one was of those who believed the future depends on local capital resources, 57 per cent of which believed multinationals would go in the case of a recession.[28] These views show a degree of consistency in the opinions of this sample which, furthermore, seems divided between those who believe the region is dependent on foreign capital and multinationals for its future and those that do not trust multinationals and believe the future to lie with local resources and entrepreneurs.

It is noteworthy, as well, that although Crete is below the Greek average per capita income the political elite finds Crete to be better off than the rest of Greece. In replies to a question asking whether their region is in a worse position than the nation 75 per cent of those who replied to this question found Crete to be in a slightly better position, while 17 per cent believed Crete to be in a much better position than the rest of Greece. At the same time 50 per cent believed MPs to have a longer term perspective while 42 per cent believed MEPs to have a longer term perspective. All of those who believed their region to be much better off than the nation believed that MPs have a longer term perspective.[29]

It could be argued that Cretans perceived themselves in a better position than the nation, because of renewed interest in the region as the first one in Europe to have an Integrated Mediterranean Programme implemented.[30] Furthermore, the fast growth and increased prosperity due to the increase of agricultural incomes and tourist revenue in the 1980s must be partly responsible for the optimistic outlook of the regional elites.

The connection between their belief in their prefecture being better off than the nation and their trust of national MPs economic foresight, indicates confidence in the region's growth at the same time regional politician's dependence on the centre. And although all respondents in this sub-sample belong to local political bodies, it is impressive that they demonstrate no trust to their own economic foresight. In that respect it would be interesting to examine whether calls for decentralisation and autonomy are led by a business elite that is driven by economic expediency and resisted by a political elite deeply embedded in the national clientelistic web.

So I examine how respondents see the relation of MPs with local authorities. Replying to a question on whether they think MPs are considered accountable for decisions taken by local authorities, 86 per cent of respondents thought this not to be the case. On answering whether MPs are held more accountable for regional development than local Councillors, 57 per cent declare this not to be the case, while 21.5 per cent say this is the case and a similar proportion do not know. There were no respondents who were positive on both questions while 50 per cent of this sample was negative on both.[31] It seems, thus, that MPs are held in high esteem, they are not considered accountable for decisions taken by regional authorities, and they are less accountable for regional development than Councillors. These results are consistent with a positive role of MPs in the region that I would not expect in a centralised state.

On their replies to the question of whether Councillors are more receptive than MPs to pressure from businessmen in their area 50 per cent replied positively and 41.7 per cent negatively. Sixty-seven per cent of those that found Councillors more attentive than MPs believed their regions' prosperity to depend on local entrepreneurs, while 60 per cent of those that found Councillors less attentive than MPs believed the future of their area to lie with companies from outside the region.[32] In this light, appreciation of local government can be related with appreciation of local entrepreneurs while disaffection with local government could be linked with trust of an 'out of region entrepreneurial effort'.

Inquiring whether they have been lobbied for the change of legislation and cross-tabulating to assess whether they believe MPs are receiving most of the lobbying, 66 per cent of respondents to both questions said they have not been lobbied and MPs indeed receive most of the lobbying for regional issues.[33]

I next examine the relationship between their perception of the most prominent local authority and the relevance they think local Councillors have with regional problems. A total of 57 per cent find Councillors possessing the most accurate 'mental map' while 75 per cent of those find the local Council to be dynamic. In total 71 per cent find the local Council dynamic which indicates the City Council is considered to be a significant political force by the local political elite. The strong concentration of positive replies for the Council and Councillors could be explained by the occupation of the respondents, being themselves Councillors or presiding over local Council bodies. I cannot thus determine whether their esteem for Councillors is dependent on their impression of Councillors possessing a more accurate mental map. A high correlation between their replies on the state of the Greek and Cretan economies shows replies to correspond on views of the economic conditions between the regional and national economy.[34]

Controlling for whether local entrepreneurs or outside companies are most important for the region's prosperity and on regional preparedness for 1992 there appears to be no apparent divergence in their replies. This suggests there is no connection between respondents preference for local entrepreneurs and their views on the Greek and Cretan economy.

I proceed to investigate their views towards national policy. Seventy per cent of those who thought the region to be better off than the nation also thought that national policies have failed. So a large proportion of those who believed the national authorities to have failed believed the region to be better off regardless. It seems they do not connect the well-being and progress of the region to national policies. At the same time they have a very positive image for local MPs. One is inclined to think that such a position is either relating to a political apathy with state institutions and policies or in a belief that the system cannot be changed and the local MPs are utilising it to the best of its capabilities.

I next try to identify to what extent the elite from the prefecture differentiates itself from the region and the nation. The first indication of divergence is between those that support the premise that there are no differences between the people of the prefecture and the rest of the region and there are no differences between people of the region and the rest of Greece, who represent 36 per cent of the sample, and a group of equal size (36 per cent) who support the premise that there are differences both within the region and between the people of the region compared with the rest of the country. 28 per cent of the sample support the premise that there are no differences within the region but there are differences between the region and the nation. The whole sample can be thus divided to those that: a) find there are no differences whatsoever between all Greeks (36 per cent); b) find people from Chania to the rest of the region and Greece (36 per cent); c) believe people from Chania differ only from the rest of the Greeks (28 per cent). The second (b) and third (c) groups comprise 64 per cent of the whole sample. So I deduce that these groups represent those who see cultural or other differences between their region and Greece. The first group (a) is intransigent in its belief that Greeks have all the same characteristics cultural or otherwise.

Further attempting to qualify respondents position towards Europe, I see that in the question asking whether respondents believe there are more opportunities or risks in a united Europe, 71 per cent reply that they believe there are slightly more or more opportunities, while another 21 per cent reply that there are the same level of risks and opportunities, with only 7 per cent replying that there are many more risks.

Trying to identify trust for multinational enterprises as it compares with their trust for local entrepreneurs I trace a weak relationship since a majority (71 per cent) of respondents who believe multinationals will stay in the case of a recession also believe the region depends on local entrepreneurs. Concurrently, a large proportion (60 per cent) of those who believe multinationals will go, seem not to trust local entrepreneurs.[35] The size of the sample does not allow a generalisation of this relationship. So, although there are indications for the existence of this relationship, trust in local entrepreneurs cannot be linked with trust on the presence of multinationals in the region.

To conclude, Cretan politicians trust local entrepreneurs and multinationals but show little appreciation for local political effectiveness. Furthermore they are optimistic towards the regions' prospects in Europe.

Notes

1   A good geographical analysis of the prefecture can be found in the *Report to the School of National Defence* by the then prefect S. Tsirkas (1975).
2   In interviews with Chania prefecture economic specialists it was noted that although in individual infrastructural projects there is a requirement for a feasibility study there is no overall development plan linking smaller projects and assessing their collective impact (Chania, July 1990 and September 1991).
3   Statistics on industrial plant size are found in *Epilogi*, August 1991, pp.44–6.
4   An extensive analysis on the state of the tourist economy in Crete is given in a special section on 'Crete and Tourism' of *Tourismos ke Oikonomia* [Tourism and Economy Monthly], No. 151, June 1991, pp.94–146.
5   A number of studies have been published on the impact of the Greek accession to the EC. Most of the early ones foresee difficulties but point to balance of payment benefits (Drakos, 1986; Kefalas, 1986; Manassakis, 1986), or see relatively limited effects (Tzoannos, 1986;

Van Frausum, 1986). There is further a call for structural changes in the Greek economy or even a need for '... the modernisation of political and institutional structures as a precondition for their successful participation in a new, more competitive environment' (Tsoukalis, 1991, p.302).

6   For a discussion of eliteness and elite functions see Welsh (ch. 8, 1979).

7   The relevant Spearman correlation coefficient confirms this strong association exhibiting a value of 0.689 (sig. 0.001).

8   The need for decentralisation and the perceived 'gross inefficiency' of the Greek state to address the problems of the locality was a prevalent theme of almost all interviews with prefecture and development agency representatives in the region. (Interviews in the summer of 1990 and 1991)

9   A high association between the two variables with a Spearman correlation coefficient value of 0.447 (sig. 0.374) for executives and a value of -0.408 (sig. 0.188) for entrepreneurs. Apparently executives relate more SMEs with a positive development for their firm, while entrepreneurs with a negative development.

10   The Spearman correlation coefficient has a value of -0.305 (sig. 0.191), which points to a moderately high association between an attitude that SMEs are related to a devolved economy and that business hold a negative view on autonomy.

11   This association is not as pronounced in the relevant statistics since the value of the Spearman correlation coefficient is only 0.182 (sig. 0.431).

12   The electoral system for the European elections allows for one national list of representatives from each party. In that sense there are no MEPs that stand in Crete alone. There are a number of MEPs however who have their political roots on the island. Because of the difference in the electoral systems and the wording of the Greek translation to this question, there are limits in our ability to cross-reference this question with answers from the Scottish sample.

13   Participation in political life is here given the characterisation 'forced' exactly because of the totality in which the state is geared to serve the political machine. Clientelism is a facet of citizens everyday interaction with the state machine, particularly so in remote provinces like Crete. See Mouzelis (1987), Christopoulos (1998) and Lyrintzis (1984).

14   The only strong association between the three attitudes exists between questions QB11 and QB13. The Spearman correlation coefficient has a value of 0.545 (sig. 0.019), suggesting that those respondents that found Councillors more fervent also found them to be more receptive and vice versa.

15   The Spearman correlation coefficient for this relationship has a value of -0.226 (sig. 0.324) which gives a mild association between a dynamic view of the Council and receptiveness of local Councillors.

16   A high Spearman correlation coefficient of 0.630 (sig. 0.002) points to the high association between answers in the two questions.

17   Cretan political customs are investigated by Hertzfeld (1985), while an insight into modern Greek political history is provided by Woodhouse (1968) and Clogg (1986).

18   A characteristic remark was 'the lone sheep is eaten by the wolf'. There are no recent claims on Crete from Turkey, but for the sample interviewed the danger appeared very real. It could be explained in part from the long fight of the Cretans to free the island of Ottoman rule, which was only achieved in the latter part of the nineteenth century.

19   Independence from Greece has never been a goal presented by any party in the regional or national level. It has been voiced however as a fringe movement of autonomy at various times.

20 Indeed many federalists, Altiero Spinneli (1972a) among others, argue exactly the opposite.
21 Note should be made that bureaucrats perspective could be closer to calls for deconcentration rather than decentralisation or devolution.
22 Details of estimates of net expenditure by the Greek state are given in the earlier analysis of economic conditions in Crete. The most important result of that analysis is that Crete is a net contributor to the state, although its regional per capita income is below the Greek average.
23 A weak Spearman correlation coefficient of 0.150 (sig. 0.609) points to the 'problematic' association between the two questions.
24 A comparatively strong Spearman correlation coefficient of 0.365 (sig. 0.243) points to the strong association between the two variables.
25 The very high Spearman correlation of 0.837 (sig. 0.000) points to the very high association between the two facets of this issue for Cretan interviewees.
26 A Spearman correlation coefficients of 0.519 (sig. 0.057) points to a higher correlation between sources of capital and skill than sources of capital and a company's base of operations (coefficient at 0.351, sig. 0.218).
27 The Spearman correlation coefficient (questions QD2 and QC5) being rather moderate at 0.230 (sig. 0.427) I have to assume that there is no overall association between the two variables.
28 There is a strong negative association (questions QD2 and QC7) with the relevant Spearman correlation coefficient taking a value of -0.382 (sig. 0.178) supporting the assumption that multinationals are linked with support of out of region capital.
29 A Spearman correlation coefficient of -0.405 (sig. 0.192) points to a strong association between preference for MPs and a belief that the region is better off than the nation.
30 The implementation problems of the Integrated Mediterranean Programmes in Greece is covered by Papageorgiou and Verney (Papageorgiou, 1992), while a general critique is given by Bianchi, (1992).
31 A Spearman correlation coefficient of -0.028 (sig. 0.923) points to no association in the way respondents replied between the two questions.
32 There is a mild statistical association between the two variables since a Spearman correlation coefficient takes a value of 0.245 (sig. 0.442).
33 This relationship attains a Spearman correlation coefficient value of -0.258 (sig. 0.418) which points to a mild association between on the one hand having been lobbied themselves and MPs receiving most of the lobbying.
34 A very high Spearman correlation coefficient of 0.751 (sig. 0.002) signifies the strong link between their perceptions of the regional and national economies, which are considered highly intertwined.
35 The Spearman correlation coefficient denotes a low statistical association (questions QC4 and QC7) at a value of 0.162 (sig. 0.579).

Chapter Six

The Prospect of Devolution

Elite Attitudes: The Broader Picture

In this chapter I initially explore the relationship between regional elites' perceptions of Councillors and elites' aspirations to autonomy. I use a composite indicator of elites' aspirations to autonomy. This entails certain limitations since this is an index of nominal rank between elite groups. So, inferences made, are limited by the nominal character of this index.

I proceed by investigating the proposition that elite attitudes on devolution have an effect on the perceptions of business prospects in a region. In this context I employ a number of working hypotheses that examine among others perceptions of importance for SMEs among political actors. The inclusion of this variable is considered imperative since SMEs have been considered essential to regional development and, some argue, to regional autonomy.[1]

In the latter part of this chapter the analysis becomes exploratory. I attempt an investigation of whether concordance of attitudes between political and business elites in a region affects regional growth prospects. This hypothesis has been an integral part of the exercise at the beginning of this research effort. Very early in the operationalisation process it became apparent that proof for such a hypothesis was beyond the resources available. Instead of dismissing it however, I have proceeded with an exploratory analysis. This is done in order to use the great wealth of data collected that pertain to this hypothesis. Hopefully, this effort may be instructive to a course of future research.

Perceptions of Regional Elites: The Effect of Aspirations to Autonomy

The main hypothesis examined here is whether:

H 1: attitudes towards regional political actors vary according to an elite's region of origin.

I refine this theme by using two working hypotheses. There is an attempt to provide an indication of whether the region of origin of the two political and business elites' influence their perceptions of regional political elites. It is of course the case that the evidence presented here will not necessarily cover all possible intervening or antecedent variables. To put it differently, there are a number of other reasons, beyond their different region of origin, that could be the cause of any observed variance between the two regional elites investigated. It is the case, however, that most variables, that could affect such a diversion in attitudes, have been identified and accounted for. I am also confident that the relationships identified are real and that the logical sequence connecting them is causal.

So, the question arises of qualifying the interaction between business and political elites:

Working hypothesis (WH): elite businessmen perceive the regional political elites to be more receptive to them than the national political elites.

This is a test of whether the independent variable level of political representation affects the dependent variable of perceived receptiveness of politicians to businessmen in their area. The assumption of the working hypothesis is that local politicians will be more receptive than national politicians to the local business elite.

Possibly the interlockingness between the business and political elites in the two regions could be the most significant intervening variable. From an analysis of the data as covered in chapters preceding I conclude that there is limited interlockingness. In the case of the Cretan political elites 50 per cent declare some business interests holding at least 1 per cent equity in one of the local companies 18 per cent of the Scottish sample make the same assertion. Businessmen on the other hand were vetted for their political activities and when found to have some function in the political community, were placed in the political elite category.[2] To put it plainly, businessmen in the sample cannot have a political function and the only effects of interlockingness exist to the degree that political elites have a prominent business function, which is not the case for the present sample.

It is also possible to consider the intervening effect of stronger clientelistic ties, in the relationship between the regional political and regional business elites, than between the national political and regional business elites.[3] Having a very small national sub-sample (consisting of three cases) in the Strathclyde political elite and no national sub-sample in the Cretan political elite it is impossible to comprehensively examine such a premise. From evidence presented earlier however it is apparent that businessmen in Strathclyde and Crete seldom lobby the local political elites.[4] From their questionnaire replies it emerges that 67 per cent of the Strathclyde and 75 per cent of the Cretan local politicians declared that they have not been lobbied by businessmen. By comparison all of the local MPs and MEPs in Strathclyde declared they have been lobbied by local businessmen.

To investigate this hypothesis I proceed by examining for replies to question QB13, which inquired on how receptive businessmen found regional elected representatives compared with MPs. Using the respondents' respective region of origin as a criterion of comparison, I identify a difference in the pattern of replies of the Scottish and Cretan businessmen.

Strathclyde business personalities thought the local and national politicians in their region to be equally receptive to their views. Cretan businessmen tended to find local politicians receptive more often, as 55 per cent said local Councillors were 'more' or 'much more' receptive; this compares with 32 per cent of the Strathclyde sample that had the same position.

In order to understand which subgroups of the respective elites support or refute the relevant hypothesis I control for their respective rank. This measure subdivides the business elites into three categories: a) the small business owners; b) the business managers; and c) the directors.

Table 6.1   Receptiveness of Councillors collapsed and controlled for categories rank and ID

Elite identification by rank and ID	Councillors are more receptive	Councillors are equally receptive	Councillors are less receptive
Cretan small business owners	29%	29%	42%
Strathclyde business managers	67%	–	33%
Cretan business managers	100%	–	–
Strathclyde business directors	26%	53%	21%
Cretan business directors	50%	33%	17%

Note: Responses to the question: 'How receptive do you think regional Councillors are to your views compared with Members of Parliament?'

Members of group a claimed that national politicians were equally or more receptive by a margin of 71 per cent. Managers in both Crete and Scotland would strongly support the premise that regional Councillors are more receptive than MPs. The bias, against local Councillors' receptiveness, can be traced to the group of directors in the two regions.

Directors in Strathclyde were symmetrically centred around the equally receptive option for which 53 per cent of their subgroup opted. Cretan directors were more appreciative of regional representatives' receptiveness, 42 per cent claiming they found them much more receptive.

A possible explanation for this difference could lie with the difference respondents gave to question QB6 in which 62 per cent of the Scottish business elites declared they did not know their regional elected representative, compared with a unanimous Cretan business sample who claimed they knew their local elected representative. Such a discrepancy could lead to the assumption that in the *comparatively* devolved region of Strathclyde, regional politicians are held in lower esteem among the local business elites than in the nationally controlled prefecture of Chania, where all businessmen know the local politicians and consider them rather receptive.

The construction and tests for this working hypothesis were based on the assumption that regional political elites possess a more accurate mental map of their constituency than national political elites.[5] It has not been possible to test this assumption as such but the working hypothesis tested should provide an indication that this may indeed be the case. Both business elites seemed to be in support of the premise if a control was applied for replies from the business directors subgroup. So, evidence analysed up to this point, supports the premise of the working hypothesis.

The analysis, so far, has concentrated on quantitative evidence of a receptiveness of the political elites, as viewed by businessmen. I proceed with an examination and analysis of their qualitative replies in the survey.

In the examination of replies to the question of receptiveness there are two trends among Cretan businessmen. According to the first prevailing view 'Councillors do not count'[6] and 'local Councillors are ornamental and bear little weight'.[7] This attitude ties in with the prevalent view that 'an MP can do a lot'[8] which points to strong existing clientelistic relationships of local businessmen with MPs. The opposite view among Cretan businessmen was that Councillors have been receptive 'within the last decade' [9] and they are more receptive than MPs 'relative to their [limited] contribution'.[10]

Scottish businessmen have an almost uniform appreciation of local Councillors' work, with some reservations however. They think Councillors are 'receptive enough but have no clout'[11] or that 'regional Councillors being in opposition are more receptive'.[12] Overall their view is rather positive as they claim that 'Councillors pay more heed'[13] to them.

From this exposition the pattern of businessmen's perceptions suggest that Councillors in Chania have no real clout and are held in low esteem, while MPs are perceived to hold the levers of power. In Strathclyde businessmen think that Councillors pay more heed to them, providing indications of a high level of interaction with the local political elite, who in turn appear to play a more integral part in the political process.

Comparing the response patterns from the quantitative and the qualitative elements, it is immediately evident there is a dichotomy between businessmen's perceived receptiveness of regional political elites (high in the case of Cretan businessmen and low in the case of Strathclyde businessmen) and the esteem in which they are held. Cretan businessmen believe Councillors are more receptive but at the same time, that they have no clout. Strathclyde businessmen believe Councillors are not as receptive as MPs but seem to pay more heed to them. This leads me to a conditional acceptance of the working hypothesis since businessmen perceive regional elites to be more receptive than national political elites. There is evidence that the two business elites have a different perspective on regional politicians' receptiveness.

In the next working hypothesis the premise that regional politicians have a longer term perspective and the economic interests of the region more at heart is given further consideration when I inquire whether:

WH: regional politicians will be perceived to favour long term economic policies in the region more than national politicians.

The dependent variable here is the perceived commitment of regional political elites to regional welfare. The level of representation of the two political elites is expected to affect their perceived commitment to their region.

Replies to this working hypothesis could be conceivably affected by elites' educational level but since this variable was considered 'intrusive' for some elites it has not been included in the questionnaire and cannot be controlled for. My personal estimate of the literacy level of the two political elite samples is that Cretan politicians seemed less educated in regard to standard qualifications, but as worldly as the Strathclyde politicians, a good number of the latter apparently possessing higher academic qualifications.[14]

Another variable that has to be considered is the possibility that regional political elites are not, by definition, considered relevant to macroeconomic planning. This could be true particularly in the case of the Cretan sample where the local government had very limited powers since the unification of the island with mainland Greece.[15] The particular question inquires whether local or national politicians have a longer term perspective when proposing policy. I believe that such an antecedent variable will only become relevant if there is a genuine bias against the local political elites, a matter which to an extent is investigated within the following analysis.

The basic premise of this working hypothesis holds true for the Scottish political elite who appear to support the proposition that regional politicians and MEPs have a longer term perspective than MPs when proposing economic policy. Replies of the Cretan political elite diverge from the Scottish pattern of replies in that they believe national and European elected representatives have a longer term perspective than regional representatives. A full analysis of their replies is given in Table 6.2.

Differences in the opinions of the two groups could be related to Greek elites' low esteem for local authorities. This I understand as an attitude stemming from the limited competence of regional political elites in Greece.[16]

The breakdown by occupational category (variable Rank) of the elite replies reveals some trends that are interesting and can elucidate the analysis

Table 6.2   Analysis of replies on long-term perspective controlling for political elites' identification by rank

Elite identification by rank	Elite preference for		
	Regional representatives	MPs	MEPs
Strathclyde activists/ administrators	–	–	3
Strathclyde City Councillors	1	–	1
Strathclyde Regional Councillors	3	–	2
Strathclyde Members of Parliament	–	1	–
Strathclyde Members of European Parliament	–	–	1
Cretan Presidents of local communities	1	2	1
Cretan City Councillors	–	2	1
Cretan Mayors	–	–	3
Cretan activists/administrators	–	2	–

Notes

1   Question: which of the following do you believe have a longer term perspective when proposing economic policy: regional, national or European representatives?
2   Number of respondents replying is 24, missing values (comprising 'do not know' or refusals to reply) equal 13 cases.

further. Councillors in the Scottish sample are almost equally split between supporting the view that it is either themselves or MEPs that have the interest of the region more at heart. In the Cretan sample it seems that Councillors believe it is MPs who have a longer term perspective, while all Mayors in Greece seem to think that it is MEPs who have the longer term perspective.

In the interpretation of replies of the Cretan elite I can only assume that the antecedent variable of perceived competencies of the local elites affects respondents replies. This view is reinforced since there is a high indication of regional grievance towards the national government. The Cretan political elite has been earlier identified as the one with the highest grievance indicator towards their national government. Local politicians see the national politicians not as having the interest of the region more at heart but probably as more competent in macroeconomic policy (which presumably is beyond their reach). It is also possible that the question used forms an inadequate measure for the Cretan sample, given their assumed lower educational level as compared with the Scottish sample.

Having completed the first level of analysis (for quantitative data) I can only conditionally accept the premise that 'regional politicians are perceived to favour long term policies' and that to hold only for the Strathclyde political elite. Qualitative data should further elucidate Cretan sample results. An examination of politicians' perspective on whether regional, national or European representatives have a longer term perspective effectively inquires which political elite subgroup respondents hold in higher esteem.

The Cretan respondents, belonging to the regional elite themselves, had a very low esteem for the local elite. This is apparent in the support for the national and European political representatives. They exhibited a very high esteem for MPs' role attesting that 'MPs will be elected and re-elected, they do not have just a four year perspective',[17] while 'MPs have the growth prospects of the region more at heart, while MEPs cannot focus on the region'.[18] Views on MEPs where consequently split between a mildly negative view that 'we do not know what the MEPs are doing'[19] to the more positive 'MEPs living in Brussels have a wider perspective'.[20] Very few took the view that 'the local Councillor has a stronger interest [in the region] than anybody else'[21] while the attitude that Councillors 'have a very limited perspective'[22] was prevalent.

Strathclyde politicians took a rather different approach to MPs' contribution to the region. They claimed that 'MPs are led by short-termism',[23] while 'strategic plans are produced by the regional Council, MPs do not have a regional impact'.[24] This support for the Council was not as readily converted into support for the regional Councillors however, since 'long-term planning is done by the Council but it does not concern the Councillors'.[25] MEPs received more uniform support, expressed as a belief that 'MEPs have a strategic view'[26] and particularly since 'the economies of Europe are tied-up [together]'.[27]

From this evidence it becomes apparent that the two political elites have a very different perspective. Cretan politicians seem to hold MPs in very high esteem, while showing an equivocal opinion on MEPs. Strathclyde politicians seem to have a very negative opinion of MPs while holding a uniformly positive opinion of MEPs.

Regarding their perceptions of the regional elites, the Cretan political elite seems to hold Councillors in very low esteem, while the Strathclyde political elite has a rather good opinion of Councillors.

Analysis of their qualifications reinforces the initial quantitative analysis between the political elites. It becomes apparent that on the present evidence the working hypothesis holds true for the Cretan elite. Qualitative replies also elucidate the reasons behind the Cretan opinion to be based on the low level of competencies of regional elites.

On the evidence from the two working hypotheses examined, it becomes obvious that the two regional elites have a distinctly different pattern of reply. It appears, as well, that their different origin has a relevance to the pattern of replies they have. To that effect I accept hypothesis *H I* as true for this sample. Their region of origin seems to be relevant to the way an elite perceives their respective regional political elites.

As is further evident from analysing the qualitative data, the varying level of devolution (or decentralisation) of the two regions can have an effect on elite perceptions.[28] It can be argued that the low competence of Cretan political elites is the actual cause of their perceived low receptiveness to businessmen. Furthermore elite replies show a remarkable covariation with the intervening variable of positive attitudes towards regional autonomy (Table 6.3).

The two elite groups with the highest positive attitude towards regional autonomy have the best opinion of regional Councillors. Strathclyde businessmen and Cretan politicians who hold Councillors at the lowest esteem also have the least positive attitudes towards regional autonomy. I have to assume on the basis of this evidence that aspirations to autonomy have an effect on perceptions of regional political elites receptiveness and their long-term commitment to their region.

Consideration should be given to the unlikely possibility that perceptions of regional elites is the independent variable, having an effect on aspirations

Table 6.3 **Comparison of the way regional political elites are perceived and regional elites positive attitudes towards regional autonomy**

Elite identification	Composite index: aspirations to autonomy	Perceptions of Councillors' performance
Strathclyde politicians	35.4	Positive
Strathclyde businessmen	-19.7	Negative
Cretan politicians	8.3	Negative
Cretan businessmen	28.6	Positive

to autonomy. I am not able to discount that possibility totally, for lack of specific measures that can test the direction of this relationship. It is reasonable to assume, however, that in the belief system of regional elites issues of regional welfare and autonomy come before those of elites' attitudes on Councillors' performance as examined here.[29] If this hierarchy is valid then it is reasonable to assume that aspirations to regional autonomy must influence perceptions of regional elites.

Does the Level of Decentralisation Influence Growth Prospects?

It has been repeatedly suggested in editorials of the *Financial Times* that the prospect of devolution in Scotland would affect business confidence, by presuming that a tax yielding Scottish Parliament will be likely to increase business tax rates.[30] Whether this would be done to cover the increased costs of a devolved government or whether it would cover an increase in social welfare policies, the message had been clear. The British business press in the early 1990s suggested that business would be apprehensive of Scottish devolution. According to this view there was a link between the prospects of devolution in Scotland and business prospects for the region.

Elite attitudes on devolution could be considered relevant, in turn, since they are directly linked with the indicators of business confidence. It could also be the case that elite attitudes on devolution have a direct causal influence on the business prospects in a region by affecting business confidence, which is the next hypothesis investigated:

H II: Elite attitudes on devolution affect the perceptions of business prospects in a region.

Elite attitudes on devolution is considered as the independent variable, while business prospects in a region is the relevant dependent variable. In the examination of this hypothesis the assumption is made that the more similar business and political elites attitudes are, the higher the growth potential for that region. I am using this premise assuming it to hold true at this juncture, and examine it in detail at the next chapter.

My test will consider three working hypotheses in an analysis of quantitative data and then proceed with an exposition of qualitative replies that can give evidence of internal validity. I first examine whether:

WH: the level of devolution/decentralisation in a region influences perceptions of SMEs importance among regional elite groups.

Table 6.4   Future of SMEs in their region

	Do you foresee more SMEs (QB3)		Positive on more SMEs (QB4)		More SMEs lead to an economy more (QB5)	
	Yes	No	Yes	No	Devolved	Dependent
Strathclyde businessmen	*19*	*5*	*14*	*2*	*19*	*4*
	79%	21%	87%	13%	83%	17%
Cretan businessmen	*12*	*8*	*15*	*4*	*13*	*4*
	60%	40%	79%	21%	76%	24%

Notes

1   Question QB3: do you foresee the development of more small-medium enterprises in your region?
2   Question QB4: will such a development create a positive environment for your firm?
3   Question QB5: do you think that a shift in the economy towards small-medium enterprises will aid in the creation of: a) a more devolved economy; or b) a rather dependent economy?

For this working hypothesis the level of devolution between the two regions investigated is the independent variable while the perceived importance of SMEs to the regional economy is the dependent variable. Effectively replies between elites of the two regions will be compared in relation to their attitudes towards SMEs importance. In this working hypothesis I have made the assumption that a higher level of devolution is linked to a stronger trust in SMEs and local entrepreneurs as compared with MNL enterprises.[31]

Table 6.5   Spearman correlation coefficients matrix for business elites' replies on the future of SMEs

	Scottish	Cretan	Scottish	Cretan
QB4	0.429	-0.152		
	sig 0.098	sig 0.546		
QB5	0.314	-0.119	0.423	0.464
	sig 0.144	sig 0.629	sig 0.116	sig 0.052
	QB3		QB4	

Note: As with other association statistics in this survey issues of validity limit the inferential value of these figures. The 'negative' category is collapsed with the 'do not know' category to facilitate correlations.

Table 6.6   Confidence on SMEs vs. multinational enterprises

	Question QC4 Prosperity depends on:		Question QC5 SMEs likely to:		Question QC7 MNLs likely to:	
	Local	MNLs	Stay	Go	Stay	Go
Strathclyde politicians	*8*	*7*	*14*	*1*	*2*	*10*
	53%	47%	93%	7%	17%	83%
Cretan politicians	*9*	*5*	*13*	–	*7*	*5*
	64%	36%	100%	–	58%	42%

Notes

1   Question QC4: do you believe your region's prosperity depends more on: a) local entrepreneurs; or b) companies with headquarters outside the region?
2   Question QC5: in the case of a recession do you believe small-medium sized business that will survive the recession are more likely to maintain operations in your region or shift to another region?
3   Question QC7: in the case of a recession, do you believe multinational business are more likely to maintain operations in your region, or shift to another region?

To test this working hypothesis I compare respondents' replies specific to the business and political elites. Questions inquiring on the importance of SMEs to the regional economy (QB3, QB4, QB5, QC4, QC5, QC7) were cross-tabulated controlling for the respondents region of origin. This is a comparison of the distribution of replies between the elite groups of the more devolved Scotland and the less devolved Crete.

As becomes apparent, from the examination of Tables 6.4 and 6.6, there is no significant difference in the distribution of replies to the questions investigated, between the regional elites. There are some differences in the correlation coefficients (Tables 6.5 and 6.7) which could be relevant to a different perception of development among the elite groups and possibly between the two regions.

Table 6.7   Spearman correlation coefficient matrix confidence on SMEs vs. multinationals

	Scottish	Cretan	Scottish	Cretan
QC5	0.037	0.372	–	–
	sig 0.889	sig 0.190	–	–
QC7	0.075	0.162	0.571	0.452
	sig 0.782	sig 0.579	sig 0.021	sig 0.104
	QC4		QC5	

Note: The standard qualifications on validity considerations apply here as well. The Negative category is collapsed with the 'do not know' category to facilitate correlations.

The higher value of the Cretan from the Strathclyde political elites correlation coefficient for questions implying confidence on local companies (Table 6.7) can be related to the Cretans' stronger support for local entrepreneurs, rather than MNL enterprises.

The difference between the two political elites' distribution of replies on the question of whether MNLs are likely to 'abandon' the region in the case of a recession is the most pronounced one. This I believe is relevant to the different experiences of industrialisation between the two regions, which makes the Strathclyde politicians more sceptical on the role of MNLs.

The Scottish business elites' high values on correlations on the questions examined at Table 6.5, relate to their positive attitude on the impact of SMEs on devolution (QB5), while they also tend to believe that more SMEs will be positive for their firm (QB4). An opposite attitude pattern is true for the Cretan businessmen, who relate more SMEs (QB3) with a negative competitive environment for their own business (QB4), and believe SMEs make a region more dependent on outside imports (QB5).

The pattern of elites replies, although divergent, does not follow the pattern assumed by the working hypothesis. The Scottish businessmen, by exhibiting more trust, and the Cretan businessmen, by being more apprehensive of SMEs, broadly abide by the assumption of the premise. The Cretan politicians, by their unconditional support, and the Strathclyde politicians by holding an equivocal position do not support the premise. With the measures employed so far, my assumption of trust of SMEs and distrust of MNLs in those regions that have a higher level of devolution cannot be supported. The argument could further be put forward, that existing elites in power will not want a change that could have an effect on the status quo. If this is the case it can be also argued that the particular elites interviewed are the least likely ones to want to instigate any such change.[32]

It could be true as well that, my categorisation of Strathclyde as more devolved than the prefecture of Chania, (although reasonable taking account of the respective regional competencies), may not concur with relative local views of the political system. For this reason I have used indirect measures by asking questions on SMEs and not on autonomy, in order to guarantee minimum bias on their replies. It could still be the case, however unlikely, that their perception of the degree of regional devolution in their region is in relative terms lower from that of Cretan elites.

In conclusion it is apparent that, although SMEs and regional entrepreneurs will be trusted more than MNLs in both samples, the pattern of their replies does not follow the one anticipated by the working hypothesis. Consequently, differences in attitudes between the elite groups in the two regions cannot be ascribed to the different level of devolution/decentralisation between the two regions. Which leads me to reject the working hypothesis based on the quantitative evidence and proceed to examine the qualitative replies of interviewees.

In the case of business interviewees there is no apparent difference on the qualifications they provide to their responses on the future of MNLS and SMEs in their region. The only minor difference was in replies to whether respondents foresee the development of more SMEs, in which the Cretan respondents seemed more preoccupied with such a scenario. Typical responses centred around the theme of a market with a high level of competition where 'the market is saturated'[33] and 'there is no space [for further SMEs developing]'.[34] This slight divergence of Cretan businessmen is understandable as they see the development of more SMEs as a direct threat to their own livelihood.[35]

In the case of the political elite groups the only variation in their replies can be traced to the question inquiring on the likelihood of MNL enterprises to go or stay. Beyond the fact that the issue investigated is marginal to the working hypothesis, apparent differences can be traced to the different experiences of industrialisation between the two regions. In the Cretan case the prevalent view was that '[MNLs] will not go because they are currently developing the [Cretan] market';[36] while in the case of Strathclyde elites the predominant view is that 'multinationals have branch plants externally controlled in the region'.[37] I take this difference in perspective to point to the significant difference in attitudes towards multinationals. It should be noted as well that, there is an underlying distrust in statements on MNLs activities from both elite groups.[38]

So the qualitative data analysis, by not adding any significant insights in the similarities or disparities of opinion between elite groups, leaves the analysis inconclusive relating to the working hypothesis. The possibility that perceptions of the level of devolution are more important than a quantifiable categorisation of devolution make any results in this working hypothesis tentative. It is further the case that attitudes of two regional elites support and two refute the premise. This indicates that it is not the level of devolution, but the perceived level of devolution, that affects elite responses.[39] This consequently has a bearing on the subsequent working hypothesis. The next premise examined is that:

WH: Those regional elites that aspire to more autonomous rule will be more positive on SME prospects in their region.

Here I attempt to introduce a measure for the regional elites aspirations to devolution. This becomes the independent variable with the importance elites place on SMEs, as the dependent variable. As with the preceding working hypothesis I have retained the assumption here that aspirations of elites to regional autonomy are linked with a trust of local entrepreneurs and SMEs and a distrust of MNLs.

To proceed with a test of this working hypothesis I employed a measure of devolutionary aspirations that applies to all four elite subgroups. To that effect I have constructed a composite index on a regional elites' positive attitudes towards regional autonomy. This will provide the basic measure I will use here. This measure employs replies to questions inquiring whether macroeconomic policies should be controlled at the regional, national or international level, whether federalism in Europe is viable and whether respondents believe business perceive autonomy positively.

In Table 6.6 pertaining to the political subgroups, there is strong evidence that the working hypothesis is supported by the data. In the question that inquires whether SMEs that survive a recession where likely to stay in their region 93 per cent of the Scottish and 100 per cent of the Cretan sample that gave an answer replied in the affirmative.[40] Responding to whether they believe regional prosperity depends more on local entrepreneurs or MNLs their replies show a trust for local entrepreneurs which is as high as 53 per cent for the Scottish and 64 per cent in the Cretan regional politicians.[41] This underlies their trust of SMEs which almost by definition are local. It would also be the case that for this particular question even a weak support for local entrepreneurs would be considered important since it would go against the popular wisdom of big MNLs being perceived as the driving force of growth.[42] The two business elite groups have replies that are concordant with each other on the particular issue of SMEs' importance and prospects, as demonstrated in Table 6.4. More specifically, 79 per cent of the Scottish business elite foresee the development of more SMEs in their region, while 88 per cent believe that such a development will be good for their own business. In the Cretan sample 60 per cent of respondents declared they foresee the development of more SMEs while 79 per cent believed this will be positive for their own firm.

Table 6.8   Elite attitudes towards SMEs compared with their attitudes towards regional autonomy and their anticipated attitudes as hypothesised

	Composite measure on regional autonomy direction and value	Recorded attitudes on SMEs (QB3, QB4, QC4, QC5)	Hypothesised attitudes on SMEs
Strathclyde politicians	Positive 35.4	Positive	Positive
Strathclyde businessmen	Negative -19.7	Positive	Negative
Cretan politicians	Neutral 8.3	Positive	Neutral
Cretan businessmen	Positive 28.6	Positive	Positive

Notes

1   The construction of the composite measures is covered on the next chapter.
2   Question QB3: do you foresee the development of more SMEs in your region?
3   Question QB4: will such a development create a positive environment for your firm?
4   Question QC4: do you believe your region's prosperity depends more on local entrepreneurs or companies with headquarters outside the region?
5   Question QC5: in the case of a recession do you believe SMEs that will survive the recession are more likely to maintain operations in your region or shift to another region?

A further test for the business elites perceptions is a comparison in their replies as analysed in Table 6.4. Cross-tabulations show that 83 per cent of the Scottish and 76 per cent of the Cretan business elites believe that a shift in the economy towards SMEs will lead to a more devolved and autonomous economy. This control proves that businessmen recognise a power in SMEs to 'generate autonomy' and at the same time have a positive opinion about them. This result is significant if it is combined with the Strathclyde elites' perceived hostility towards regional autonomy and contradicts earlier assumptions of this working hypothesis.

To provide a final test for the working hypothesis I compare elite attitudes towards SMEs with their attitudes on regional autonomy in Table 6.8. It is apparent that for two of the elite groups the relationship holds true and for two of them it does not. It could be argued that attitudes on SMEs are not related with regional autonomy and that is why the results are inconclusive. The evidence here suggests that a great percentage of the business sample believe that autonomy and SMEs are related.

According to the working hypothesis, elites that are more positive towards regional autonomy are going to be more positive towards SMEs' prospects. In Table 6.9 I look at how responses of the two political and the two business elites compare.

Table 6.9   Expected and observed affirmative responses

Expected according to the working hypothesis	Observed %
QC4 SCOT.POL.> CRET. POL.	53% < 64%
QC5 SCOT.POL.> CRET. POL.	93% < 100%
QB3 CRET.BUS.> SCOT.BUS.	60% < 79%
QB4 CRET.BUS.> SCOT.BUS.	79% < 88%

Note: Spearman correlation coefficients between these variables are presented in table 6.5 and table 6.7.

In all relationships that could be investigated with the present data the observed relationship has an opposite direction from the expected one according to the working hypothesis. It is the case as well that the evidence is weaker for the political and stronger for the business elites. This result by implying a weak association leads me to an exploration of the alternative rival working hypothesis (AWH) that:

AWH: those regional elites that aspire to more autonomous rule will be more negative on the prospects of SMEs in their region.

On a review of the qualitative replies of the business elites it becomes immediately apparent that most respondents share a great concern over SMEs future in their region. Cretan businessmen say that 'SMEs are closing'[43] and 'they need greater state support'.[44] While Strathclyde businessmen claimed that more SMEs 'increase our potential customer base'[45] but that their increased numbers 'might pose competition'.[46] At the same time a Cretan executive claimed that 'a big corporation needs many SMEs in its environment'[47] and a Strathclyde executive claimed that 'there is a relation between SMEs and economic growth'.[48] Overall evidence suggests that Cretan businessmen are rather negative on SMEs' prospects while Strathclyde businessmen, by contrast are rather positive.

The political elites in Crete claimed that 'if the local entrepreneurs invest, we don't need outside investors at all'[49] while also stating that the future of the region depended 'mainly on local businessmen who are involved in tourism'[50]. The Strathclyde politicians claimed that 'the prospects are not good [since there is] no strong entrepreneurial spirit',[51] also claiming that 'local entrepreneurs [will be important] in the long term'.[52] Apparently the Strathclyde politicians' perception of SMEs prospects is more negative than that of their Cretan counterparts.

Evidence from the qualitative analysis suggests that the alternative rival hypothesis is supported by the replies of elite groups. So, overall, the Cretan politicians were positive, while the businessmen were negative on SMEs' prospects. The Strathclyde politicians were negative, while the businessmen were positive on SMEs' prospects for their region. These attitudes are discordant with their views on regional autonomy (index used in Table 6.8). This contradiction reinforces support for the alternative rival working hypothesis.

I finally examine whether:

WH: positive attitudes towards devolution in a region are related to a positive perception of business prospects for the region.

Respondents' attitudes towards devolution is the independent variable. This working hypothesis attempts to measure the existence of an effect of the independent variable on elite perceptions of the business prospects for a region. I have made the assumption that elites which are positive on devolution will be positive on the business prospects for their region. This assumption was based on the observation that 65 per cent of those who gave a positive reply on businesses perception of autonomy had a concordant reply on the preparedness of their region for 1992.[53] Effectively this test attempts an investigation of whether regional elites' business confidence relates to their devolutionary aspirations.

In a cross-tabulation of respondents' replies, between their perception of business concern over further devolution and their regions' competitive position, I found no apparent distribution variations between the political elites. The two variables appear unrelated for these subgroups.[54] This implies that either the measures used are inappropriate or that this relationship does not hold true for political elites. The reasons that this relationship cannot hold true for the political elites can be traced to a number of causes that are relevant to the particular samples. In the case of the Cretan political sample the fact that 86 per cent believe autonomy would not be perceived positively by business limits the potential for analysis. Similarly in the case of the Strathclyde political elite the fact that 88 per cent find the regional economy unprepared for the challenges of 1992 limits the relevant inferences that can be made about the relationship this hypothesis attempts to investigate.

In examining the pattern of replies for the Cretan political elite I found a high degree of concordance in their replies to the two questions. They exhibit a high consistency in that 81 per cent of their replies are either negative on both or positive on both questions investigated. This I take as an indication of a degree of correlation between the two questions, even if their frequency distributions reveal no apparent patterns.[55]

Inevitably I have to conclude, however, that for the measures at my disposal, no inferences can be made about the political elites. From the analysis of data for the business elites, a relationship becomes evident which is summarised in Table 6.10. The business elites in Crete confirmed my initial assumption that a positive view of higher devolution is related to a positive view of regional prospects. The Scottish business elite however, showed a different pattern of replies, since most of those believing that business would perceive autonomy positively also stated that their region is not prepared for 1992.[56] Overall, the evidence is stronger in the case of the Cretan businessmen and inconclusive in the case of the Scottish businessmen.

This response pattern is sustained when analysing respondents' views on whether macroeconomic policies should be controlled at the regional, national or international level, cross-tabulated with their replies on the preparedness of the regional economy for 1992. Again a similar pattern between the two business elites emerges. Scottish businessmen are divided into two groups. Those that believe macroeconomics should be controlled at the national level and tend to be pessimistic about the region's prospects in 1992. And those believing that macroeconomics should be controlled at the international level, are also more likely to believe that their region is comparatively prepared. Cretan businessmen tend to again take a contrasting perspective. Most of those that believe macroeconomics should be controlled at the regional level being more likely to believe that their region is comparatively prepared, while most of those believing macroeconomics should belong to the international domain also believing that their region is not prepared.

Table 6.10 Regional business elites' collapsed responses between views on autonomy and regional competitiveness

QD6 by QD1	Strathclyde businessmen		Cretan businessmen	
	Business positive on autonomy	Business negative on autonomy	Business positive on autonomy	Business negative on autonomy
Region not prepared	5	8	2	12
Region prepared	2	5	4	2
Region well prepared	–	1	–	–

Notes

1 Question QD1: do you believe that if your region were to become more autonomous business would perceive this as a generally positive development?
2 Question QD6: do you believe that the Strathclyde/Cretan economy is ready for the 1992 competition challenge?
3 Refusals to reply and 'do not know' answers accounted for three cases in the Strathclyde and three cases in the Cretan sample.

I could thus divide the Scottish business elite sample into two main groups. Those that believed their region was prepared for 1992 tended to have a negative view on business perception of autonomy and at the same time believed macroeconomics should be controlled at the international level. Those that believed their region was not prepared for 1992 also believed business had a positive view of autonomy and that macroeconomics should be controlled at the national level. The Cretan business elite can also be divided into two main subgroups. Those that had a positive view of the preparedness of their region towards 1992 also tend to believe business will view autonomy positively and that macroeconomics should be controlled at the regional level. Those that had a negative view of the region's preparedness towards 1992 also believing business would perceive devolution negatively and supporting the view that macroeconomics should be controlled at the international level. It is apparent from the analysis, that there can be no irrefutable proof that the relationship between the two variables is true for the direction assumed in the beginning of the analysis. It is indeed possible that it is not attitudes on devolution that affect elites' perception of economic prospects, but economic prospects affecting devolutionary attitudes. The working hypothesis inquires into the existence of a relationship rather than its direction however, and therefore any strong indications to that effect will be considered adequate proof. Furthermore, employing a set of composite indexes there is evidence of the strong associations present. Table 6.11 demonstrates a comparison between attitudes on regional autonomy and regional competitiveness.

Table 6.11 Comparisons of views on competitiveness and autonomy

Elite identification	Regional autonomy (cumulative mean of Q1+Q2+QD1)	Preparedness towards 1992 (cumulative mean QD5+QD6)
Strathclyde politicians	35.4	-48.4
Strathclyde businessmen	-19.7	-39.6
Cretan politicians	8.3	-35.7
Cretan businessmen	28.6	-61.9

Note: The construction of these cumulative indexes is explained in the next chapter.

The two elite groups with the highest absolute scores on the measure of 'autonomy' and 'competitiveness' are the Strathclyde politicians and the Cretan businessmen. Both groups had the highest positive scores on the first and the most negative scores on the second. This could signify a relationship between a positive attitude for regional autonomy as linked with a negative attitude on economic preparedness. Strathclyde businessmen and Cretan politicians recorded comparatively modest scores for these measures.

This evidence is proof against the basic hypothesis that positive attitudes towards devolution are related to a positive perception of business prospects for a region. The evidence even warrants the creation of an alternative rival hypothesis on exactly the opposite premise that:

AWH: positive attitudes towards devolution in a region are related to a negative perception of business prospects for the region.

Since the analysis of the quantitative data support the alternative rival working hypothesis, qualitative replies are employed in order to provide a final test. From evidence so far, there seems to be a division of the elites I am investigating into two groups. The first group consists of the Strathclyde political elite and the Cretan business elite and their particular characteristic is their extremity of views on the issues of this working hypothesis. I will identify them as 'radical'. The second group consists of the Strathclyde business and the Cretan political elite who are more 'moderate' on the issues raised. On their qualitative replies on whether business perceive autonomy positively it becomes apparent that the 'radicals' have a stronger opinion on the issue. Strathclyde politicians say that business 'ought to be [positive on devolution but] they will not be',[57] while suggesting that 'business favours the status quo'.[58] At the same time Cretan businessmen suggest that 'maybe autonomy would be good if political and economic guarantees are given [by Greece]',[59] while showing apprehension that 'there is total dependence on the rest of Greece'.[60]

The 'moderate' elite groups had, overall, more balanced replies but at the same time shared similar concerns with their respective 'radical' counterparts. The Scottish business elite was rather negative on autonomy claiming that it will bring 'an increase in taxation'[61] and concern that 'in [the rest of] UK they will have a different attitude [towards devolution]'.[62] The Cretan political elite was split between those that claimed there was a great danger in autonomy by stating they will accept 'autonomy under no circumstances and for no reason'[63] and those that claimed that 'there exists [a high level of] sensitivity on the issue'.[64]

I proceed with an investigation of elite replies on whether the regional economy was ready for 1992. From the group of 'radicals' a Scottish politician claimed that '[regional elites did] not know what 1992 is',[65] while a Cretan businessman said that Crete was not prepared because 'the Greek economy is undisciplined'.[66] The concerns of the 'moderates' were not much different. A Strathclyde businessmen claimed that 'Scotland is in a recession for hundreds of years'[67] while another that 'Strathclyde is opening-up a regional route to Brussels'.[68] The Cretan politicians showed concern over the role of the national bureaucracy one of them claiming that the regional economy is not ready because 'the decision making is done in Athens and we have no direct connection with Brussels'.[69] As is evident, there are no apparent trends in elite replies. The same themes of distrust of the national bureaucracy for the Cretan and apprehension towards 1992 for the Strathclyde elites were eminent here as they were in their replies to earlier questions.

I hypothesise that one of the reasons that two elite groups seem moderate and two seem radical relates to their respective degree of acceptance of the status quo and their consequent propensity to initiate change. The two 'radical' elites have their own reasons for discontent. The Scottish regional politicians predominantly belong to the opposition parties, where they have been since 1979. They do not accept the UK government's interference, while they see its policies as disruptive and detrimental to their region.[70] The Cretan business elite is systematically hindered in its activities by a centralised and unresponsive national bureaucracy.[71] Both groups can foresee great benefits from change.

The 'moderate' elites have invested interests in the status quo, that are to an extend threatened by change. Strathclyde businessmen are alarmed by the prospect of devolution and higher taxes more than they are of increased competition from Europe.[72] Similarly, the prospect of autonomy[73] for the Cretan political elites is an *anathema* which contrasts with their understanding of the need of the region for devolution from Athens.[74] The two moderate elites are thus apprehensive of devolutionary change and the effect it may have to their elite position and benefits in their respective regions.

A comparative examination of the results in testing the three last working hypotheses gives a profile of the elites investigated relevant to their attitudes on devolution and their perceptions of business prospects for their region. In particular, the fact that the two regional elites come from regions with a different level of devolution for local government appears to have an equivocal impact on perceptions of SMEs importance; those regional elites that aspire to more autonomous rule will be more negative on the prospects of SMEs in their region; and positive attitudes towards devolution relate to a negative perception of business prospects in a region. It is apparent that for the case of the particular elite samples and regions there is evidence to support the hypothesis that there exists a relationship between attitudes on devolution and perceptions of business prospects. Finally it should be noted that the assumptions that support this research also limit its universality. Particularly relevant to the hypotheses presented here is that aspirations of higher devolution relate to expectations of higher prosperity and also that centralised national control of the local economy is perceived as inefficient.

Notes

1   References on the importance of SMEs for regional development can be found on a number of European Commission Documents (1989c, 1991a). Gerry Sweeney has argued that in regions where there are large firms 'there is a lower level of entrepreneurial vitality' (1987, p.21), while also claiming that 'autonomy in decision-making within a region ... supports entrepreneurial activity' (1987, p.124), which suggests that entrepreneurial vitality is positively related with the existence of decision making autonomy and negatively with the existence of multinationals. The role of local authorities in promoting SMEs seen as a measure of promoting endogenous growth is covered by a report of Nuttal (1986) for the Council of Europe. Coincidentally, it was one of the basic contentions of the Scottish National Party (SNP, 1992) that Scottish economic independence can be based on local firms and the development of local SMEs.

2   Exception to this rule was one distinguished Cretan businessman (Case 42), who was also a member of the City Council. The decision to include him in the business elite sample was taken because of his prominence in the business community.

3   It is interesting to examine the relevant bibliography on Greek patron-client political ties which includes articles by Sotiropoulos (1994), Kouvertaris and Dobratz (1984) and Lyrintzis (1984). They all point to strong and pervasive patronage ties that they relate to underdevelopment or political culture. The relation of centre vs. periphery, within the existing political structures, gets a mention only relating to the 'macro' level of international politics (Kouvertaris 1984, p.36). All commentators identify the highly centralised character of the Greek state, which is heavily politicised along party lines (Sotiropoulos, 1994, p.359). These studies do not specifically investigate the relationship between business and political elites or patronage networks between regional and national political elites. It is assumed that patronage networks are vertical with localities at the 'receiving' end of central political institutions patronage. See also Christopoulos (1998).

4   For a detailed anthropological account of a Cretan communities' perceptions of clientelism and patronage see Herzfeld (1985), while a very interesting account of an earlier study of a Greek pastoral communities' perceptions of clientelism is found in Cambell (1964). Work by Clapham (1982) and Gellner (1977) can be useful, by providing a typology with which to examine patron-client relations in the Mediterranean context.

5   A discussion on the assumptions I made regarding mental maps is given in chapter one, while a further analysis from the perspective of behavioural geography can be found in Gould and White (1986) and Gold (1980).

6   Case 45. Business manager. Date of interview: 24 September 1991.

7   Case 62. Business proprietor. Date of interview: 16 September 1991.

8   Case 51. Business proprietor. Date of interview: 16 September 1991.

9   Case 52. Managing director. Date of interview: 17 September 1991.

10   Case 54. Business proprietor. Date of interview: 17 September 1991.

11   Case 38. Managing director. Date of interview: 20 May 1991.

12   Case 26. Company chairman. Date of interview: 5 June 1991.

13   Case 27. Company director. Date of interview: 5 June 1991.

14   This is an intuitive assessment of their level of education.

15   The unification of Crete with mainland Greece took place in 1913 after a long series of revolts against Ottoman rule and a period of autonomy under the auspices of the Greek

monarchy (1898–1913). Hopkins (1977) and Woodhouse (1968) provide concise accounts of modern Cretan and Greek history.

16 It is also the case that in the period between the second world war and the 1967 coup d'etat, local authorities in Crete had very restricted competencies, while during the years of the dictatorship (1967–74) local authorities where effectively appointed, further discrediting the institution. Relevant analysis can be found in Featherstone and Katsoulas (1987) as well as Clogg (1986).

17 Case 75. City Councillor. Date of interview: 26 September 1991.

18 Case 68. City Councillor. Date of interview: 9 September 1991.

19 Case 64. President of local community. Date of interview: 26 September 1991.

20 Case 76. Mayor. Date of interview: 23 September 1991.

21 Case 66. President of local community. Date of interview: 25 September 1991.

22 Case 65. President of local community. Date of interview: 26 September 1991.

23 Case 1. Regional Councillor. Date of interview: 26–28 June 1991.

24 Case 5. Regional Councillor. Date of interview: 1 July 1991.

25 Case 11. Activist. Date of interview: 10 November 1991.

26 Case 16. Regional Councillor. Date of interview: 19 June 1991.

27 Case 10. Regional Councillor. Date of interview: 28 October 1991.

28 A very interesting case study analysis of devolution versus deconcentration in the decentralisation experience of some low income countries as given by Crook and Manor (1995).

29 The interrelationship of individuals' feelings and expectations with their environment is analysed in *Behavioural Geography* (Gold, 1980), while *Political Behaviour* (Jaros and Grant, 1974) has interesting insights into belief system attributes and the hierarchies of opinions, attitudes and belief systems. Under this typology I assign elites' perceptions on autonomy as part of their ideology and belief system, while their perceptions of Councillors performance belong to the 'inferior' opinion and attitude level (Kavanagh, 1983, pp.14–15).

30 The British Prime Minister opposed the idea of devolution for Scotland on the grounds that it would mean higher taxes and less investment (*Financial Times*, 12 January 1991 and 14 November 1991), while the Scottish CBI members opposed the creation of a Scottish Parliament with tax raising powers (*Financial Times*, 26 April 1991).

31 The relationship between local development, regional autonomy and small business is covered in a series of case studies by Vazquez-Barquero (1990); while the role of local authorities in the development of SMEs is examined by Nuttal (1986).

32 I do not consider elite change as it may be linked with broader process of economic and social change. A discussion of the link between micro (elite) and macro (society) inter-dependence in change of elites are discussed by Welsh (1979, ch. 8).

33 Case 50. Business proprietor. Date of interview: 19 September 1991.

34 Case 59. Business proprietor. Date of interview: 14 September 1991.

35 Cretan business are predominately small. An analysis of the size distribution of this sample compared with the Cretan business as a whole can be found in chapter three.

36 Case 74. Mayor. Date of interview: 21 September 1991.

37 Case 9. Activist. Date of interview: 15 October 1991.

38 A number of researchers have consistently investigated political attitudes towards multinational enterprises including La Palombara and Blank (1976), Fayerweather (1982) and Taggart (1993).

39 I note here that according to Anthony Smith 'ethnic nationalisms do not generally correlate with economic trends' (1995, p.73).

40 On these questions I have attempted a measure of respondents acceptance of SMEs as important factors of growth in the region and I take respondents replies to be a testament to that effect.

41 When a filter is used on the national politicians of Scotland, excluding the views of the three MPs, the Scottish support of local entrepreneurs was up to 62 per cent. The three MPs views can be excluded since the subject matter of the hypothesis permits such a treatment, while for reasons of compatibility of the two samples (i.e. the Cretan sample lacks national MP interviewees) such a filter could be considered desirable.

42 There is extensive literature referred to throughout this thesis on the importance of MNLs as potential engines of regional development and the relevant studies conducted at the international and European level (Yannopoulos, 1976; Young, 1993).

43 Case 54. Business proprietor. Date of interview: 22 May 1991.

44 Case 45. Business manager. Date of interview: 24 September 1991.

45 Case 31. Company director. Date of interview: 30 May 1991.

46 Case 18. Company director. Date of interview: 9 November 1991.

47 Case 55. Business manager. Date of interview: 18 September 1991.

48 Case 35. Company director. Date of interview: 23 May 1991.

49 Case 66. City Councillor. Date of interview: 25 September 1991.

50 Case 68. City Councillor. Date of interview: 9 October 1991.

51 Case 1. Regional Councillor. Date of interview: 26–28 June 1991.

52 Case 7. Regional Councillor. Date of interview: 2 July 1991.

53 The figure of 65 per cent is derived if all positive replies on QD1 are compared with replies on QD6 and all replies of QD6 that are at or above the mean value of the particular elite subgroup of QD6 are recorded as success.

54 The Spearman correlation coefficients for QD1*QD6 were 0.277 (sig. 0.338) for the Cretan and -0.150 (sig. 0.579) for the Scottish political elites. A negative view of autonomy (QD1) is correlated with a positive view of the regions preparedness (QD6) in the Cretan politicians case, while a positive view of autonomy is correlated with and a negative view of the regions preparedness in the case of Scottish politicians. The relatively small coefficients however, make any further inferences tenuous.

55 The reliability of correlation coefficients is low as there is a large number of cells that have a low expected frequency.

56 The Spearman correlation coefficient for Strathclyde businessmen was 0.279 (sig. 0.209) which links a negative view on autonomy (QD1) with a high score on their perception of their region's preparedness for 1992 (QD6). The Cretan businessmen's sample showed a correlation of -0.554 (sig. 0.009), which links their positive view on autonomy with a low score on their regions perceived preparedness for 1992.

57 Case 2. City Councillor. Date of interview: 28 June 1991.

58 Case 11. Activist. Date of interview: 10 November 1991.

59 Case 62. Business proprietor. Date of interview: 16 September 1991.

60 Case 44. Business proprietor. Date of interview: 23 September 1991.

61 Case 32. Managing director. Date of interview: 29 May 1991.

62 Case 36. Managing director. Date of interview: 22 May 1991.

63 Case 69. Mayor. Date of interview: 20 September 1991.

64 Case 67. City Councillor. Date of interview: 26 September 1991.

65 Case 14. MEP. Date of interview: 18 October 1991.
66 Case 55. Business manager. Date of interview: 18 September 1991.
67 Case 25. Managing director. Date of interview: 5 June 1991.
68 Case 33. Managing director. Date of interview: 27 May 1991.
69 Case 76. Mayor. Date of interview: 23 September 1991.
70 On an article in the special supplement of the *Financial Times* on Scotland (13 December 1991, pp.30–32) titled 'Farce and Tragedy' the views of all Scottish political parties, including the Conservatives, are reported to be in favour of some form of Scottish assembly. The views of local opposition parties in Strathclyde to Government proposals for the reform of local government, (to a single tier Council system), may be one of the reasons behind their hostility towards the incumbent Government (Glasgow City Council, 1991; Strathclyde Regional Council, 1993; Scottish Office, 1992). For a critical analysis of the views of the main British political parties on regional government see Moore (1991).
71 The extent of the Greek states' centralised structures and resistance to reform is attested by the attempt to decentralise the administrative structures legislated in 1986 (Law 1622/86), which however were not yet enacted as policy by 1991 (Pierros 1991, p.55). The role of the prefectures in the attempt to decentralise Greece is analysed by Verney and Papageorgiou (1992). Regional policy incentives combined with the need for decentralisation were identified as a hindrance to development by the *Fifth Periodic Report on the Social and Economic Condition and Development of the Regions of the Community* (Commission, 1994).
72 Three quarters of the members of the Scottish CBI, in April of 1991, opposed any form of a Scottish Assembly (as reported in the *Financial Times*, 21 February 1992, p.20).
73 Herzfeld (1985, pp.3–50) gives some very interesting insights on the hierarchy of a sense of belonging for the Cretan people and their 'concentric loyalties' between the local, the regional, the national and the European level. In his study he identifies the segmentary view of Cretan allegiances to be based on the view that 'Crete ... regards itself as an idiosyncratic and proudly independent part of the national entity, distinct from it, physically separated from it, but yet endowed with qualities that have made Crete the birthplace of many national leaders in politics, war, and the arts' (Hertzfeld, 1985, p.6).
74 The calls for political autonomy are related by Cretan and Greek Press to foreign attempts to destabilise Greece. The source of such perceived propaganda has at different times been identified as the United States who hold military bases on the island (Cretan local newspaper *Alithia*, a number of issues in July 1979); Israel, through its intelligence agency Mosad (Cretan local newspaper *Kritiko Fos*, 15 July 1979); the former Yugoslav Republic of Macedonia (national Greek newspaper *Ethnos tis Kyriakis*, 2 February 1992) and Turkey on numerous occasions (Cretan local newspapers *Chaniotika Nea* and *Kyrikas Chanion* on a number of issues in 1991). In this political climate Cretan political elites view the debate on devolution from Greece with a marked unease.

Chapter Seven

Attitudes and Economic Growth

Ranking Attitudes[1]

I have devised a set of measures that give an ordinal ranking of a number of attitudinal categories for the four regional elites. The ordinal scale has been coded to denote the highest value for the highest ranking parameter. So, 4 ranks the elite group with the strongest or most positive recorded attitude and 1 the one with the weakest or most negative recorded attitude.

I have initially intended this section to include factor analysis for groups of variables. As explained in the methodological appendix there are a number of reasons that limit the scope of using advanced statistical techniques. These are mainly due to the samples' elite character and comparatively small size. In the case of the present measures care was taken for variables not to be causally related. The data available however was not always of interval character. All, but one, of the measures constructed are based on what are effectively dichotomous variables. So, in order to group variables together an empirical assessment had to be made instead of a statistical factor analysis. I trust the measures eventually devised closely represent the attitudes they attempt to gauge and to be indicative of attitudes of the wider elites outwith this sample.

Grievance Towards National Government

From analysing replies on whether the region is in a much better position than the nation in regard to 1992 (QD7) and whether national policies have failed to create opportunities in the region (QD8) a certain pattern emerges. Both Strathclyde elite groups believe their region is in the same or worse position than the nation by a wide margin since 69 per cent of the political and 77 per cent of the business elite appear to believe so. In contrast the Cretan elites appear strongly optimistic, most of them stating their region is in a better or much better position than the rest of the nation, with 86 per cent of the political and 81 per cent of the business elite taking that position.

These replies compare interestingly with their replies on whether national policies have failed to create opportunities in their region comparable to those created in other regions of the nation (QD8). A wide margin of 88 per cent of Strathclyde politicians believe national policies have failed to do this. The reverse was true for Strathclyde businessmen, 57 per cent of whom believed that national policies have not failed in the region. Both Cretan elites believed national policies to have failed, 57 per cent of the political and 65 per cent of the business respondents taking that view.

I assigned a value of 100 to those that both said that regional policies had failed (QD8) and that their region was in a much worse position than the nation (QD7). The value of -100 was given to those replies both identifying the region to be doing much better than the nation and national policies not to have failed in the region. For those that did not give an answer or stated they did not know the answer, a value of zero was assigned.[2] This scale thus can take values of between -100 and +100, where replies closer to zero identify a neutral view point. In Table 7.1, I have calculated the mean score of all respondents to both questions for all four elite groups.

The measure (Table 7.1) shows Strathclyde politicians to have the highest level of grievance and the Cretan politicians to have the lowest. Cretan businessmen seem neutral while Strathclyde businessmen, although negative, are not nearly as negative as Cretan politicians.

The initial analysis of the frequency distributions for the two questions showed a high degree of regional grievance towards national policies for all elite groups except for Strathclyde businessmen. These latter seem to think that their region is worse off than the nation and at the same time reject the premise that national policies have failed in the region. It seems thus that overall, Strathclyde businessmen are those with the fewest grievances towards the national government, a result partly confirmed by the measure constructed.

Support for Regional Autonomy

To create a measure for this attitude I initially compare elite group replies to a question inquiring whether respondents believe federalism is viable in Europe (Q2) and whether respondents think business elites would perceive autonomy positively (QD1). I have also included a second measure by including replies to a question inquiring whether respondents believed macroeconomics should be controlled at the regional, national or international level (Q1).

To establish a measure I decided to use a technique of scaling respondents replies for the questions and then establishing a common numerical factor that if compared for each elite group could give an indication of how favourable or unfavourable they were towards regional autonomy. The scale ascribed a

Table 7.1   Regional elite's grievances towards their national government

Elite identification	Cumulative mean QD7+QD8 (standard deviations)	Ordinal rank/ Measure A
Strathclyde politicians	39.1 (39.8)	4
Strathclyde businessmen	-11.4 (57.1)	2
Cretan politicians	-17.9 (56.7)	1
Cretan businessmen	-3.6 (49.6)	3

Notes

1   Question QD7: do you find that your region is in a worse position than the nation in regard to 1992?
2   Question QD8: do you believe that national policies have failed to create the opportunities in your region that have been created in other regions of Britain/Greece?

value of -100 to replies that were negative on regional autonomy, 0 to those that refused to answer or claimed they did not know and +100 to replies positive on regional autonomy. The group means for the two groups of questions and all four elite groups are compared in the following table.

In Table 7.2 the highest mean score represents the highest sympathy level for regional autonomy by the respective elite. Consequently, Strathclyde politicians and Cretan businessmen high score indicates a strong positive attitude for the questions examined. A lower score indicates a comparatively neutral attitude, which may indicate that there are equal numbers amongst a subgroup of the sample that support and refute a proposition or that most respondents chose a neutral answer.[3]

The inclusion of question Q1 alters responses for three of the subgroups. This variable, because it is primarily indicating anti-state sentiments is conceptually similar but not the same as those of variable Q2 and QD1. Strathclyde businessmen become more negative towards autonomy, while Cretan politicians and businessmen become more positive.

An explanation could lie in the trust of the national state by Strathclyde businessmen, which supports the assumption that they are primarily against further autonomy. Remarkably, Strathclyde politicians are unaffected by the measure, remaining the most positive subgroup on regional autonomy.

Both Cretan elites become distinctly more positive on autonomy by the introduction of the QD1 variable. This could be related to my assumption of the Cretan regional elites overall distrust of the national government and a

**Table 7.2   Ordinal ranking of variables indicating regional elites'
positive attitudes towards regional autonomy**

Elite identification	Cumulative mean Q2+QD1	Cumulative mean Q1+Q2+QD1 (standard deviations)	Ordinal rank/ Measure B
Strathclyde politicians	35.3 (60.6)	35.4 (43.0)	4
Strathclyde businessmen	-6.8 (69.5)	-19.7 (62.3)	1
Cretan politicians	-17.9 (54.1)	8.3 (51.5)	2
Cretan businessmen	16.7 (48.3)	28.6 (45.1)	3

Notes

1   Question Q1: Do you believe that macroeconomic policies should be controlled at the
     regional, national or international level?
2   Question Q2: Do you believe a federal structure for Europe can be viable?
3   Question QD1: Do you believe that if your region were to become more autonomous,
     business would perceive this as a generally positive development?

possible underlying sentiment that may become apparent in future demands
for regional devolution. Such an attitude if true could be relevant to future
political developments in the region.

Finally it should be noted that this measure is intended as a gauge of
positive attitudes towards regional autonomy and I do not believe it can be
taken to indicate a positive relationship to any political party's agenda.[4]

Perceived Difference from the Rest of the Nation

To create this measure I examine elite replies from a question inquiring whether
respondents perceive differences to exist between people in their locality and
those in the rest of Scotland/Crete (QD9). This is compared with whether
they perceive a difference in people from their region and those in the rest of
Britain/Greece (QD10). This measure is also relevant in establishing whether
regional elites perceive people in their region and by inference themselves to
be different from people in the rest of their nation.

There was relatively little variation in the replies between the four elite
groups. The Strathclyde political elite agreed with the two premises more
strongly than any other group 56 per cent attesting that they are different from
people in the rest of Scotland (QD9) and 81 per cent saying that the Scottish
are different from the rest of the UK. The Strathclyde business elite was also

strong in its identification of difference from the rest of the nation with 83 per cent of respondents answering in the affirmative (QD10) but only 43 per cent of respondents believing the same difference to hold between their region and the rest of Scotland (QD9).

Table 7.3   Regional elites' perceived differences between people in their region and people in the rest of their nation

Elite identification	Cumulative mean QD9+QD10 (standard deviations)		Ordinal rank/ Measure C
Strathclyde politicians	35.3	(70.2)	4
Strathclyde businessmen	27.1	(73.7)	3
Cretan politicians	26.2	(83.1)	2
Cretan businessmen	0.0	(87.7)	1

Notes

1   Question QD9: overall do you find there are great differences between people in your region and those in the rest of Scotland/Crete?
2   Question QD10. overall do you find there are great differences between people in your region and those in the rest of Britain/Greece?

The Cretan elite samples also strongly identified their regional peoples' as separate. The Chania business elite had the stronger indication of this attitude since 71 per cent show people in their locality as different from the rest of the Greeks (QD10) and 55 per cent believed the local people to be different from the rest of the Cretans. The Cretan political elite was the one who perceived the least differences between the peoples in their locality and those in the rest of Greece 64 per cent attesting to that effect, while only 36 per cent of them perceived differences between themselves and the rest of Crete.

I will not attempt a comprehensive explanation of the possible reasons for the divergence in attitudes here. Strathclyde politicians showed the highest score in this measure attesting to their perception of a high degree of separateness between people in their region and people in the rest of Scotland and UK. Strathclyde businessmen and Cretan businessmen follow closely behind, while Cretan politicians show a neutral overall position. This difference of Cretan politicians I assume to be partly due to associating separateness of people with calls for autonomy.[5]

Preparedness Towards 1992

To establish this measure I inquire whether the national and regional economy is ready for the competition that the creation of a common market in 1992 is bound to bring.

Responding to the question of whether their national economy was prepared for 1992 (QD5) 81 per cent of the Strathclyde politicians, 67 per cent of the Strathclyde businessmen, 79 per cent of the Cretan politicians and 100 per cent of the Cretan businessmen replied their nation was rather unprepared or not at all prepared.

Responding to the question of whether their regional economy is prepared for 1992 (QD6) 86 per cent of the Strathclyde politicians and 67 per cent of the businessmen believed their region to be slightly or not at all prepared. Similarly, 57 per cent of the Cretan politicians and 71 per cent of the businessmen believed their region to be slightly or not at all prepared.

In both these questions a Likert scale was employed which for the purposes of this measure is converted to a scale of -100 for the most negative attitude to the proposition up to 100 for the most positive attitude for the proposition. The middle value in the Likert scale is given a value of zero, while intermediate values 4 and 2 are given values of -50 and 50 respectively.

Apparently all elite groups believe their regional and national economies not to be prepared for 1992 (Table 7.4). The elite group with the lowest perception of preparedness towards 1992 is the Cretan business elite. Interestingly the Cretan political elite is the one with the most favourable opinion of regional preparedness.

The opposite pattern is apparent in the Strathclyde elite groups. Politicians think their region and nation is not as prepared for 1992 as businessmen whose opinion is not as pessimistic on regional preparedness.

To the degree that these results could be generalised for the broader elite groups investigated I could infer that on this particular issue, elite groups in the two regions seem to have diverging attitude patterns or even value systems. Politicians in Strathclyde are more pessimistic than businessmen, while businessmen in Crete were more pessimistic than politicians.

Attitudes Towards European Integration

Replying on whether they find federalism in Europe viable (Q2) 86 per cent of the Cretan business elite, 76 per cent of the Strathclyde political elite, 71

Table 7.4 Preparedness of the regional and national units towards 1992

Elite identification	Cumulative mean QD5+QD6 (standard deviations)		Ordinal rank/ Measure D
Strathclyde politicians	-48.4	(30.9)	2
Strathclyde businessmen	-39.6	(38.2)	3
Cretan politicians	-35.7	(36.3)	4
Cretan businessmen	-61.9	(29.2)	1

Notes

1 Question QD5: do you believe that the British/Greek economy is ready for the competition that the 1992 integration will bring?
2 Question QD6: do you believe that the Scottish/Cretan economy is ready for the 1992 competition challenge?

per cent of the Cretan political elite and 63 per cent of the Strathclyde business elite answer affirmatively.

Answering whether more risks or opportunities exist in a united Europe (QD13), 76 per cent of the Cretan politicians, 71 per cent of the Cretan businessmen, 65 per cent of the Strathclyde politicians and 63 per cent of the Strathclyde businessmen replied they believed there will be more or many more opportunities in a united Europe.

The introduction of the recoding and computation of the new measure follows the same rules as above with -100 signifying an extremely negative attitude to the proposition, 0 signifying a neutral attitude to the proposition and 100 signifying an extremely positive attitude to the proposition.

The strongest positive attitude towards European integration is expressed by the Cretan businessmen (Table 7.5). Cretan politicians and Strathclyde politicians also show strong but slightly milder support for European integration. Strathclyde businessmen are those with the smallest support indicator for European integration.

Attitudinal Profiles

Certain trends emerge in replies of the four elite groups on all five constructed measures which summarise the findings. It may be significant to note at this stage that average standard deviations (empirically estimated at a value close

Table 7.5   Regional elite attitudes towards European integration

Elite identification	Cumulative mean Q2+Q13 (standard deviations)		Ordinal rank/ Measure E
Strathclyde politicians	44.1	(62.2)	2
Strathclyde businessmen	27.1	(54.1)	1
Cretan politicians	48.2	(57.6)	3
Cretan businessmen	69.0	(48.7)	4

Notes

1   Question Q2: do you believe a federal structure for Europe can be viable?
2   Question QD13: do you believe there are more opportunities or risks in a united Europe?

to 50) are observed in most mean values of measures employed. High standard deviation values are only observed in the case of Measure C (difference between people in their region and the rest of the nation) signifying relative disagreement among members of an elite group, while in Measure D (preparedness towards 1992) a high concentration in their replies produces small standard deviation values.

The *Strathclyde political* elite shows a great sense of grievance towards their national government (Measure A), believes the people of the region to be very different from the people in the rest of the nation (Measure C), has a positive view of regional autonomy and European integration (Measures B and E) and believes the region not to be prepared in the run-up to 1992 (Measure D).

The *Strathclyde business* elite has a positive opinion of the national government (Measure A) and believes their region to be unprepared for 1992 but by a smaller margin than any other elite (Measure D). They also find the regional people significantly different from people in the rest of the nation (Measure C) and have a comparatively negative view of regional autonomy and lower support for European integration than any other group (Measure B and E).

The *Cretan political* elite shows the most support for their national government (Measure A), have the strongest negative view on regional autonomy (Measure B) and at the same time seem keen on European integration (Measure E). They believe their region is rather unprepared for 1992 (Measure D) and are equivocal about whether there are differences between the people in their region and those in the rest of the nation (Measure C).

The *Cretan business* elite do not show signs of grievance towards the national government (Measure A), are comparatively positive on regional autonomy (Measure B) and very supportive of European integration (Measure E). They believe people in their region are rather different from people in the rest of their nation (Measure C) and have very strong doubts as to whether their region is prepared for the Single European Market (Measure D).

Interpretations for the divergence among elites in these attitude measures should be supplemented by the 'qualifying' qualitative input of the relevant interviews.

Influence of Attitudes on Regional Growth[6]

I have included here a discussion of one hypothesis I aspired to test at the beginning of this research effort, but for which there could be no conclusive measures devised for the particular sample and research resources. The advantage of proceeding with a purely exploratory investigation lies in the existence of a wealth of information in my survey, that could give some indication for its validity and possibly assist in future research efforts.

I investigate whether:

H III: the greater the similarity of attitudes among the political and business elite in a region the better the regional growth prospects.

I have used this hypothesis as an assumption in a number of occasions, on the logical deduction that cooperation is a more effective form of societal interaction than friction. Although logical on the surface this premise is not necessarily true in the everyday experience of elite interaction. Difficulties in providing a proof for this hypothesis are compounded by the difficulty of inferring an influence on the 'macro' level (regional competitiveness) by the 'micro' level (elite interaction).

I have identified the similarity (or diversity) of attitudes between the business and political elites as the independent variable and regional growth prospects as the dependent variable in each region. I anticipate that the region with a greater similarity in attitudes among two elite groups has better growth prospects. It can be argued that depending on how well a region is doing, we can infer a regional elites' success in promoting regional development. So, as a measure of comparison I include data on the performance of Crete and

Strathclyde as they compare with regions of similar development level and position in the economic cycle.

Because of a great number of antecedent and background variables this investigation cannot provide a quantifiable element on the relative importance of the variable investigated. Furthermore I have to account for the possibility of spuriousness, particularly since an indication of similar responses between elite groups is not necessarily a proof of harmony in their relationship.[7] It could also be argued that, to the degree that there is interlockingness among the two elite groups in each region, they would be expected to hold similar opinions. I believe that for the samples investigated the degree of covert interlockingness is rather small, as uncovered in a number of previous hypotheses.[8]

To provide a measure of discordance in the replies of the two regional elites, I have devised a composite index.[9] In particular I quantify the absolute difference in the scores of the regional elite groups on a set of measures eventually adding them up to calculate a regional elites 'discordance in attitudes score'. I subsequently convert this absolute difference into a new index to facilitate the interpretation of results. Since I measure absolute difference, a high index score signifies a high degree of difference and a low index score a low degree of difference. This index can take a minimum value of zero if the two groups are completely concordant and a maximum value of 100 if the two groups are completely discordant. By examining Table 7.6 it becomes immediately apparent that Strathclyde and Cretan elite groups are quite disparate.

This is apparent in both the level and the variance of their discordance. Cretan political and business elites appear to have a constant and consistent discordance across the spectrum of the measures employed. Strathclyde elites portray a very different picture however. In measures A (grievance towards their national government) and B (positive attitudes towards regional autonomy) they show a high level of discordance. Reasons for this discordance can be sought in the high degree of grievance by Strathclyde politicians compared with a relative satisfaction with Westminster government by businessmen (negative score on grievance). At the same time there is a positive attitude towards regional autonomy by politicians compared with a negative one by businessmen. This discordance can be related to the high priority the particular issues hold on the political agenda and their highly 'emotive' content in the political debate. By comparison, there is a comparatively small discordance in measures C (difference of local people) and D (preparedness towards 1992).

Table 7.6   Index of discordance as revealed by the difference in attitude scores between the business and political elites in Strathclyde and Crete

	Measure A	Measure B	Measure C	Measure D	A+B+ C+D	Discordance index D
Strathclyde politicians	39.1	35.4	35.3	-48.4		
Strathclyde businessmen	-11.4	-19.7	27.1	-39.6		
Difference between Strathclyde elites	50.5	55.1	8.2	8.8	122.6	15.3
Cretan politicians	-17.9	8.3	0.0	-35.7		
Cretan businessmen	-3.6	28.6	26.2	-61.9		
Difference between Cretan elites	14.3	20.3	26.2	26.2	87.0	10.9

Notes

1   The algebraic equation used to produce the absolute difference score a, when one of the 'measure' scores is negative and one is positive, has the following form: $|a| = |b| + |c|$. When both 'measure' scores are either positive or negative it becomes, $|a| = |b| \quad |c|$.

2   The discordance index D is calculated as the sum of the absolute difference values divided by eight $D = |a_A + a_B + a_C + a_D|/8$.

Two alternative and rival explanations can be offered in interpretation of Strathclyde discordance. The first one is that Strathclyde region will be doing better (than a comparable region) because regional elite discordance centres along politically emotive issues that are not vital to elite interaction. Such an interpretation would assume high levels of local corporatism. In that respect it will not be able to affect the interaction between the political and business elites who can have an active collaboration, evident from their concordance on non-politically sensitive issues. An alternative explanation could point to the politically sensitive nature of the measures of high discordance and suggest that elite interaction will depend on the existence of non-divisive issues among elites and that therefore Strathclyde is bound to do worse (than a comparable region).

In the Cretan case again two alternative rival explanations can be offered. In the first instance it can be hypothesised that the relative concordance influences elite interaction positively, and that by reflection it has a decisive influence on regional development. In that case Crete would be expected to be doing better than a comparable region. The alternative explanation would be that political elites will not interact successfully with business elites because they have consistently different perspectives as evident from a small but constant difference in their attitudinal measures.[10]

A comparison of the discordance index scores between Strathclyde and Crete points to a higher discordance score for the Scottish than the Cretan elite. If the two regions could be directly compared I would expect Chania influenced by a comparatively concordant regional elite, to show a better relative performance than Strathclyde. Such a comparison would assume however that agreement in all measures is of incrementally equal importance to elite cooperation.

A final word of caution in the interpretation of the attitudinal results. In the case of the Strathclyde elites' relative discordance, it can be partly ascribed to presumed different political affiliations between elite groups as most politicians tend to be on the left of the political spectrum and most businessmen tend to be Conservative supporters.[11] On the other hand, the degree to which the measure constructed identifies value orientations, political affiliations can be considered irrelevant. The criticism can also be levied that Cretan elites are relatively concordant because there is a limited impact local political elites' power has on business elites.[12]

I believe that in spite of all such intervening or antecedent variables, the examination of the evidence will give a good indication of the input of the regional elites to regional performance.[13]

I proceed to examine data on the growth rate of the two regions between 1990 and 1992 expecting to find how well the two regions performed compared to the regions of Merseyside and Notio/Vorio Aigaio.[14] I assume that elite membership in regions investigated (Crete, Strathclyde) were the same (or if different displayed similar attitudes and behaviour), for the period investigated.[15] Regional elites in the 'null hypothesis' regions of comparison (Aigaio, Merseyside) are presumed not to have the characteristics that make Strathclyde and Crete unique.

It is, of course, the case that I cannot provide an exact measure of how significant the regional elites' input is to the respective regional performance. It could also be the case that over the period examined, external events, irrelevant to the input of the respective regional elites, had influenced the performance of the respective regions. I could also identify a number of structural constraints on the influence of elite interaction on regional growth. These would stem from previous rounds of capitalist accumulation and the 'uneven' character of capitalist development between Strathclyde and Crete. Comparing the performance of Strathclyde vis-à-vis Merseyside and Crete

**Table 7.7   Composition of GVA by sector for Strathclyde/Dumfries/
Galloway with Merseyside; and of Crete with Vorio and
Notio Aigaio**

	Agriculture	Industry	Services
Strathclyde+	1%	30%	69%
Merseyside	0%	27%	70%
Notio Aigaio	9%	27%	64%
Vorio Aigaio	25%	17%	57%
Crete	25%	26%	49%

Source: *Portrait of the Regions*, Vols 2 and 3, Commission of the EC, Luxembourg, 1993.

vis-à-vis Vorio and Notio Aigaio is an attempt to alleviate that condition. [16] Finally results from the regional rate of performance can provide a broad measure of comparison between the two regional elites.

Both regions under investigation appear to be doing better than their regions of comparison (Graph 7.1). Strathclyde appears to be doing remarkably better than Merseyside, while Crete appears to be doing marginally better than Notio and Vorio Aigaio. [17] As apparent from Table 7.7 Strathclyde and Crete do not have an economic profile that can allow a direct comparison, Merseyside and Vorio and Notio Aigaio respectively, seem to provide a fair match however.

Coming back to the possible explanations of their discordance I have to conclude that the Strathclyde elites have 'performed better', as is evident from the favourable disparity in regional growth with Merseyside. It is reasonable to assume that the comparative discordance among elites in Strathclyde was focused on political issues with a marginal effect on their cooperation. The evidence here suggests that their cooperation was not hampered by their discordance on politically 'sensitive' issues.

In the case of Crete, it can similarly be argued that although attitudinal discordance is evident in all measures constructed, this discordance does not appear to hamper the growth prospects of the region. It is also the case, however, that the combined regions of comparison appear to be doing just as well. It can be deduced that a small level of discordance influences elite interaction if it is assumed that it points to a varying but not necessarily divisive perspective of the relevant elite groups. Results for the Greek regions are made more tenuous by the limited level of decentralisation of the Greek state at the time of survey. This would suggest that regional political elites are less

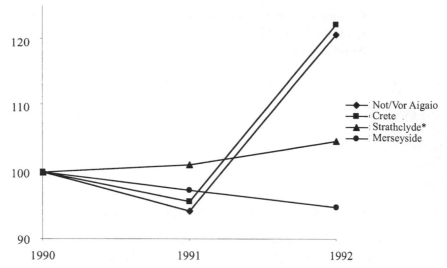

Graph 7.1   Regional GDP at market prices for Strathclyde and Merseyside; Crete and Notio/Vorio Aigaio measured in PPS, for 1990=100

*   The weighted PPS value of 100 for the two regions is provided from the formula $a= 100/b$, where b equals the respective PPS value of the base year for each region. In the case of Crete $a_C= 2.22$ and in the case of Strathclyde $a_S= 1.162$.

Source: PPS data are available in the Eurostat: *Basic Statistics of the EC/EU*, Luxembourg, 1992–95.

significant to regional development as regional elite interaction cannot be seen to be instrumental to development.

An exercise of the possible reasons behind attitudinal concordance or discordance can be offered however, based on the two regions for which data exist. Strathclyde politicians assessing that they are in the periphery of Europe and suffering from a declining industrial base were preoccupied with supporting entrepreneurship and regional development (Keating, 1988; Jensen-Butler, 1996).[18] Their approach was pro-active as they strove to develop links with the local business community and establish a 'policy network', that would allow them to tap into European financial resources (Bomberg, 1994).[19]

In the case of Crete the region was suffering under strict centralisation of all regional development schemes, and the regional political elite lacked the impetus to produce solutions for the business of the region. The networks existing in Crete were clientelistic with the national bureaucratic and political elite at the nexus of those networks. This lack of independence for the local political elites does not eliminate their significance however. Local enterprise councils and communal entrepreneurial initiatives, in which the local political elites were highly active created a local 'entrepreneurial milieu'.[20]

According to Table 7.6, regional elites appear more concordant in Crete than they do in Strathclyde, at the same time regional elites in Strathclyde were comparatively successful while there is no strong evidence to suggest the same for Crete. Except from noting the limited compatibility of the two regions, in terms of the policy making freedom of the relevant political elites, I can offer an explanation that refers to their respective political culture. It is possible that in regions where civil society can only accept a 'meritocratic' dissemination of political patronage, elite concordance is vital to regional development. On the other part of the spectrum where clientelistic networks are prevalent elite concordance, although important, is not essential. Regional elites in the latter case, although not openly interlocking are likely to be part of a single network.[21] Evidence for these relationships should lie with elite interaction in each region.

In an attempt to determine which are the factors that play the determining role in the interaction between business and political elites in Strathclyde and Crete I analysed their qualitative replies on a number of questions inquiring on the level and intensity of this interaction (QB6-QB13 and QC4-QC13).

The qualitative data analysis on their value orientations can be summarised in that, Strathclyde business and political elites do not show the singularity of purpose exhibited by elite groups in Chania.[22] At the same time political elites in Strathclyde seem keen to cooperate with business and facilitate business expansion. This evidence would support the premise that regional elites in Crete although not always cooperating appear to share the same vision for their region. Regional elites in Strathclyde although relatively discordant on politically 'sensitive' issues make a conscious effort at cooperation, even when they do not share the same vision for their region's future. It is apparent that there are significant differences in the political culture of interviewees in the two regions investigated.[23] It is however beyond the scope of the present volume to investigate that conjecture and determine to what degree it is the differences in the civic and political culture that can be responsible for the different way elite attitudes appear to affect regional elite interaction. A factor of spuriousness in this analysis could be that higher growth rates for Crete are relevant to its higher potential for growth. Crete starting from a lower level of productivity and an economy based on agricultural production has a higher potential for development.[24] Data for that period however show that the expected trend to industrialisation cannot account for Crete's higher growth.

Table 7.8   Gross value added in market prices by sector for Scotland and Crete

| | Crete | | | Scotland | | |
	Agriculture	Industry	Services	Agriculture	Industry	Services
1986	36.0%	19.9%	44.1%	2.1%	38.6%	59.2%
1991	45.0%	15.9%	39.1%	3.1%	30.4%	66.5%

Source: Eurostat publication: *Basic Statistics of the Community*, Luxembourg, 1987 and 1994.

As is apparent from Table 7.8, in the Cretan economy an increasing amount of value added is produced in agriculture in a remarkable nine percentage points change between 1986 and 1991.[25] Scotland is moving in the predictable trend of most post-industrial economies by a shift of resources away from industry and into services.[26] So, industrialisation cannot be relevant to the difference in the growth performance of the two regions.

So does attitudinal concordance among elite actors affect regional performance? Or even more topically, do regional elites agree? And what is the significance of this agreement or disagreement?

In the evidence I have uncovered regional elites' concordance appears to be related to the performance of a region. This happens despite a presumed negative attitude of a Labour dominated local authority to business (Strathclyde) or of a state 'controlled' local political elite (Chania/Crete). In both regions investigated there appears to be a *modus vivendi* between the local and national political elites under which although the locality may be on the receiving end of state *caprice,* cooperation over 'practical' development issues prevails. Such an 'understanding' certainly suits local business elites as it typically serves their interests. It could be argued therefore, that regional political elites are significant for business, even in comparatively centralised states, by the degree to which they subjugate their own interests to those of business in their area.[27] It would be interesting to determine the degree to which political elite actions are guided by a sharing of 'values' with the business elite.[28]

It is also topical at this stage, to note that the debate on the relevance of the interaction between regional business and political elites acquires significance only in the context of contemporary local elite interaction.[29] Within the context of contemporary modern (or post-modern for some) political interaction and under the effects of market globalisation local business and political elites roles change. The emergence of the welfare state to a degree emancipates local political elites from dependence on business or landowning interests. At the same time integration of international markets creates a new production and consumption space. The wide scope for the onomatopoeia of this new topography of what Swyngedouw (1992) calls the 'glocal' while Coffey and Bailey (1996) call 'micro-global' points to problems with its definition. With the growth in importance of 'place productivity' (Jensen-Butler, 1996) at the expense of the principle of absolute advantage for an area, urban or economic regions become increasingly more important as the new production engines in Europe and the world (ERECO, 1993).

In conclusion, initial examination of the data would support the premise of *HIII* as higher attitude concordance among elite groups in Crete is matched by their higher growth than Strathclyde. When the two regions are compared with the 'equivalent' regions of Vorio/Notio Aigaio and Merseyside, Strathclyde's performance is more remarkable, however. Lack of evidence on elite concordance on the regions of comparison precludes any conclusive evaluation of the premise. There is some degree of confidence in saying that higher concordance of attitudes in Crete correlates with a higher likelihood of agreement and a sharing of values among elite groups than is the case in Strathclyde. However, as unravelled through the examination of data in this section, agreement among regional elites does not necessarily lead to 'productive' cooperation. Evidence analysed here offers support to the alternative hypothesis that only concordance on certain attitudes is significant for elite interaction (relevant to regional competitiveness). Strathclyde elites appear more concordant than Cretan one's on Measure D (preparedness towards 1992). If this measure is indicative of other similar attitudes that could be grouped under an elites' concern with a market's efficiency[30] it would lend support to the premise that only certain values are important for effective regional elite cooperation.

I can juxtapose, that the sharing of values among elites facilitates what regional economists call the 'entrepreneurial milieu' although I cannot test the null hypothesis for this argument. The existence however of elite concordance would be in accord with arguments presuming the emergence of governance in the European regions, along neo-corporatist lines. If it can be proven that regional elite cooperation depends only on sharing of values relevant to regional development and happens in spite of or regardless of their sharing of values on issues in the political or social agenda, this would provide support to one of the basic tenets of neo-corporatism.

My initial hypothesis (*HIII*) could be thus refined to examine whether regional elite attitudinal concordance on issues of economic efficiency (as opposed to issues of social equity or political governance) promotes regional growth prospects.[31] The academic discourse surrounding such an investigation is examined in the next chapter.

So, with conditional support for the hypothesis that attitudinal concordance among elites affects regional development in different ways in both regions investigated, I now turn to a re-evaluation of the whole research exercise, examining the relevance of my conclusions to the current academic debate.

Notes

1 In this section I have to specifically acknowledge extensive advice from Professor William L. Miller (University of Glasgow). It is naturally my interpretation of that advice that entails any weakness in the indexes that follow.
2 In none of the questions employed here 'neutral' scaling (do not know – refuse to answer) represents more than 14 per cent of the respective sub-samples.
3 A low value in the standard deviation would support the proposition of a concentration of replies close to the mean value, while a large standard deviation would allude to a wide spread in responses. Such an interpretation of the standard deviation assumes normal or bell shaped distributions of replies that are not necessarily feasible in small samples.
4 It is apparent that political interviewees may be rehearsing political standpoints instead of personal attitudes. The use of three questions with a partly indirect way of inquiring on this topic is meant to alleviate that possibility.
5 Issues of political autonomy are extremely emotive for Cretan political elites who appear to consider any such debate as seditious, separatist and motivated by foreign propaganda. Many examples of this are apparent in the editorials of local newspapers (i.e. *Kyrikas Chanion*, August–September 1991).
6 I have proceeded to the investigation of these issues with the presentation of two papers so far, the first co-authored with Stephen Herbert (Christopoulos and Herbert, 1996) focused on institutional transformations in Strathclyde, while the second is a comparative study of the impact of elite concordance on growth prospects in Strathclyde and Crete (Christopoulos, 1996a). I have to thank reviewers and commentators at the 1996 Annual PSA Conference and the 1996 ECPR Annual Session of Workshops for very constructive comments and ideas that have helped me advance these arguments.
7 Alternative methods of investigating actor interrelations, including social network analysis (Scott, 1991; Wasserman and Galaskiewicz, 1994) or a sociometric application to decision making networks (John and Cole, 1996) I have considered inadequate as they typically give limited importance to the sharing of values among actors in their analysis. Most importantly for a sociometric approach I would have needed 'complete' data on the networks examined. The nature of elite interviews unfortunately precludes that possibility.
8 Welsh (1979, p.27) has identified Greece as a country where interlockingness is 'periodically' prevalent due to the 'traditional oligarchies' of the country. A discussion on the tests and identifiable interlockingness of elite groups is presented earlier as well as comprising part of the analysis in earlier chapters. It is my conviction that positional interlockingness is of minor significance for this sample.

9   Indexes of a number of questions that have conceptual relevance have been grouped to aid in this process. Thematically these relate to: a) grievance towards their national government; b) positive attitudes towards regional autonomy; c) difference of local people from people in UK/Greece; and d) preparedness of their region towards 1992.

10 It should always be born in mind that particularly in the era discussed, regional elites in Crete had a limited input on regional development and planning, being rather dependent on national elites. Andrikopoulou (1992) refers to the failure of 'regionalising' the Greek budget and giving power to local political elites in Greece. Furthermore, in attaining a truly comparative measure the region of comparison should be of similar size to the one from which attitudinal data were examined, in this case for instance the West of Crete (Nomos Chanion) with one of the eastern prefectures (Nomos Irakliou). Dearth of statistical data preclude that possibility.

11 Small variance of attitudes can be linked to differences in an elites' perception or viewpoint (Rickets, 1990; Brittan, 1990).

12 I have argued in this book that Cretan political elites are relevant to the political process (even though they belong to a less devolved region than Strathclyde) because they are tied to the national political elites. Their role could be linked to what Kouvertaris and Dobratz (1984) identified as the 'vertical clientelistic relationships' on the pyramid of political patronage and favouritism. Of course this raises the possibility of the particular local elites holding only 'positional' and not 'functional' eliteness in their exercise of power (as discussed by Welsh, pp.166–7). I have empirically perceived their 'functional' elite power, in their locality, to be significant however. Finally, local political elites are definitely relevant to local business interests by their controls on planning permissions and licensing of business. Research on Spanish regional elites (Vazquez-Barquero, 1990) has pointed to the close ties between business and political elites that are fostered under a local development strategy.

13 Valid attitudinal comparisons should entail regions of similar size, endowments, economic development and stage in the economic cycle. Regions like Strathclyde and Merseyside can be considered of roughly similar socioeconomic background and offer good grounds for comparison.

14 Crete has a similar economic profile with different sectors of Vorio and Notio Aigaio, so combining the two appears to provide the best mode of comparison. Table 7.8 provides a comparison of the regional economies by sector.

15 Regional elites 'personnel circulation' and 'social circulation' data (as defined by Welsh 1979, pp.25–6), are not available for the Cretan regional elites.

16 Ideally this test would be performed on regions of similar size, endowments, economic development and stage in the economic cycle.

17 It should be noted that statistics published in relation to regional growth denote a fall in the average growth of GNP for the 12 European Community Member States commencing from 1988. This trend was consistent until 1993 (Commission, 1994).

18 It has been recently pointed out that the effect of the Single Market on Scotland has not been particularly significant (Raines et al., 1995). On the other hand the Strathclyde Regional Council using data compiled by Cambridge Econometrics suggest that the region has greatly benefited by European Structural Funds, predicting an impact of an additional 34,500 jobs by the year 2000 (Strathclyde Economic Trends, 1995).

19 The actions of Scottish elites have been well documented (Keating and Midwinter, 1981; Stoker, 1991; Kellas, 1989).

20 Or what Bailly and Lever (1996) among others call 'regional milieux'.

21 Piatonni (1996) in her model of 'virtuous clientelism' suggests that there are certain conditions under which clientelism can induce development, which implies an efficient allocation of resources within a clientelistic network.

22 This does not imply that there have not been notable success in the interaction between the public and private sector in Strathclyde. An obvious example is *Glasgow Action* that successfully dealt with organising the '1990 European City of Culture'.

23 Differences in political culture are examined in earlier chapters.

24 This potential for development has failed to materialise within the last 15 years. This I believe relates more to the economic performance of Greece as a whole rather than to a failing of the region. Certain reasons for the deteriorating competitiveness of the Greek industry are analysed in the relevant report of the Organisation for Economic Cooperation and Development (OECD, 1993).

25 The Cretan economy's shift to agricultural production and tourism is attributed to the specialisation of the local economy away from an 'integrated and self-sufficient economic unit' (Manolikakis, 1963) to a peripheral unit, geared towards European production needs.

26 A more complete discussion of economic trends for the two regions is presented in Chapter Three.

27 This argument assumes that local politicians associate more closely with issues of 'equity' and 'resource use externalities' than 'efficient use of resources' arguments. For a comprehensive debate of the trade-offs of urban economic policy Jensen-Butler (1996) gives an excellent account, while Pickvance (1996) deals with its political dimensions.

28 It is indeed relevant to the examination of elite interaction within 'policy networks' of whether those elites share the same values. In this respect, value concordance is an essential determinant of what can be termed the 'quality' of elite interaction and could provide a better understanding (instead of a simple investigation of elite interaction) of how closely policy networks coincide with networks of power.

29 Slaven and Kim (1994) among others have noted the extensive interlockingness among business and political elites in Scotland between 1860 and 1960.

30 Efficiency considerations can be linked to policy efforts to supplement the workings of the market when it fails to attain a 'Pareto optimum' efficiency as well as attempts to introduce 'structural efficiency' by the support of 'urban entrepreneurialism' within the context of inter-regional competition (Jensen-Butler, 1996, pp.262–79).

31 Efficiency and equity as defined by Jensen-Butler (1996).

Chapter Eight

Regional Elite Behaviour

Introduction

I have argued throughout this volume that regional elite interaction may be one of the causes behind differentials in regional performance. It should be apparent however, that precise measurements of elite interaction and their exact influence on regional development are quite difficult to gauge. Hence a number of important limitations to my hypotheses arise.

In setting out to investigate the interaction of European regional elites, my attempt had been to study the influence of their attitudes and interaction to the regional polity. I have also attempted to 'question' the relevance of those attitudes to a number of preconceived notions on what regional elites do and what they believe while also revealing possible inconsistencies between their professed attitudes and their actual behaviour. I have in other words conducted a study of attitudes with the intention of understanding behaviour. The two main themes investigated dealt with 'regional autonomy' and 'European integration'. A number of secondary or supportive issues examined included 'grievances towards respondents national government', perceived 'regional difference from the national body' and 'preparedness of their economy towards 1992'. These issues were examined in the interview questions and led to the construction of attitudinal indexes that were subsequently employed in a control function of the main themes investigated.

It has been evident, throughout the analysis presented here, that on most issues investigated there can be no conclusive evidence. A number of very significant issues raised were addressed however, leading to a number of novel hypotheses that are expounded in the last section of this chapter. Validity considerations, arise out of the nature of an elite survey, while further restrictions arise from the implementation of a limited scale questionnaire and should be taken into account while interpreting results. These limitations however, are endemic to small scale research projects and do not deduct from the originality of the research approach or the relevance of the conclusions.

The variety of individual answers to questions raised in the interviews were effectively processed by a combined use of quantitative (in codified statistical analysis) and qualitative (recorded responses to open-ended questions) techniques of analysis. The use of both methods in tandem provides potential gains in the reliability of the data, particularly in such a small size, case intensive and cross-sectional elite survey.[1] The divergent profiles of the four elite subgroups emerges from their replies to the multitude of questions posed. Their rather diverse attitudes became apparent early on and serve to identify each of the four groups in their idiosyncracies. In the course of testing hypotheses, differences within and between regions become apparent as well.

It comes as no surprise, for instance, that devolution and business prospects are correlated. The direction and strength of the correlation however, did not prove as self-evident and required careful interpretation[2] which in conjunction with a number of other working hypotheses leads to the support of the premise that a relationship exists between attitudes on devolution and business prospects in a region. In this as in all other hypotheses, the analysis is based on a number of assumptions. These assumptions limit the universality of findings and point to inherent difficulties in interpretations of attitude surveys.[3] To counteract these hindrances in interpretation I will proceed with an exposition of findings and a parallel analysis of relevant sources of research and theory, particularly as it relates to my own conclusions. Surveys of similar context provide a partial test of criterion validity. I will be also attempting an evaluation of certain of my conclusions by comparing them with assumptions or conclusions of other relevant academic work.

Finally, I explore whether my analysis supports the assumption of an emergence of regional behaviour as a facet of an increasingly interdependent and integrating European political landscape. I aim to determine a degree of content validity, although I am aware that not all aspects of the relevant research questions have been covered in this exercise.

Evaluating Findings

Attitudes investigated in tested hypotheses address a number of issues for which references in the international bibliography are rather limited. In particular, issues addressed pertain to the existence of a differentiation in attitudes related to a regional elites' origins (*HI*); the relationship between attitudes on devolution and business prospects for a region (*HII*); and the relationship between concordance of attitudes between elite groups and regional growth prospects (*HIII*). To investigate these hypotheses I employed a number of working hypotheses. These tests have led to a number of interesting conclusions that relate to the samples investigated.

From the analysis of respondents replies I have been able to determine variance both 'between' and 'within' regions in terms of attitudes among the regional elites investigated. I found businessmen to perceive regional political elites as more receptive than national ones', although I could identify a number of different causes for this divergence in the two regions investigated. It becomes evident as well that regional politicians are perceived to favour long term economic policies more than national politicians, although there are significant variations in this premise which relates to the occupational category of each elite group. From this section of the analysis a possible relationship is identified between aspirations to autonomy and perceptions of regional Councillors performance. If such a relationship exists, it could be assumed that 'autonomy' would precede 'Councillors performance' in a regional elites value system. It is hypothesised therefore that aspirations to autonomy have a positive effect on Councillors perceived performance. Overall, I was able to detect that regional elites' region of origin is relevant to their appreciation of the role of regional political elites.

The different level of devolution among the two regions investigated seems to have no significant impact on their attitudes towards SMEs importance. By comparison those regional elites with a higher aspiration to autonomous rule will be more negative on the prospects of SMEs in their region. In conjunction, positive attitudes towards devolution relate to a negative perception of business prospects in a region. This indicates that even if the measures used are inadequate there is strong evidence to support the proposition that there is a relationship between attitudes on devolution and perceptions of business prospects in a region among local elites.

Finally, I explore the possible link between the concordance of attitudes between political and business elites in a region and regional performance. On the level of investigation permitted with the data available, it appears that there is a relationship between high concordance of attitudes between elite groups and growth performance for a region. For the two elite groups investigated, there are a number of intuitive comments that can be made regarding their differences in attitude. Strathclyde business and political elites seem to have a high discordance among each other for issues relating to grievance towards their national government and their attitudes towards regional autonomy, while they appear comparatively concordant on all other issues indexed. By comparison Cretan elites, appear equally divergent across the spectrum of measures investigated, but without any acute (or divisive) differences. I initially offered the alternative hypothesis that Cretan elite groups, although holding consistently different attitudes, do not have divisive differences on issues investigated and can thus be constructive in their cooperation. By comparison, Strathclyde subgroups, although highly appreciative of each other, appear to be discordant on issues of political salience.[4]

My final test consisted of comparing the performance of Strathclyde with Merseyside and Crete with Vorio/Notio Aigaio. This comparison points to a remarkably better performance by Strathclyde compared to Crete. By a closer examination of the data it becomes apparent that Strathclyde elites are concordant on issues of 'structural efficiency' but are relatively discordant on issues of 'social equity'. To put it differently, they appear concordant on attitudes that can determine their effective collaboration on regional development, but discordant on 'purely' political or social equality attitudes. Furthermore there are limitations on inferences that can be made on the effectiveness of local elite interaction in Crete since it is positioned on the receiving end of a vertical clientelistic relationship with the national executive. In the case of Strathclyde it appears evident that discordance based on politically contentious issues has not hampered elite interaction, while strong concordance on the condition of the regional economy seems to be in tandem with a high willingness among elites to cooperate. This can be viewed as a form of local neo-corporatism among elite groups. It can be deduced therefore that regional elites need to share the same views on issues of economic efficiency for a region to perform well.

It is difficult to compare other research for an element of criterion validity without engaging into secondary analysis of their data. From current published research however it appears that a number of studies in Europe touch upon issues I have investigated. Particularly issues relating to the emergence of regional elites and their relevance to regional growth have started receiving attention.

Research by Dupoirier (1994) focuses on the development of political elites in France and not on their relationship with business elites.[5] In that respect it provides some insights into the relationship between the local/ regional elites and the national political elites. She concludes her analysis claiming that 'the first regional elites have indeed been bearers of regional autonomy' (Dupoirier, 1994, p.32). In this respect her account points to a process of regional socialisation that according to her, follows institutional decentralisation. Or to put it differently, she accounts for the emergence of a regional elite as a result of institutional change. These regional elites in turn generate 'regional autonomy'. Such a view can be limited, for not taking account of generic or external factors to the 'creation' of regional elites as well as the importance of pre-existing power structures surviving the process of institutional change.

Leonardi and Garmise drawing from primary research on a number of European Union states (Italy, Greece, Spain, Portugal, and Ireland), point to the 'possible connection between regional government and economic growth' (1992, p.247). They base their arguments on an 'analysis of the economic data [which] suggests that centralised nation-states have been less successful in mobilising resources ... than their more decentralised counterparts in Europe' (1992, pp.265–6). And although it seems that the argument they put forward is primarily one of decentralisation, as this relates to further efficiency, they recognise the significance of regional elites by pointing to 'the fact that regional elites do not see the single market as a zero sum game' (1992, p.252) and therefore are optimistic about regional prospects. Their sub-national elite survey points to significant differences among regional politicians on among others the 'state of the regional economy', 'impact of the single market', and 'functions of the EC'. These taken in conjunction demonstrate, according to the authors, that 'the ongoing European integration process has established deep roots in the local body politic' (1992, pp.257–8). Regional political elite attitudes are implicitly assumed to account for regional prospects and development. The relationship of the political with the regional business elites is not specifically considered, however.

Vazquez-Barquero (1990; 1992a) gives an account of the interaction of local political and business elites in Spain when faced with the challenge of local development strategies.[6] He attests that local political leaders 'show themselves ready to cooperate and collaborate with other local groups' (1990, p.371). He finds that local development programmes depend, among others on a 'tacit or express acceptance of the local development strategy by the local entrepreneurs' (1990, p.372), signifying the importance of the interaction between political and business elites in the regions. He concludes his analysis by claiming that 'we are witnessing in Spain for the first time the definition of local development strategies which condition the behaviour of the public and private, local and external actors' (1990, p.372).[7] So, in conditions of 'incipient autonomy' local development projects with their importance for autonomous regional development produce regional cooperation and consensus. This consensus is viewed by Vazquez-Barquero as quintessential for an autonomous development. The question, posed therefore is whether it is the prospect of regional development that produces cooperation, or consensus that produces regional development.

In an analysis of research on regional elites conducted over two decades Putnam reports that there are changes in the political culture in Italian regions. This has resulted in 'open partisanship' and the 'building' of new regional institutions.

> The first two decades of the regional experiment witnessed a dramatic change in political climate and culture, a trend away from ideological conflict toward collaboration, from extremism toward moderation ... from abstract doctrine toward practical management (Putnam, 1993, p.36).

Accounting for these changes, three hypotheses are proposed: 'electoral replacement', 'national politics' and 'institutional socialisation'. With the use of a series of panel surveys he supports the conclusion that electoral replacement played no contribution to the change; national political trends played a modest role; while institutional socialisation has the highest effect on the moderation of political views. The significance of this study is that it points to the 'fostering of a tolerant, collaborative pragmatism' (1993, p.38) among members of the new political elites.[8] This pragmatism could affect their attitudes and interaction with the local business elites. Putnam concludes by claiming that 'social context and history profoundly condition the effectiveness of institutions' (1993, p.182) assuming that different civic traditions are the basis of regional success. Civic community or civic virtue could provide a conducive background to the development and interaction within contemporary regional society but I contend that they are not necessarily the driving forces behind elite interaction.[9]

Overall, I have found a number of examples in recent regional elite research to lend support to some of the conclusions I reached. In this respect I have provided some validation to my results, even though other regional elite surveys are not always directly addressing the same issues that I do and cannot therefore provide a direct test of criterion validity.

Inferences

A number of inferences can be made from testing the hypotheses. It has been demonstrated that the interaction between business and political elites in the two regions, is marked by structural differences. A number of secondary tests constructed point to issue involvement of different elite groups, in accordance with their perceived regional interests. So, unexpectedly, it appears that Strathclyde political and Cretan business elites are more concordant with one another on issues of autonomy than with their respective regional counterparts! Moreover, it appears to be the case that this similarity in attitudes does not correspond to their respective occupational categories. I have explained this discrepancy as 'issue involvement' together with a presumed division between 'moderate' and 'radical' elites. This latter classification refers to the degree that elite groups investigated welcome or fear change, as it pertains to European integration and regional autonomy.

It seems to be the case as well, that aspirations for enhancing devolution are linked with expectations of higher prosperity (and possibly social justice in the case of Strathclyde). Furthermore, some members of regional elites are objecting to the centralisation of the nation state in its present form. Which will signify that their support of regional autonomy may be based upon an objection on principle to state centralisation.

I have hypothesised that differences in attitudinal patterns by affecting elite interaction will be directly related to the 'endowment base' of a region. This will be the case if the assumption is accepted that regional elites are of paramount importance to regional development. The investigation of this premise in the last section of my analysis points to a relationship between concordance of attitudes on certain key issues and regional performance. This is linked to evidence in support of the premise that a higher degree of concordance, between a region's elite groups, indicates better development prospects for a region.

The importance of European regional elites and their significance in the European political arena is expounded by Harvie (1994). While Keating (1992) notes that the emergence of a 'variable geometry state order' directly affects European regional interaction. Taken one step further this notion could imply that regions will be 'emancipated' within a European space of regional units. In this way regions will become significant political actors as part of the formation and implementation of EU policy.[10]

The roots of 'regionalisation' of European Union members can be traced beyond the current preoccupation with regional welfare.[11] It is suggested that European funding institutions favour a 'regionalisation' of member states that would enhance efficiency, bypassing national governments and dealing directly with the regions. On the other hand it is suggested that 'the EU does not intend to play the role of "universal liberator" of subnational government' (Van der Knaap, 1994, p. 96) while at the same time it has been suggested that 'the Commission seeks to increase communication and contact with subnational groups and regional bodies on the periphery' (Bomberg, 1994, p.58). These analyses point to the fact that policies and motives towards regions by European Commission policy makers are ambivalent. Do EU policies really empower European regions? Is that the result of a conscious attempt to do so by the European Commission? I have great doubts to that effect. The process witnessed here seem to be the outcome of generic processes that transform the nature of interaction within the 'multi-perspectival' European political landscape. These processes cannot be attributed to the will of any one actor.

In the case of the Scottish regional elites it can be argued that at the time of the survey the Labour controlled Strathclyde Regional and Glasgow City Councils had a positive and constructive relationship with the local business community. It was further the case that most businessmen had a very positive image of the local political elite.[12] Major differences between the two groups centred around attitudes towards regional autonomy, grievance towards their national government and attitudes towards European integration.

In the case of the Cretan regional elites it can be assumed that they exhibit a sharing of purpose that takes them beyond perceived differences in their views on autonomy and European integration. Both Cretan elite subgroups seem to share a sense of what comprises common goods, while at the same time appear divided along party political lines, in a much more categorical way than is the case in Strathclyde.[13] The Cretans seem to differ consistently in all attitudes measured and indexes constructed. Their views on regional autonomy, being overall negative, seem to be undermined by their very strong sense of regional identity on all issues raised. They seem unwilling (or it could be argued unable) therefore to construct a mature case for autonomy as they lack an autonomy inspired 'cultural elite'.[14]

So the two regional elites although living in regions with a strong regional (if not nationalist ethnic) identity, do not share similar aspirations to autonomous rule.[15] In particular the Scottish *ethnie*[16] seems comparatively emancipated, compared with the Cretan *ethnie* that appears subsumed to a greater Hellenic national identity.[17]

It is unfortunate that I cannot determine the degree to which local elite attitudes reflect public opinion. It appears that elite perceptions coincide more with politically over-participating groups and the middle class than they do with the disenfranchised (Nie and Verba, 1975). It could thus be assumed that political elites have a close attitude concordance with the middle classes (most of this sample could be considered as middle class). If that is the case, views held by politicians on European integration for instance, could be considered relevant to a wider audience.

From the exposition of findings it becomes apparent that subnational elites in the two regions have indeed different attitudinal patterns and perceptions.

It is not apparent however, whether subnational elite groups have separate behavioural patterns than national ones. Since the samples investigated did not contain specifically national elites or other elite 'control groups' no inferences can be made on that front. Evidence from all research quoted in this chapter provide relevant support to both my conclusions and my inferences. Theoretical assumptions of other researchers are broadly in accord with the results I present here. In this respect an element of construct validity is successful, as attitude measurements complied with the theoretical predictions of hypotheses constructed. Furthermore, it is assumed that cultural and ethnic characteristics indeed separate the Cretan and Scottish regional elites from their respective nation states. I can make no direct assumptions however on the degree to which the national political and business culture subjugates the respective regional cultures. There is some evidence to suggest that regional culture, if not predominant, is at least significant in attitude formation in the two regions investigated.[18]

The question finally arises of whether I have demonstrated the existence of regional behaviour, that is distinct from national behaviour, for the relevant regional elites investigated. As this is a comparative inquiry, I can attest that the empirical findings separate the elites investigated according to their attitudes between the two regions. I have come to no conclusions as to what extent these regional elites have distinctively separate attitudes from their respective national elites not having a national sample to compare each region. I will proceed with a purely exploratory inquiry of this topic in the following section.

Regional Elite Behaviour?

Generalisations made here focused, on purpose on two regions with different cultural and socioeconomic character that share however, certain identifiable common political attributes. The use of two regions not within the confines of a single nation state was based on my assumption that in the emerging European polity, even the most disparate of regional units will be likely to share a number of common features. One of these could be the behaviour of their regional elites, particularly if we accept that in the context of globalisation elites will exhibit similar value systems and consequently behaviour (Lasch, 1995). I will argue here that 'regional behaviour' (beyond the culturally defined expected difference in behaviour among regions with different ethnic backgrounds), will be one of the by-products of European integration. It could be further implied that it is one of the major intangible assets of a region.

The basic arguments on globalisation[19] and the emergence of an identifiable political class at the regional level I have assumed would be related to the existence of an identifiable regional behaviour. Post-modernity may be relevant to the vision of Anthony Giddens who predicts that it 'would not be a world that "collapses outward" into decentralised organisations but would no doubt interlace the local and global in complex fashion' (1991, p.178).[20] To the degree that this signifies the emergence of new forms of polity, the relationship between the local/regional units will become the arena where most political decisions, affecting everyday life, will be taken. This perspective transcends the view of the emergence of regional democracy, as a response to the need of the contemporary overburdened nation states for increased legitimacy, as I will be arguing further on. In this context, regionalism within post or radicalised modernity (as defined by Giddens, 1991, p.150) and the focus on a Europe of the Regions among European elites are not necessarily related. The latter has more to do with the democratic deficit of European Union institutions and a nation-based regionalism.[21]

The institutional antagonisms within the EU are also relevant to the emergent importance of regions.[22] The European Commission 'in order to increase its political autonomy ... is looking for "new partners" against the omnipotent Council' (Van der Knaap, 1994, p.90).[23] On the other hand local elites as part of 'territorial communities' that affect decisions taken at the EU institutions are not necessarily 'agents of change' or 'champions of oppositional interests' (Bomberg, 1994, p.56). In the French case Dupoirier (1994) asserts that the emergence of regional elites has fostered an increased awareness on the role of new regions, which in turn has led to an increase in regional autonomy. A similar case is made for Germany where 'the success of "co-operative federalism" was partly due to the emergence of regional political elites' (Harvie, 1994, p.59).[24] It is the same case in Spain where 'incipient regional autonomy' has 'brought about both awareness that local community work is a necessary condition for solving local problems and the willingness of local actors to co-operate' (Vazquez-Barquero, 1990, p.371). In Italy Putnam suggests that 'regional leaders exercised more independent influence' in the 1990s than they did in the 1970s while 'over the last two decades the region has become an authentic, autonomous, and increasingly distinctive arena in Italian politics' (1993, p.47). These accounts take the perspective that regional elites developed as a result of legislation establishing autonomous government in the regional level, this in turn is assumed to lead to elite formation by a process of adjustment and incorporation to the new institutional regime that has in turn produced elite 'institutionalisation'.

I have argued earlier that the regionalisation process is a 'response' to globalisation. The 'glocal' (Swygendouw, 1992) signifies both the importance of 'place productivity' as well as the increased relevance of 'information networks' (Jensen-Butler, 1996). So, the increased relevance of local economic actors to regional competitiveness and the effect of the welfare state in increasing the power and relative independence of local political actors is another factor influencing European regionalisation (Lever, 1996).

A rather idealised and glorifying perspective views the regional unit as:

> an institution whose origins are lost in the mists of time, which serves today as a bulwark against totalitarianism. The region is seen to be rooted in a natural law or derived from the theory of intermediate authorities (Kukawaka and Tournon, 1987, p.40).[25]

In the same vein there have been calls for a 'constitutional guarantee for local and regional autonomy within the Community' (Council of Europe, 1990, p.12).[26] According to this view localities, as the focus of the first level of allegiance among citizens and the founding block of democracy, are only important in promoting democratic efficiency. This can only imply, however, that their historical 'fulfilment' will come with an institutionalised decentralisation.

Identifying the EU as the first 'post-modern political unit' it is suggested that integration leads to an 'unbundling of territoriality' which 'is not located some place else: but it is becoming another place' (Ruggie, 1993, p.176). The European Union 'may constitute the first "multiperspectival polity" to emerge since the advent of the modern era' (Ruggie, 1993, pp.171–2). while as a part of a 'nonterritorial global economic region' it is significant in that it embodies 'novel behavioural and institutional forms and ... novel space-time constructs that these forms embody' (Ruggie, 1993, p.173). In other words the EU is perceived not only as related to post-modernity, but also as an *inevitable* by-product of it since 'the emergence of multiperspectival institutional forms was identified as a key dimension in understanding the possibility of postmodernity' (Ruggie, 1993, p.176). In this respect, regional behaviour, in the European context, is determined by the need to redefine identity in a local sphere that could be seen as a by-product of modernity and globalisation.[27] It is also the product of elite interaction as part of territorially based networks that increasingly bypass or even ignore the supremacy of nation state policy networks.[28] And although, as Smith points out, the emergence of a 'distinctive value and belief-system shared exclusively by the peoples of Europe' (1995, p.128) may be a chimera, the realities of globalisation are creating the conditions for reasserting regional identities.

This condition is not one that directly threatens the nation state or national identity.[29] The nation state can coexist within the concentric circles of citizens allegiances and patterns of identification.[30] It is the behaviour of citizens at their locality that can act as a point of convergence for their self-identification and serve as a focus of their identity.[31] The academic interest on regional behaviour will increase in tandem with evidence of the emergence of a 'variable geometry state order' (Keating, 1992, p.60).

In my analysis most of the difference of regional elite attitudes within the regions investigated can be explained away by party political and socioeconomic considerations. Differences between the two regions however cannot as readily be explained away by the same political or socioeconomic factors. I have uncovered some evidence suggesting that it is their occupational position as businessmen or politicians that accounts for most of the variation in attitudes within regions. While, on most attitudes investigated, Cretan and Strathclyde elites show a variation in attitude. At the same time there appears to be a higher concordance of attitudes in Crete, which is the less developed region examined, than in Strathclyde, which is the more developed region.

My perspective being 'agent-based' it may be inherently restricted, as I try to examine how regional elites influence their regional environment. In that respect, it could also be suggested that my account of the importance of 'regional behaviour', as it is related to globalisation and European integration, may be limited in the same way that neorealist and neofunctionalist accounts are in their analysis of European integration (Hix, 1994). My 'alternative' interpretation of regional behaviour as one of the forces of European integration can be related to what Wallace calls 'informal integration', which consist of 'intense interaction patterns' that are a result of the 'dynamics of markets, technology, communications networks and social change' (1990, p.9).[32]

Inferences that can be made on the general population in the regions examined are naturally limited. This is particularly the case since not all aspects of the relevant hypotheses could be examined in this work, a result of limited content validity. It is also impossible to deduce 'laws' of conduct for regional elites or infer the emergence of 'regional behaviour' throughout the EU from the comparative examination of two non-typical regions.

So, although I cannot pretend to have 're-evaluated' the role of regional elites, I have found some evidence to suggest that their role is indeed vital for the economic development of regional units. The process of European integration could be leading to the reasserting of regional identities and the re-enforcement of those codes of conduct that will lead to the recognition of 'regional behaviour' as a variable of regional development.[33] In this respect I am in agreement with Rosamond in his claim that 'there may indeed be identifiable sets of global dynamics, but their impact is entirely dependent upon the mediation provided by localities and regions' (1995, p.401). I cannot give evidence of a transformation of regional civil society as I do not engage in a longitudinal analysis, I can detect causes of strain and discontent with institutional arrangements regarding the respective nation states that could be eventually related to the emergence of 'regional awareness'. This, as I have tried to portray from my analysis of the current academic discourse, is not necessarily envisaged as an antagonistic 'sub-state nationalism'. The emergence of a politically significant and identifiable 'regional behaviour' can be partly related to the opportunities presented to regional elites by the emergence of the new European polity. [34] It can be in that sense the product of European integration under the influence of globalisation and radicalised modernity.

Investigating Networks of Interaction within Regions

There are a number of issues that I have considered relevant to this investigation and which I have not been able to test with the measures employed My inquiry has touched upon a number of these issues and I have consequently decided to give a number of *ex post facto* explanations that can be used in developing relevant research designs and hypotheses in the future. The first of these fields is the perceived role of multinational enterprises and therefore international capital in a regional economy. Attitudes towards multinationals could be linked with attitudes to regional autonomy. Secondly, attitudes on European integration may also be linked with regional elite alienation from the state centre. This may be due to the increase in grievance towards the nation state in tandem with an increase in expectations from the supranational EU.[35] Further research is also needed on the effect of elites' 'locally biased' mental maps of opportunity. These may be affecting regional competitiveness by being markedly different between regional political and business elites. This last sphere of 'distorted maps of opportunity' could be relevant to the current preoccupation with globalisation and the consequences of modernity (or post/radicalised modernity).

What I have termed 'regional behaviour' could be relevant to the emergence of a new regional affinity in defiance to, or as a consequence of, the so called laws of globalisation and capitalist accumulation. We may be witnessing the beginning of an era in which there will be a re-focusing of allegiance to more narrowly defined territorial localities/regions. Such a development will find us ill equipped in making interpretations or understanding change, if current dividing lines between fields of social science research are maintained. New challenges require new tools which can be provided only by taking a multidisciplinary perspective and by relying on a multitude of methods of inquiry.[36]

Finally, I would suggest that a regional behaviour approach can enhance one of the emerging perspectives in regional inquiry namely the policy networks approach. It is assumed that within the context of multiperspectival polities (and multi-level governance) policy networks can improve our understanding of how regional elites interact as well as how they interlink with national and supra-national ones.[37] When this is a qualitative policy area inquiry it is open to the criticism that 'if you will look for policy networks you can find them in all aspects of governance' alluding therefore to limited explanatory power. When sociometrics are employed there seems to be an inherent weakness in determining how closely policy communities and policy networks mirror power networks or indeed determining the 'currency' of interaction within networks.[38] In that respect actor 'centrality' or 'betweenness' may be inadequate determinants of interaction.[39] I suggest that elite value sharing should be considered at least as important in determining the effectiveness of network connections. In the same vein we can identify those value categories (i.e. social equity) that acquire salience in effective interaction. It should therefore be possible to determine the quality and effectiveness of exchange among actors. In this context, the possibility that collaboration between elites is conditional on sharing of certain values warrants further investigation. Elite actor concordance can enhance our understanding of transactions within regional networks as well as provide us with a better insight of the effects of such interaction on society and the regional milieu.

Notes

1   The use in this research of both techniques could be improved by devising a model in the future for case intensive quantitative elite surveys. I have used a quasi-experimental design by employing both qualitative and quantitative techniques. This design led to the introduction of a number of substantive differences in the interpretation of results. A more thorough exposition of the research design is presented in the appendix.

2   Note should also be made that the survey took place in 1991 before the proposals for the reorganisation of the Scottish local authorities were finalised (Scottish Office, 1992) let

alone the creation of a Scottish Parliament. Similarly there was no indication that legislation on Greek devolution was likely to be enacted (Law 2218/94).

3   In this respect I would mention here the effect of personnel and social circulation among political elites that point to the 'transient' character of any elite survey. These factors can be particularly significant in times of institutional change, which could influence the composition of emergent local elites.

4   From the measures compared in the index of Table 7.6 in Chapter Seven, it becomes apparent that difference in attitudes among Strathclyde elites receive high scores on issues of 'grievance towards their national government' and 'attitudes towards regional autonomy' (ranging from 50.5 to 55.1 index points) and low scores on all other measures (from 8.2 to 8.8 index points). At the same time Cretan elites show a consistent discordance but with much lower divergence on all measures investigated (ranging from 14.3 to 26.2 index points).

5   A relevant analysis of regional elite roles by Lucas (1994) makes a number of relevant conclusions that cannot however be validly considered as his analysis focuses on Kenya. He found a link between the diminishing of state capacity and an increase in elite leverage while 'factions of the [regional] elite are interested in establishing and elaborating their own identity and bases of power, distinct from the state' (Lucas, 1994, p.38). Closer to home Lecomte testifies of the emergence of a 'politically defined regional identity' (1994, p.143) in the region of Rhone-Alps.

6   In a comparative analysis of four Spanish regions' political and socioeconomic elites Morata points to 'the existence of a regional elite which is highly professionalised and with a tendentiously pragmatic and rather anti-centralist behaviour' (1992, p.215). It is easy to infer that a professionalised regional elite would facilitate interaction between the business and political elites. Evident in an identifiable 'general agreement in favour of increasing regional powers at the expense of the central government' (Morata, 1992, p.215).

7   Vazquez-Barquero also attests to the significance of the 'mobilisation of the endogenous development potential' (1992b, p.32) that would imply the active cooperation between regional political and business elites.

8   I note here reservations on some of the assumptions made by Putnam in *Making Democracy Work* as expressed by Tarrow (1996) and some appraisal by Katz (1993).

9   The seminal work by Almond and Verba (1963) *The Civic Culture: Political Attitudes and Democracy in Five Nations* is the starting point, in empirical political science, for the debate on liberal versus civic citizen values. A recent survey by Miller et al. (1995) points to the relevance of 'the moral community' in modern Britain in questions posed to local politicians and a sample of the public.

10 The role of local political elites as instigators of institutionalised cooperation across-regions is explored in an article by Perulli (1992) on the Alpe Adria Community.

11 European regional funding through the ERDF, but also through the EIB, the EAGF and the ESF are increasingly directed at the regional level (Armstrong, 1993). It is also assumed that Community Support Frameworks (CSF) are geared towards the coordination of the existing EU funds in peripheral and less developed regions (Hitiris, 1994). More importantly it has been suggested that the coordination of regional funding has in some cases (i.e. Greece) introduced 'the role of regional authorities as effective administrators of development policies' (Bianchi, 1992, p.66). Using the Integrated Mediterranean Programmes as a paradigm it is suggested that 'the IMPs have actively contributed to launching (Greece) or relaunching (France, Italy) the idea of regional planning' (Bianchi,

1992, p.65). This view suggests that national governments devolve and decentralise by their own design seeking efficiency gains and increased European funding.

12 In this instance I refer to their positive replies to questions QB11 (78 per cent), QB12 (71 per cent) and QB13 (74 per cent) inquiring whether businessmen found local politicians more or equally fervent, effective and receptive than local MPs.

13 The difference in values among peoples in the two regions investigated can be credibly linked to the character of the respective societies and the level of their industrialisation and development. It is possible that Cretan people are not consciously aware of the class dimension of political action in a 'mobilised' sense. Attitudes of elites are not necessarily representative of those of the greater populace. So, a connection with class political perceptions, although relevant, is not necessarily a determining factor.

14 There appears to be no significant academic, cultural or artistic discourse in support of a Cretan identity separate from the Greek one. I assume thus that although there exists an identifiable and separate Cretan identity within the concentric identities of the greater Greek *ethnos* (Hertzfeld, 1985, p.xii) there is a lack of willingness (and possibly as well, a local elite incentive) to build-up a consciousness of 'autonomy'. This does not mean that the output of local cultural elites can not be co-opted at a future date on an autonomy inspired build-up of a regional cultural identity as discussed by Anderson (1991).

15 Kellas defines ethnic groups as being 'essentially exclusive' compared with nations which 'are more inclusive and are culturally or politically defined' (1991, p.4).

16 Smith gives a concise definition of *ethnies* which are 'named units of population with common ancestry myths and historical memories, elements of shared culture, some link with a historic territory and some measure of solidarity, at least among their elites' (1995, p.57). Smith distinguishes between "lateral' or aristocratic and the 'vertical' or demotic types of *ethnies*' (1995, pp. 58–9), he further suggests that some *ethnies* are 'peripheral' in that they are determined by a core-periphery relation of alienation and subordination to dominant ethnic communities, as were the Scots to the English. A discussion of nation-building as part of 'an invented tradition' (Hobsbawm, 1983) and an 'imagined community' (Anderson, 1991) takes account of the needs imposed on nation states by capitalism and modernity. A critical account of 'post-modern' views of nationalism is given by Billig (1995).

17 Diamandouros points to the importance of the 'fragmentation' and 'geographical isolation' of Greek society under Ottoman rule 'which gave rise to an ethos of pronounced localism and parochialism that was effectively to impede national integration by placing a premium on primordial sentiments, and by producing fierce and lasting local and regional attachments' (1983, p.46). Greek nationalism during the formation of the Greek state was all pervasive, while religion was used as an 'ethnic tool' that infused 'distinctive life-styles, customs, language and ancestry myths with the capacity for self-renewal and reinterpretation under changed conditions' (Smith, 1986, p.260, n.51). In this context all divergent local identities were subdued to the dominant Byzantine-Hellenistic tradition. An anthropological account of a 'recessive' local ethnic identity in modern Greece can be found in Campbell (1964).

18 In their verbatim replies to questions pertaining to how 'separate' people are in their locality and the rest of the nation (QD9, QD10) respondents invariably expounded on cultural differences.

19 I note here that globalisation is not an inevitable condition of contemporary capitalism but is seen by some as 'no more than an argument deployed by the right to cow the left [as it] denudes the few existing international institutions of the political and financial support necessary to upgrade their capacity to shape and manage current trends' (Hutton, 1995).

20 For a critical account of the 'neoconservativeness' of postmodernity see Habermas (1987).

21 The idea of a 'Europe of the Regions' received attention during the negotiations and the signing of the Treaty of the European Union which instituted a Committee of the Regions. A critical account of the notion is given by Borras-Alomar et al. who attest that 'the utopian discourse of a harmonious, peaceful "Europe of the Regions" has practically no resemblance with current practices, nor even with probable future developments' (1994, p.21). Keating suggests that 'the Europe of the regions scenario stumbles on the awkward fact that there are no natural regions or nations in Europe' (1992, p.52). It can also be assumed that the EU needs to operate at a scale intermediate between the state and the locality for its policy initiatives to be effective.

22 A thorough account on the institutional dynamics of the EU can be found in Lodge (1993; 1995), who makes a very concise case for redressing the democratic deficit, as does Martin (1991) in a federalist inspired diatribe.

23 In this respect 'one by-product of the subsidiarity debate has been the opening up of a related discussion about expanding the role of subnational governments in EC policy making' (Peterson, 1994, p.129).

24 Although it can also be claimed that the emergence of regional elites in Germany is the product of a unique political moment in the historical development of the German state. A number of relevant arguments on German regional elites are analysed in Kuhne and Ruck (1993).

25 A narrowly defined economic argument is also put forward for the importance of emergent 'region-states [which] are the natural economic zones in a borderless world because, by definition, the demands of the global economy shape their contours' (Ohmae, 1995, p.134). It is further suggested that now 'economic activity is what defines the landscape on which all other institutions, including political institutions, must operate' (Ohmae, 1995, p.129), while 'nation states are eroding as economic actors. Region states are taking shape' (Ohmae, 1995, p.137). This view completely ignores the role of international politics by assuming that 'all politics is local', by inferring that all human motivation is economic and by supposing that local, national and international elites always aim (or should aim) at the highest economic returns.

26 A call for 'strengthening the regional structures in Europe' (Robert, 1985, p.4) is also related to the need for efficient regional development.

27 The redefinition of regional identity in the political sphere is not necessarily identical with notions of regional culture or local ethnic identity. The two spheres may be related but should not be confused. According to Keating 'there is a danger of culture becoming a residual category to explain everything which can not be explained in terms of structures or political choice' (1991, p.3).

28 In his study of 'civic traditions in modern Italy' Putnam suggests that the civic community is far from disappearing and that globalisation and modernity do not necessarily mean that 'modernity is the enemy of civility' (Putnam, 1993, p.114).

29 Indeed it has been suggested that 'The growth of initiatives and competencies on regional and European levels is accompanied, in many instances, by a reassertion of national governments and bureaucracies', while at the same time 'the place of regions in Europe is alongside that of national and non-state actors' (Borras-Alomar et al., 1994, p.24).

30 See Smith (1996) for an account of how 'concentric identities' coincide with 'concentric models of territorialised governance' in France.

31 In this context Keating also asserts that 'territorial autonomy will depend less on the acquisition by regions and stateless nations of state like attributes and competencies ... than on the constitution of their civil societies' (1992, p.59).

32 It would be further interesting to note a shift in the emphasis of the debate on globalisation to local and regional 'subnationalisms' (Featherstone, 1990) as well as the emergence of an agenda on the *Self-determination of Minorities in International Politics* (Heraclides, 1991).

33 It has further been argued that 'national and subnational identities are reimagined as awareness of external, globalizing "threats" takes place' (Rosamond, 1995, p.401).

34 Wallace claims that the EU is better understood as 'a semi-developed political system than as a highly interdependent regional international system' (1994, p.272), the EU is still on the formative phase of its institutional and maybe as well of its social development.

35 For instance the question arose whether a higher level of devolution is correlated with higher aspirations to autonomy. Evidence gathered suggests that Strathclyde politicians have a high positive attitude towards regional autonomy while, the only other group with a high positive attitude are Cretan businessmen. The two subgroups would reasonably be expected to give answers on opposing sides of that scale. Since there is no corroboration and the data appear inconclusive this question has to remain open in this thesis.

36 I have borrowed concepts and dealt with both theoretic and empirical material beyond those of purely political science or European integration studies from among others, political geography, political sociology, social anthropology, regional economics and political economy. I note here the results of a round table organised under the aegis of the Journal of Common Market Studies, where it was stressed that studies of European integration need to be interdisciplinary, while there was also a call for an integration of empirical and theoretical work (Bulmer and Scott, 1994).

37 Noting the limitations expressed earlier on employing policy networks as more than an investigative tool (Kassim, 1995; Peterson, 1994).

38 Social network analysis methodology in Scott (1991) and Wasserman and Faust (1994), while political networks are analysed by Knoke (1990).

39 For an excellent empirical investigation with the use of sociometrics see John and Cole (1996).

Appendix

On Methodology and Validity

A Framework for Surveying Regional Elites

The survey employed researches attitudinal characteristics of two key elite groups in each region investigated.[1] Attitudes from elite groups are juxtaposed in an effort to reveal inter and intra region (within and between) variances of elite perceptions. The use of regional elite groups, comparatively, on a cross-national survey is not tantamount to assuming that regional elite groups vary from national ones. A more extensive survey should include the national elites as a control for a presumed regional distinctiveness of regional elites a feat which is not attempted here.[2]

The number of factors that can influence attitudinal responses and the number of measurements relevant are vast. I have attempted a measurement of direction and intensity of attitudes in a thorough manner.[3] I have also tried to take account of issue salience, inconsistency of responses and degree of inclusiveness without however making them a central element in my analysis.[4] Certain important conditions that affect response patterns are taken into consideration although I have attempted to steer away from an extensive analysis based on behavioural psychology focusing instead on political behaviour.[5]

The survey I conducted has a number of limitations relating to the size and the selected subsets of the particular elite populations, these could, in many respects, characterise this as a comparative rather than a pure survey analysis.[6] In selecting and defining type of questions that can be asked and elite groups that can be successfully approached I understood that 'the procedures still involve a considerable amount of ad hoc choice in order to cope with the complexities of the real world' (Moyser, 1987, p.15) which in turn make the use of elite interviewing techniques imperative in order to 'reveal information about underlying attitudes, interactions and intentions ' (Moyser, 1987, p.18).[7]

I had initially aimed to attain a nomothetic explanation with this project, it became apparent early-on however that a number of restrictions, arising from sampling bias and the idiosyncrasies of the particular regions investigated limited the scope of generalisations and theorising.[8] Internal and external validation have been attempted in the concluding chapter.[9]

Evidently this work cannot attempt a dynamic interpretation of possible relationships revealed.[10] The aim instead is to give, to the degree possible, a snapshot picture of the regional elites investigated. Relationships revealed are used to test hypotheses.[11] Exploratory tests attempted provide some evidence of trends in certain attitudes of regional elite groups. In the final chapter the proposition of whether elite interaction influences regional prospects, is considered.[12] However, the temporality of the data stream and limitations in the sample size, do not allow a genuinely predictive interpretation, but limit this work to an exploratory and predominantly inductive investigation.

It must always be borne in mind that this is a cross-sectional survey of the particular regional samples. Attitudinal responses aid in elaborating an analysis of regional actors attitudes, which with the aid of qualitative data can be used to partially determine their influence in the political and economic affairs of their region.[13] It can be deduced that the attitude measures constructed indicate elite value systems or what Van Deth and Scarbrough call 'underlying value orientations' when they suggest that we can 'infer values from data about attitudes' (1995, p.37).[14] Although value systems and orientations of the elite groups investigated are inherently interesting, particularly as these relate to their cultural background, there has be no attempt here to construct a 'values profile' further than the one that can be inferred from their general attitudinal profile. However, by presuming that regional elites will be influenced by their different institutional and cultural backgrounds (their separate value systems), there has been an expectation to find variations in the attitude of individuals that are resonant with their background when comparing samples from the two regions.[15]

The use of a structured survey was employed to aid in the codification of a comparatively large number of elite interviews. Failure to codify from the beginning would have resulted in a big loss of data or producing data particularly susceptible to interviewer and analysis bias. Codification itself however entails some loss of data particularly in the cases where data series have to be collapsed in order to create meaningful statistics.[16] An ultimate test of the hypotheses is provided by juxtaposing standardised data with respondents' qualifications or explanations on issues raised by the questionnaire.[17] This alludes to what I have earlier called a 'linked data analysis' between quantitative and qualitative data. This technique can enable mutual confirmation or corroboration in the analysis of data, assist in elaborating the relevant themes and draw attention to paradoxes in the data.[18]

In the analysis of the quantitative data SPSS-PC and SPSS for Windows software has been employed while in the analysis of qualitative data there is an application of comprehensive transcript briefs of each question to the questionnaire. In dealing with over one hundred interviews (76 are part of the attitudinal analysis) I can bear witness to the limitations of qualitative research analysis. I anticipated using the QSR.NUD*IST software but it has eventually proved unnecessary.[19]

Approaching Political and Business Elites in Strathclyde and Chania

Having the distinct task of identifying the business and political elite groups within their respective civil society, I had to deal with a number of considerations of research validity. As mentioned already I share one of Welsh's concerns on political elites that could apply to business elites as well:

> it seems dubious to assume that any individual who holds membership in a prominent decision-making body actually exercises influence on political outcomes. His colleagues may be influential, but it does not necessarily follow that he is (Welsh, 1979 p.166).

So, initially one has to deal with the problem of an individual holding positional but not functional 'eliteness'. While the possibility exists as well, that 'elites may occupy formal positions for nonfunctional reasons' (Welsh, 1979, p.166).[20]

Beyond procedures and measures, analysed in the following section, a bias arises from the fact that personal judgement on who does or does not hold functional or reputational eliteness, partly influenced who I chose to approach for an interview although their positional eliteness was the decisive factor in attempting to interview. This is particularly relevant for most of the Cretan survey, where approaching interviewees was less structured and based more on a 'snowballing' technique, that is fraught with reputational bias.[21]

Equally, I recognise the possibility that a particular elite member is an extremist, a maverick which has no influence among his peers, society or over decision making structures. In this volume admittedly, I cannot resolve issues dealing with a 'reputational definition of eliteness', but I felt inclined to consider problems of identification of individuals in the 'elite proper' category.

In the business samples surveyed there is an attempted to 'limit our definition of economic elites to those exercising allocative control' (Whitley, 1974, p.115). An effort to that end was of interviewing managing directors or owners-entrepreneurs in the companies approached. Failing to secure an appointment with the managing director I tried to interview one of the executive directors, never interviewing non-executive (or ceremonial) directors. The sampling method for the business sample identified suitable companies first (based on a number of criteria on size by number of employees and turnover) and their managing directors second. In the case of Glasgow/Strathclyde I used a register of companies out of which by random selection a letter was sent asking the company managing director for a forty minute interview stating the cause of this research.[22] In the case of Chania I used a register of trading companies supplied by the local Chamber of Commerce together with a list of all registered companies from which a random sample of address and telephones was used to contact prospective interviewees.

The mailing in Chania produced no replies and so each company was approached individually by telephone.[23] The character of the contact thus was much more impromptu and it could be argued that the Greek sample is biased by the personal response interaction to the interviewer. There seems no way I could eliminate that bias, if it exists, impromptu surveying being the standard practice in Greece.[24] After a series of phone calls an interview time and date was agreed which in many cases did not necessarily mean the individual in question would adhere to appointments in 'submitting' to an interview.

Overall, I eliminated companies with fewer than five employees in Greece and ten employees in UK from the sampling. Proprietors of such small companies usually falling within the self-employed category and with typically a very small chance of belonging to the local business elite.[25]

For the political samples I targeted individuals in the local and national executives of elected officials in both countries. As mentioned above however, I could not secure any interviews from the Greek national executive. This fact is limiting the scope of this research and the consequent hypotheses that can be effectively examined. Furthermore, as is apparent in the profile of elites interviewed (developed in chapter five) in Crete most of the interviewees were entrepreneurs, while in Strathclyde most were executives.

In Strathclyde, political elite interviewees came from the following bodies:

a) the City Council of Glasgow;
b) Strathclyde Regional Council;
c) the UK Parliament (elected in Glasgow);
d) the European Parliament (elected in Glasgow);
e) political candidates or activists in above bodies.

In the prefecture of Chania political elite interviewees came from:

a) local Community Councils (Presidents);
b) small Town Councils (Mayors);
c) Chania City Council (Mayor and Councillors); and
d) political parties (influential activists in Chania).

My approach on the political sample was very similar to the one used on the business one. I used a mailing for arranging an interview in the case of the Scottish sample, while I came in touch with the local community liaison officer in the Chania City Hall who introduced me to a meeting of the local mayors. Additionally a list of elected officials provided from the office of the prefecture served as reference for approaching local community mayors. In this respect there are both elements of 'snowballing' and random selection in the Cretan sample. Unsuccessful attempts to interview the Cretan members of the Greek parliament were made both by a mailing and by personal contact in the House of Parliament (*Vouli ton Ellinon*) in Athens.

In both samples interviewing activists and individuals with political importance were pursued after referrals to the particular individuals by some of the office bearing interviewees. In this sense their selection is not random and their replies have to be considered in this light.

Another issue that arose was that of interlockingness. In some cases I found interviewees to belong to both elite groups simultaneously. This likelihood was closely scrutinised. The inclusion of a question inquiring on politician's business links (QC14) is meant to explore precisely that possibility. To determine whether business respondents had an elite position in the political world I specifically asked whether they held an elected position to a public body.

In two cases in the Greek sample and in one in the Scottish sample I found political personalities that also had an influential function in the business world. In those cases they were asked to answer the whole of the survey (including both business and political sections). I hoped to be able to make particular inferences from their responses but opted instead for eliminating one from the business and the other from the political analysis in the Greek case (reasoning explained in Chapter Five) and keeping the Strathclyde respondent within the political sample. I further avoided in the business sample the inclusion of heads of governmental agencies or organisations, academics or consultants, as I believed this could spoil the 'purity' of the sample.[26] I made a point of interviewing a number of them (as a pilot and not as part of the survey) in both regions and found they provided me with a very good understanding of local culture and civil society. These groups obviously belong to the wider elite structure, but I have attempted here to narrow the sample to the absolutely necessary groups in order to increase the significance of my conclusions.[27]

Response Rate in Approaching Key Actors

The diversity of cultures between Scotland and Crete also determined the approach I could employ to interview the respective elites. It became apparent very early on that the Greek samples had to be approached differently than what could be considered standard code of practice in Britain.

In the case of the Scottish political elite, all Glasgow MPs and MEPs were approached, together with a number of the local regional and City Councillors. Two MEPs (out of three) responded and were subsequently interviewed, while three out of 11 MPs responded and were subsequently interviewed. The Councillors contacted were selected randomly from the list of Councillors of the two bodies (City, Region). There are 66 elected Councillors in Glasgow City, while there were 103 Councillors in the Strathclyde Regional Council.[28] Regional representatives with a constituency outwith Glasgow I considered part of the local elite, since their decisions are bound to influence local affairs, and have not been therefore excluded from the sampling.

A rough estimate of the membership of the local political elite will include all those presently in office, together with those that could most seriously challenge them in the next election (the elite-in-waiting).[29] It will also include their most trusted advisors, and the senior bureaucracy of the Councils, the local arm of the national bureaucracy (i.e. the Scottish Office or the office of the Prefecture) and the Regional Development agencies.[30] Assuming a strong local political culture, I could also consider as members of the local political elite, editors of local political papers, senior political activists within party hierarchies and prominent intellectuals that influence or challenge political thought and concepts in the region.[31] Resource limitations did not permit the thorough investigation of all sections of the local political elite. In my Strathclyde political sample I have interviewed 21 elected representatives out of the 182 holding office in the relevant political bodies (a 12 per cent sample) and three from the non-elected regional elite, which my arbitrary estimate brings to 500 individuals.

There were a series of mailings to attain interviews for the Scottish business elite based on a catalogue of business based in Glasgow (ICC, 1989), from which companies with the desired characteristics of number of employees (over nine) and turnover (over £100,000) were randomly selected. This means that business in both industry and services were selected.[32] The mailing of letters requesting interviews was conducted in waves, while all positive responses were followed up. There was a total of six batches with the first one in March and the last one in May of 1991. In total 139 letters were sent-out that led to 24 interviews. That represents a response rate of 17.3 per cent of those approached.[33]

In the case of the Cretan political elite I have used a list of the local Mayors (seven cases), provided by the office of the prefecture, and presidents of local communities which included 152 cases. Since MEPs are elected on a national, rather than a regional constituency, their relevance to regional political life can only be limited; so, I do not consider MEPs a part of the regional elite. There are 21 councillors elected in the Chania City Council, which is the largest and most influential local authority. There are further, four MPs elected to the national parliament from Nomos Chanion. This brings the local elected elite to 184 cases of which I have interviewed 12, or 7 per cent. I have also interviewed two individuals belonging to the non-elected local political elite, which similar to all the regional elite categories described for the Strathclyde political elites, I speculate it consists of 300 individuals.[34]

To identify the Greek business elite I used a list of members to the Chania Chamber of Commerce and Industry (*Emporiko Ke Viomihaniko Epimelitirio Chanion*) as well as from a list of members of the Crafts and local trade associations. I also used a list of 72 exporting companies from the region, targeting the managing directors.[35] My sample of 21 cases represents 20 per cent of that population. There were 2,551 registered enterprises in the prefecture,[36] which could only be an indication of entrepreneurship however, since Labour Statistics are notoriously unreliable in the Greek state. I consider the lists used to offer a close approximation to the size of the local business elite.

So, overall I have interviewed 12 per cent of the Glasgow elected local elite and 7 per cent of the one elected in Nomos Chanion. A token sample of the non-elected political elites was included for both regions. From business elites I have interviewed an estimated 1.2 per cent sample of directors and managers of small, medium and large enterprises in Strathclyde and a 20 per cent sample in Nomos Chanion. These samples being relatively low, affect the inferential value of most statistics employed but by being closely focused on the elite groups identified earlier in this thesis (the influential within a locality) present a fair picture of elite attitudes.

And as for the Weaknesses ...

Issues of validity are often mentioned throughout this work. There is a variety
of reasons why this is the case. As mentioned earlier a small sample coupled
with a restricted population size are main limiting factors. A number of factors
that could compromise the universality of the results are identified and listed
below. For reasons of expediency the limiting factors have been grouped into
six general categories.

1   *Different business conditions* between the two regions surveyed is a factor
    limiting this research. Their divergent state of development was one of the
    criteria for selecting the two particular regions, but it also creates problems
    in the analyses and interpretation of data.
    i)   The possibility (indeed probability), that companies active in the locality
          are not registered there. This could be particularly relevant for the
          Scottish sample. The sampling process in Scotland, of approaching
          locally registered companies, might limit the representativeness of
          the elite sample if a significant part of the local elite operates in non-
          locally registered premises. From empirical evidence – in the data
          collection stage – I consider this factor not to significantly distort the
          sampling as it is expected that most companies whose executives are
          active in the region have a registered office there as well.
    ii)   The average respondent in the Strathclyde business sample could be
          identified as a comparatively successful operator, while unsuccessful
          or companies under liquidation were not likely to be part of the sample,
          as indeed none responded. This bias on successful companies and
          their executives was to some extend the case in Chania as well, since
          the two lists that were used to approach interviewees are of exporting
          companies and the commercial association's members list, which is
          safe to assume include relatively successful enterprises.[37] It could be
          argued that the unsuccessful or temporarily set-back members of the
          economic elite will be more disgruntled and negative towards their
          national government or other institutions they blame for theirs' or
          the markets' failings. There is no concrete indication however that
          this is the case and that the less successful members of the economic
          elite significantly diverge in attitude from their more successful
          counterparts, not to mention the obvious that a pervious member of
          the economic elite that has lately been unsuccessful may not qualify
          to be considered a member of the local business elite.

iii) Cretan businessmen perceive a dependence on resources to the mainland which may bias their answers to the effect that it would be inconceivable for them to express support for autonomy if it meant being cut-off from mainland resources. This I consider to be a psychological barrier to their thinking and it is be given some attention in the analysis.

iv) The most important limiting factor, for comparing businessmen's attitudes is the diverging degree of development of the two regional economies. The maturity of the Strathclyde economy compared with the agriculture/services based Cretan economy is affecting the outlook of the respective elites.[38] Questions on local versus outside investment for example, are directly relevant to the perceived nature of those investments which relate to the degree of development of the local economy. This divergence, is however, part of the reason these questions are significant for a comparative study. In interpreting results this divergence has to be appreciated for the limits it imposes.

2 *Differing political conditions* in the respective regions can have an effect as interviewees may have a different frame of reference and the analysis can be influenced if consideration is not taken of relevant deviations. Many of the limitations pertinent to the political interviewees are also relevant for the business ones and vice versa.

i) The Regional Council of Strathclyde was a local authority with an impressive track record, while its range of services to the local community is wide and varied. By comparison the Regional authority of Nomos Chanion in Crete was for all practical purposes an office of a government appointed prefect (*nomarhis*) with a mandate to oversee government policy. Local government comparisons had to be made between the Strathclyde Regional Council with Nomos Chanion and Glasgow City Council and the City Council of Chania. This reduces comparability of replies of the two elites. The Scottish one having the experience of interaction with a local authority which is very active on the regional level, the Greek one having considered the prefect (nomarhis) as an appendix to the government and the local politicians closely tied with the national political system.[39]

ii) With different competencies of the two countries local authorities, opinions on the fervour and effectiveness of the two groups are less compatible. This affects questions which ask business elite respondents to rate the effectiveness and fervour of Councillors vis-à-vis MPs.

iii) The different structure of local authorities in the two regions could also be 'responsible' for certain attitudes, for instance, institutional structures could be affecting approachability of local Councillors (QB9–QB13). This consideration may be relevant to Greece, where party politics and clientelism further erode direct approach to elected members.

iv) Differences in the electoral systems of the two countries reduce the validity of certain comparisons. Particularly in the case of MEPs who are elected on regional constituencies in the UK, while they are elected on a nation wide party list in Greece.

v) To the degree that the state has an all pervasive superstructure in Greece certain answers can be considered biased since any research, particularly from more senior elite members, may be linked consciously or subconsciously with the maintenance of 'personal files' by the state.[40]

vi) The perceived dependence on out of region resources may bias results to questions relating to autonomy. This may be particularly the case for Crete where qualifications to the quantitative part of the questionnaire suggest a strong perceived but limited real dependence on the mainland.[41]

vii) The difference in size of the relevant economies could support the argument that on the smaller Cretan economy a greater interlockingness of elite positions should be expected, as indeed is the case. This point should be taken into consideration when examining differences in the political culture of the two regions.

viii) As with the business elite's bias of successful companies responding to this survey, in the case of the political elites there might exist a bias of getting responses from elected representatives of parties with a clear political agenda on European issues. It seems to be the case in Strathclyde, where pro-European Liberal Democrats, had a 75 per cent response rate, far surpassing any other political group.

3 *Sample size* related factors are given a more thorough exposition here. Statistical significance cannot be attained for most samples, although the population sizes are comparatively small. In the Strathclyde political sample the MEP population subgroup consists of three cases, this survey includes two of those which would have made it sufficiently significant, it is however the case for most other subgroups that a 50 per cent level of the population size is not attained.

i)   Institute specific hypotheses can not be tested since it would have meant further dividing already small sample sizes. Such questions can only be investigated in an exploratory fashion as part of the qualitative element of this research.

ii) Party specific hypotheses can not be tested for the same reason as above. Again, those hypotheses that are instrumental in the research design will be investigated as part of the qualitative element.[42]

iii) Female, ethnic or other special elite group variations cannot be tested for sample size limitations.

iv) In both regions business samples, executives with ethnic roots outside the region constituted too small a subgroup to effectively test relating hypotheses. Their small overall number provides some evidence in support of some of the hypotheses relating to elite origin, but their small numbers also mean they cannot be used as a control group for the ethnic (i.e. Cretan or Scottish) participants. A similar case holds true for the Strathclyde political sample, where the non-Scottish interviewees are too few. In the Cretan political sample none of the respondents acknowledge out-of-region ethnic roots.

4 *Attitudinal or etymological variations* between the two samples or between the Greek and English version of the questionnaire are dependent on cultural differences between the two countries and semantic differences between the two languages. The extent of these is difficult to assess and every effort has been made to limit relevant bias.[43]

i)   Entrepreneurship has proved more controversial than initially anticipated. Admittance to being an entrepreneur seem to denote a special status which some respondents in the Strathclyde sample seemed to shun. In the Greek language the equivalent word '*epihirimatias*' is close in meaning to the word for businessman but also carries a connotation of small operator. Larger company entrepreneurs would prefer been called executives, since this denotes a higher social status. The question asked: 'whether they consider themselves as entrepreneurs or executives' (QB10F) may have been too simplistic if one wanted to investigate the true nature of their perceived role. More than one questions would have been necessary to achieve that, which I feel lies beyond the scope of this research.

ii) Remnants of an authoritarian state machine create problems in the relationship of the interviewer and interviewee in Greek surveys. One of these is the treatment of the survey as a test for which they try to give correct answers, which to some extent is true about Scottish interviewees as well.[44]

iii)   When expressing an opinion about local Councillors or MPs, some of the evidence from cross-referencing replies suggests that respondents may refer to the institutions rather than the individuals.

iv)   Opinions on individual Councillors or MPs may also be affected by their grievance with the existing institutional structures (i.e. their belief in the need for greater autonomy might affect their perception or response to the existing local authority) and have nothing to do with the individual representatives.

v)   A difference in the functions of the local political authorities means that the reference to the local political institutions have a differing significance for Strathclyde and Chania. These last three factors are partly an expected by-product of a cross-national survey, consideration should be given, nevertheless, of their ramifications when interpreting information comparing the two groups.

5   *Interpretation of results* can be a limiting factor in the validity of the testing, particularly since this research is based on a combination of qualitative and quantitative responses.

i)   Standardisation of results is limiting the explanatory value of many of the hypotheses.

ii)   The mainly ordinal character of data from the quantitative part of the questionnaire limits both the applicability and the spread of possible testing.

iii)   The process of including qualitative replies to the explanation of the hypotheses testing is selective. The judgmental character of the process makes the possibility of error higher. Certain replies will have to be qualified by this factor.

6   *Questionnaire construction and survey implementation* has affected the validity or applicability of certain of the hypotheses tested. An initial round of fact finding exploratory interviews (13) was conducted in 1989 in Scotland among officials in regional agencies which was not based on the questionnaire used in 1991 (76 administered and analysed questionnaires). Resource and time considerations precluded the use of a pilot survey questionnaire. However, preceding as well as shortly after the main series of elite interviews I conducted a number of interviews with senior local government administrators, academics, national government bureaucrats and party activists in both Greece/Crete (16 interviews) and Scotland/Glasgow (11 interviews). These were semi-structured 'informed subject'

interviews that helped me identify issues pertinent to my investigation. In that respect they assisted me to orient the survey questions and direct my analysis. Validity considerations remain in that:

i)   it has become apparent in certain occasions that the investigative tools are inadequate for a complete and thorough investigation of the hypotheses. For instance, there are no adequate measures to establish or refute a link of nationalism with xenophobia. Although this was of secondary importance to the survey, investigating such a link for this particular sample would have aided with the testing of other relevant hypotheses;

ii) the order of the questions, although designed to produce a certain impact, may influence replies to certain questions in such a way that subsequent tests will be affected adversely;

iii) certain questions are not applicable to both countries, in particular question QD11, inquiring whether respondents in Chania believe there are great differences between people in their region and people in the rest of Europe, was only employed in the Greek sample;

iv) Scottish business and political elite interviewees replied to a letter requesting an interview, which as mentioned above has the drawback of successful businessmen or favourably minded politicians taking part. In the Greek sample, lists from appropriate collective bodies were supplied (primary bias) and all those successfully contacted participated. This difference in the implementation of the questionnaire, creates problems with the applicability of certain hypothesis which assume the sample to be homogeneously (if not randomly) sampled;

v)   certain of the questions have to be practically eliminated from the testing of the hypotheses due to an unexpected optimism in replies to certain questions. This is the case for question QD12, in which all members of the Greek business sample replied that they thought Europe represented a challenge for their region. This condition weakens the quantitative tests of some of the hypotheses.

Suggestions on Questionnaire Design

In the course of this research effort one of the main difficulties has been data collection. Existing survey formats are too loose and are based on an intuitive understanding from the researcher of the strengths and pitfalls of particular understanding from the researcher of the strengths and pitfalls of particular questionnaire designs. More significantly, however, the two basic questionnaire designs are not often linked and there are rare instances of a combined use (method triangulation) of quantitative and qualitative survey approaches.

In comparative local elite surveys, which can encompass a large number of informed subjects, it is desirable to conduct surveys that both tap into the need for efficient quantitative analysis and to the possibility of knowledgeable insights from the subjects. In this research I have used a variant of both methods by employing questions that can provide quantifiable measurements (i.e. Likert scale) as open ended questions as well. The quantitative data provided the orientation, while the qualifications to replies provided the insights that can be reasonably expected from an in depth elite survey. Furthermore, although in the name of efficiency quantitative surveys are considered a more precise and accurate solution, they are embedded in validity limitations exactly because it is impossible to evaluate all relevant parameters while constructing a questionnaire. It is not possible, in other words, to know beforehand concerns a regional Councillor may have towards European integration and by asking any number of prearranged questions it is not certain that the most relevant issues will be explored or that their strength will be correctly gauged. This condition makes the use in tandem of both quantitative and qualitative tools desirable, if not imperative.

Given the resource limitations there are very few elements, that could have been improved on the research design.[45] In retrospect I would have eliminated some questions that did not belong to the indexes I constructed.[46] Furthermore, I would not have separated and distinguished parts B and C of the questionnaire to be exclusively asked to the business and political sub-samples. Although the issues pertaining to each elite group are different this solution diminishes the comparability of a number of their replies.

Notes

1   This survey – from which the data stream emanates – investigates attitudinal responses. Behavioural patterns are not investigated as this survey does not attempt to construct complete belief systems for each interviewee. An analysis of the importance of 'belief systems' for political leaders is given in ch. 7 of Kavanagh (1983).

2   The distinctiveness of the political culture is a presumption based on the difference in the cultural heritage of the Scots and Cretans from their respective national cultures (Kellas, 1989; Midwinter et al., 1991; Allbauch, 1953; Herzfeld, 1985). Recent survey data analysis however, suggests that there are insignificant variations in the value systems (and by extension political culture) between the regions of Great Britain (Miller et al., 1996).

3 For a comprehensive analysis of attitudinal measures see chs 7 and 8 of *Political Behaviour: Choices and Perspectives* by Dean Jaros and Lawrence Grant (1974).

4 Salience is taken to be the measurement of relative importance at a given time, inclusiveness to be the degree of complexity of an attitude and inconsistency to be the tendency to reply randomly. See Jaros and Grant (1974, p.248).

5 Certain important premises of social psychology had to be taken into account as are issues relating to the 'false consensus effect' raised by Ross, Greene and House (1977); while the analysis of problems in survey questions made by George Bishop (1987; 1990) and William Belson (1981) created important considerations for my research.

6 In the words of William Miller 'As the number in the survey decreases there comes a point where the researcher is using a Comparative Method rather than a Survey Method' (Miller, 1983, p.5) which points inevitably to the limited scope of using quantitative methods of analysis when the sample size is small.

7 A vast amount of research has been conducted on elite interviewing of which *Leaders and Elites* by William Welsh (1979) covers the methodological problems of survey research on elites. A number of surveys also tackle the different methodological issues that arise. In Business and Economic elite surveys interesting are the one's by Samuel Brittan (1973; 1990), R.E. Pahl and J.T. Winkler (1974), John Winkler (1987) and Martin Ricketts and Edward Shoesmith (1990). In political elite surveys methodological points are covered by Geoffrey Pridham (1987), Neil Nevitte and Roger Gibbins (1990), and J.H. Taggart (1993). Methodology on other European elites are covered by Helge Hveem (1972) and Ch. W. Nam, G. Nerb, and H. Russ (1990). This is by no means an exhaustive list, but one that refers to research relevant to my own.

8 See de Vaus (1991, chs 2 and 3) for an analysis of limits to research design and scope.

9 Questions of validity in survey research are thoroughly covered by William Belson (1986).

10 Since the data collected have a temporal character they do not lend themselves for any kind of dynamic interpretations. See Tufte (1974) for a more thorough account of data analysis and research design. Mannheim and Rich (1991) also develop the limitations of using temporal data.

11 A number of analytic strategies are covered by Miller (1983, pp.42–6). Case analysis is used here although certain assumptions on the causal structure of the data is more extensively covered in the main text.

12 In the concluding chapter I am attempting an interpretative analysis of the data utilising a number of insights that could not be part of a causal analysis. Limitations apply however as analysed in chs 2 and 4 of Mannheim and Rich (1991) and ch. 3 of de Vaus (1991). I have elsewhere attempted an investigation of the link between attitudes and regional prospects (Christopoulos, 1996b).

13 Survey research methodology is analysed in the *Handbook of Survey Research* (Rossi, 1983), *Surveys in Social Research* (de Vaus, 1991) and in *Empirical Political Analysis: Research Methods in Political Science* (Mannheim, 1991).

14 A comprehensive study of the contemporary interrelationship between values and culture can be found in Inglehart who attempts an analysis of the 'linkages that culture has with both politics and economics' (1990, p.15).

15 William Miller also gives two other possible multinational attitudinal survey goals further than the one used here. The first is 'to measure the influence of individual attitudes and behaviour upon political institutions' and the second is 'to establish a degree of generality of a finding by showing how little it was affected by the social and political setting' (1983, p.163).

16 For a thorough analysis of data codification and analysis see Mannheim and Rich (1991) ch. 15 and de Vaus (1991) chs 14–19.

17 It has been suggested that responses of open and close ended question systems should not be combined as this can lead to problems of validity of the response distributions (Belson, 1986). In this thesis statistical analysis is limited to closed ended questions.

18 For a comprehensive exposition of reasons for linking quantitative with qualitative data see Miles and Huberman (1994).

19 A number of sources proved helpful in dealing with qualitative data. I have found Taylor (1983), Altheide and Johnson (1994) and Denzin and Lincoln (1994) particularly relevant. Qualitative data management and the use of specialist software such as QSR.NUD*IST are elucidated by Richards and Richards (1994) and Huberman and Miles (1994).

20 Functional eliteness can be also linked to 'issue determination' or 'agenda setting' individuals within elite structures (Bachrach and Baratz, 1970).

21 A very informative account on the 'ethnography of local community elites' is presented by Hunter (1995), while snowballing in the context of qualitative research is discussed by Devine (1995).

22 A register of companies used included a Regional Company Survey that provided comparative size and profitability data for companies in Western Scotland (ICC, 1989).

23 This does not constitute classic 'snowballing' as most of the businessmen interviewed were selected from lists provided by the local chamber of commerce. The main bias exists in the reputational approval – or possibly disapproval – of my research that helped in securing interviews or could have been the cause of denials.

24 A recent example of an excellent elite survey that uses 'snowballing', is the one by Sotiropoulos (1994) on the Greek bureaucracy.

25 I take the point made by a number of academics (see Garmise, 1996) that local business elites have to be part of 'policy networks' or be involved in 'governance'. It is however my conviction that business elite *attitudes* can be correctly gauged if one concentrates on the attitudes of the wider business elite (of those holding substantial portions of allocative power) instead of investigating a nexus of power of regional businessmen, or identifying those with most frequent interactions to the political elite or considering those in business representative organisations as most significant.

26 In the Scottish political sample a senior bureaucrat was included as he has a very instrumental position in policy implementation. Two Regional Councillors in Strathclyde are also academics, they were expected however to express views under their political function.

27 In a sample questionnaire on similar hypotheses with the present one which I constructed and implemented between April and October 1989 aiming particularly at consultants, head of governmental agencies and union officials, results did not appear particularly conclusive and one of the reasons was obviously the heterogeneity of the elite groups surveyed.

28 The number of SRC Councillors was nominally 104 (before the abolition of Strathclyde).

29 Although in the case of the SRC and Glasgow City, these 'challengers' would be expected to come not from other parties but from within the Labour Party.

30 I consider senior bureaucrats (of which one is interviewed) of the local authorities and the national executive to be members of the local political elite. Furthermore, all those that can influence decision making, could be considered as part of the political elite. These according to Lasswell (1965, p.16), include those 'adherents of a counter ideology that are influential with the established order', those that held office and still are influential, highly influential people such as advisers and close family members of elected officials.

31 A number of individuals belonging to what I could call 'tangential elite groups' (such as journalists or academics), can be considered relevant to regional political interaction, by affecting political consciousness on what is desirable, and what is politically feasible.

32 No enterprises exclusively occupied with agriculture were part of the random sample, although a number of industrial companies were engaged with processing of agricultural products.

33 According to European Commission (1990) statistics 9.91 per cent of enterprises in the UK are Medium or Large according to employment figures. There were approximately 2,000 business in that category registered for VAT purposes and filing accounts (according to ICC, 1989), which suggests interviews here represent a 1.2 per cent sample. A more recent publication puts the total number of VAT registered business in Glasgow at 12,000, a 10.3 per cent share of Scottish business (Glasgow Development Agency, 1995).

34 My estimate of the local non-elected political elite in Chania is higher than that of Strathclyde, if the population of the respective regions is taken into account, but reflects my understanding of the high involvement with politics of the local elites (bearing a relevance to clientelism as well). I also believe that there is a 'minimum figure' in the constitution of a local political elite, i.e. there is a minimum number of individuals, even in the smallest regions, that comprise an active local body politic.

35 My initial attempt to use the register of companies resident in Nomos Chanion proved unsuccessful because, at the time of my research, this information was not part of a data bank, was not updated and contained no vital information on the registered companies. Consequently, a great number of companies were inactive while most were personal craft or trading enterprises. Similarly unsuccessful was my attempt to use a register of Limited Companies, Corporations and Cooperatives, provided by the local Labour Ministry Department (*Epitheorisi Ergasias*).

36 Data existing for Greece (Commission, 1990) puts micro enterprises (1–9 employees) at 92.8 per cent of the total. Assuming that there are 2,500 active enterprises in the region (and not taking account of the probability that the average size of enterprises in Chania is bound to be smaller than that of the rest of Greece) I would expect to find 29 enterprises with over 10 employees in Chania. This is an indication that my estimate of 105 individuals comprising the local business elite must be close to the true figure.

37 It is a standard accusation of business surveys that their sample is biased by successful operators (Pahl, 1974). Some of the media has also made similar claims, with the *Financial Times* stating that CBI surveys are unreliable because they focus on successful operators (*Financial Times*, 6–8 July 1992).

38 The local economy outlook is analysed in chapter three, it is sufficient here to note that in 1983 Cretan gross regional product (GRP) was standing at 43.5 per cent of the European Union average, while Scottish GRP was standing at 100.3 per cent of the EU average.

39 The system of local government analysed here is the one relevant during 1991. Changes in local government structures that have materialised since have not been taken into account.

40 The monitoring of political beliefs by the creation of 'files' was endemic in Greece during the Metaxas dictatorship, on the aftermath of the Civil War and at the time of the Colonels dictatorship.

41 The Cretan economy is comparatively self-sufficient in that it is a net exporter of goods and services.

42 It is obvious from the previous section that party political hypotheses have been eliminated from the analysis.

43 Among others Belson (1981) discusses the issues that arise out of the semantic interpretations of language in survey questions.

44 Miller (1983) and Sheatsley (1983) analyse the dangers from misconceptions in the implementation of surveys, while McCrossan (1991) refers to the approaches the interviewer must take when initiating an interview. In this series of interviews, in order to limit any such bias, respondents where introduced to the interview by the assertion that there are no correct replies and their names would be protected in the publication of results.

45 I would have liked to consider the possibility of a panel study or of a longitudinal survey in the regions and for the topics I have researched, but I know this to be unfeasible.

46 I also note here the changes that have occurred since I have conducted my survey which include the introduction of a single tier in Scottish local government in April 1996 (discussed by Paddison, 1995 and McAteer, 1996) and the creation of a Scottish Parliament with a remit on local government. These new institutional structures is reasonable to assume have totally transformed the political landscape. Similarly elections of regional prefects in Greece in for the first time in October 1994 and again in 1999, together with a number of measures of administrative decentralisation has altered the political landscape in Greek local politics. A discussion of pre-decentralisation attitudes of regional elites in Greece by Verney and Papageorgiou (1992) is interesting in that context. These developments have an effect on both attitudes and composition of the new regional political elites and is reasonable to assume have led to a significant reshaping of regional elites' role and possibly attitudes.

Bibliography

Agnew, John A. (1988), 'Beyond Core and Periphery: The Myth of Regional Political Restructuring and Sectionalism in Contemporary American Politics', in *Political Geography Quarterly*, Vol. 7, No. 2, pp.127–39.

Albertini, Mario (1992), 'A Draft Manifesto for European Federalism', *The Federalist*, Vol. 34, No. 1 (published in Pavia, Italy).

Alker, H.R. (1965), *Mathematics and Politics*, New York: The Macmillan Company.

Allbauch, Leland (1953), *Crete: A Case Study of an Underdeveloped Area*, Princeton: Princeton University Press.

Allen, Kevin and Yuill, Douglas (1980), *European Regional Problems and Policies: Key Issues and Research Needs*, Glasgow: University of Strathclyde.

Almeida, Louis Tadeu (1980), 'The Use of Socio-Economic Indicators to Group European Countries', in J. DeBandt, P. Mandi and D. Seers (eds), *European Studies in Development*, London: The Macmillan Press.

Almond, G.A. and Verba, S. (1963), *The Civic Culture: Political Attitudes and Democracy in Five Nations*, Princeton: Princeton University Press.

Altheide, D. and Johnson, J. (1994), 'Criteria for Assessing Interpretive Validity in Qualitative Research', in N. Denzin and Y. Lincoln (eds), *Handbook of Qualitative Research*, Thousand Oaks, California: Sage.

Amin, A. and Thrift, N. (1994) 'Living in the Global', in A. Amin and N. Thrift (eds), *Globalisation, Institutions and Regional Development in Europe*, Oxford: Oxford University Press.

Anderson, Benedict (1991), *Imagined Communities: Reflections on the Origin and Spread of Nationalism*, 2nd edn, New York: Verso.

Andrikopoulou, E. (1992), 'Whither Regional Policy? Local Development and the State in Greece', in M. Dunford and G. Kafkalas (eds), *Cities and Regions in the New Europe: The Global-Local Interplay and Spatial Development Strategies*, London: Belhaven Press.

Armstrong, Harvey (1993), 'Community Regional Policy' in Juliet Lodge (ed.), *European Community and the Challenge of the Future*, 2nd edn, London: Pinter Publishers.

Aschroft, Brian (1980), *The Evaluation of Regional Policy in Europe: A Survey and Critique*, Studies in Public Policy, University of Strathclyde, Paper No. 68.

Bachrach, Peter and Baratz, Morton S. (1970), *Power and Poverty: Theory and Practice*, New York: Oxford University Press.

Bachtler, John (1990), 'North versus South in European Regional Policy', *European Access*, December.

Bailly, A. and Lever, W. (1996), 'Conclusion', in W. Lever and A. Bailly (eds), *The Spatial Impact of Economic Changes in Europe*, Aldershot: Avebury.

Bateson, Nicholas (1984), *Data Construction in Social Surveys*, London: George Allen & Unwin.

Baumol, W.J. (1990), 'Entrepreneurship: Productive, Unproductive and Destructive', *Journal of Political Economy*, Vol. 98.

Belson, William (1981), *The Design and Understanding of Survey Questions*, Aldershot: Gower.

Belson, William (1986), *Validity in Survey Research*, Aldershot: Gower.

Berg, L. van den, Burns, L.S. and Klaassen, L.H. (1987), 'Introduction: Cities and Regions, Trends and Cycles', in L. van den Berg, L.S. Burns and L.H. Klaassen (eds), *Spatial Cycles*, Aldershot: Gower.

Bernstain, Robert Alan (1970), *International Integration*, PhD thesis, Cornell University.

Bianchi, Giuliano (1992), 'The IMPs: A Missed Opportunity? An Appraisal of the Design and Implementation of the Integrated Mediterranean Programmes', *Regional Politics and Policy*, Vol. 2, No. 1.

Biehl, Dieter (1987), 'Do National Subsidy Policies Cause Distortion of Competition?', *European Digest*, No. 55, August/September, pp.55–60.

Billig, M. (1995), *Banal Nationalism*, London: Sage.

Bisesi, Michael (1983), 'Strategies for Successful Leadership in Changing Times', *Sloan Management Review*, Vol. 25, No. 1, Fall.

Bishop, George F. (1989), 'Experiments with the Middle Response Alternative in Survey Questions', *Public Opinion Quarterly*, Vol. 51, Spring, pp.220–32.

Bishop, George F. (1990), 'Issue Involvement and Response Effects in Public Opinion Surveys', *Public Opinion Quarterly*, Vol. 54, Spring, pp.209–18.

Boisot, Max (1990), 'Territorial Strategies in a Competitive World: The Emerging Challenge to Regional Authorities', *European Management Journal*, Vol. 8, No. 3, September.

Bomberg, Elizabeth (1994), 'Policy Networks on the Periphery: EU Environmental Policy and Scotland', *Regional Politics and Policy*, Vol. 4, No. 1, pp.45–61.

Bongers, Paul (1990), *Local Government and 1992*, Essex: Longman.

Borras-Allomar, S., Christiansen, T. and Rodriguez-Pose, A. (1994), 'Towards a "Europe of the Regions"? Visions and Reality from a Critical Perspective', *Regional Politics and Policy*, Vol. 4, No. 2.

Bradley, S. and Taylor, J. (1995), 'Human Capital Formation and Local Economic Performance', *Regional Studies*, Vol. 30, No. 1.

Brittan, Samuel (1973), *Is There an Economic Consensus: An Attitude Survey*, London: Macmillan.

Brittan, Samuel (1990), 'Preface' in M. Ricketts and E. Shoesmith (eds), *British Economic Opinion: A Survey of a Thousand Economists*, London: Institute of Economic Affairs.

Brown, Callum G. (1987), *The Social History of Religion in Scotland Since 1730*, London: Methuen.

Brown, Callum G. (1993), 'The People in the Pews: Religion and Society in Scotland Since 1780', *Studies in Scottish Economic and Social History: No. 3*, Glasgow: Economic and Social History Society of Scotland.

Bulmer, S., George, S. and Scott, A. (1992), 'The Conclusions', in S. Bulmer, S. George and A. Scott (eds), *The United Kingdom and EC Membership Evaluated*, London: Pinter Publishers.

Bulmer, Simon and Scott, Andrew (eds) (1994), *Economic and Political Integration in Europe: Internal Dynamics and Global Context*, Oxford: Blackwell.

Burns, Leland S. (1986), 'On the Timing of Investment to Maximise Spatial Diffusion', in J.H. Paelinck (ed.), *Human Behaviour in Geographical Space*, Aldershot: Gower.

Burns, Leland S. (1987), 'Urban Growth and Decline as a Force in Regional Development: Issues and a Research Agenda', in L. van den Berg et al. (eds), *Spatial Cycles*, Aldershot: Gower.

Burton, M. and Higley, J. (1987), 'Invitation to Elite Theory: The Basic Contentions Reconsidered', in G. William Domhoff and Thomas R. Dye (eds), *Power Elites and Organizations*, Newbury Park, California: Sage Publications.

Camagni, R. (1995), 'The Concept of the Innovative Milieu and its Relevance for Public Policies in European Lagging Regions', *Papers in Regional Science*, Vol. 74, No. 4.

Campbell, J. (1964), *Honour Family and Patronage: A Study of Institutions and Moral Values in a Greek Mountain Community*, Oxford: Oxford University Press.

Campbell, J. (1983), 'Traditional Values and Continuities in Greek Society', in R. Clogg (ed.), *Greece in the 1980s*, London: Macmillan.

Castoriadis, Cornelios (1991), *Philosophy, Politics, Autonomy*, edited and partly translated by D.A. Curtis, New York and Oxford: Oxford University Press.

Cawson, Alan (1985), 'Corporatism and Local Politics', in W. Grant (ed.), *The Political Economy of Corporatism*, London: Macmillan.

Cawson, Alan (1986), *Corporatism and Political Theory*, Oxford: Basil Blackwell.

Cecchini, Paolo (1988), *The European Challenge 1992: The Benefits of a Single Market* (copyright Commission of the EC), Aldershot: Wildwood House.

Central Statistical Office (1992), *Social Trends 22: 1992 Edition*, London: HMSO.

Christiansen, U. (1981), 'Changes in Locational Behaviour in the Sixties and Seventies. Responses of Private and Public Institutions', in W. Buhr and P. Frierich (eds), *Lectures on Regional Stagnation*, Baden-Baden: Nomos Verlagesellschaft.

Christopoulos, D. (1996a), 'Regional Elite Concordance: The Relevance to Regional Development. Evidence from two Peripheral European Regions', Annual PSA conference, Glasgow 1996, mimeo.

Christopoulos, D. (1996b), 'Nationalism and Ethnicity: The Case of the Former Yugoslav Republic of Macedonia', in H. van den Berg et al. (eds), *Cultural Diversity in Europe: Threat or Treasure?*, Utrecht: YES-Nederland.

Christopoulos, D. (1996c), 'Business and Political Elite Networks in a Greek Region: Assessing the Potential for Corruption', presented in a conference on 'Corruption in Contemporary Politics' at the University of Salford, November, mimeo.

Christopoulos, D. (1998), 'Clientelistic Networks and Local Corruption: Evidence from Western Crete', *South European Politics and Society*, Vol. 3, No. 1, pp.1–22.

Christopoulos, D. (2000), 'Regions and the State in Southern Europe', in K. Lavdas (ed.), *Junctures of Stateness*, Aldershot: Ashgate.

Christopoulos, D. and Herbert, S. (1996), 'Elite Interaction and Institutional Development: The Case of Strathclyde Region', ECPR, 24th Joint Session of Workshops, Oslo March–April, mimeo.

Ciavarini Azzi, G. (1991), *Survey of the Current Political Science Research on the Community Worldwide*, presented in the XVth World Congress of the International Political Science Association, London: London School of Economics and Political Science.

Clapham, C. (1982), 'Clientelism and the State', in C. Clapham (ed.), *Private Patronage and Public Power: Political Clientelism in the Modern State*, New York: St Martin's Press.

Clogg, Richard (1983a), 'Troubled Alliance: Greece and Turkey', in R. Clogg (ed.), *Greece in the 1980s*, London: Macmillan.

Clogg, Richard (ed.) (1983b), *Greece in the 1980s*, New York: St Martin's Press.

Clogg, Richard (1986), *A Short History of Modern Greece*, 2nd edn, Cambridge: Cambridge University Press.

Coffey, W. and Bailly, A. (1996), 'Economic Restructuring: A Conceptual Framework', in W. Lever and A. Bailly (eds), *The Spatial Impact of Economic Changes in Europe*, Aldershot: Avebury.

Combes, David (1987), 'The Regional Policy of the European Community: A Re-examination of its Aims and Methods from the Perspective of the Periphery', *European Digest*, No. 55 August/September, Strasbourg: EPP of the European Parliament.

Commission of the EC (1973), 'Report on the Regional Problems in the Enlarged Community' (Thomson Report), *Bulletin of the European Communities*, Supplement 8/73, Brussels, pp.1–14.

Commission of the EC (1981a), '*The Regions of Europe: First Periodic Report*', 7 January 1981, COM(80), final, Brussels.

Commission of the EC (1981b), '*New Regional Policy Guidelines and Priorities*', 24 July 1981, COM(81), 152 final, Brussels.

Commission of the EC (1983), *Regional Development Programme – Greece 1981–85*, Brussels.

Commission of the EC (1984), *The Regions of Europe: Second Periodic Report*, Luxembourg.

Commission of the EC (1985), *The Tourism Sector in the Community*, Luxembourg.

Commission of the EC (1989a), *Regions Statistical Yearbook*, various editions and years 1985/1986/1987/1988, Luxembourg: 1985/1986/1987/1989.

Commission of EC (1989b), *Eurostat, Rapid Reports, Regions*, 1989/2, Luxembourg 20/10/1989.

Commission of the EC (1989c), *Evaluation of Policy Measures for the Creation and Development of Small and Medium Sized Enterprises: Synthesis Report*, Brussels.

Commission of the EC (1989d), 'Community Support Frameworks for the Regions', *Bulletin of the EC*, No. 9, Vol. 22.

Commission of the EC (1989e), *European Regional Development Fund: 13th Annual Report 1987*, 10 January, Brussels.

Commission of the EC (1990), *Enterprises in the European Community*, Brussels.

Commission of the EC (1991a), *Europe 2000: Outlook for the Development of the Community's Territory*, COM(91), 452 final, Brussels.

Commission of the EC (1991b), *The Regions in the 1990s: Fourth Periodic Report on the Social and Economic Situation and Development of the Regions of the Community*, COM(90), 609 final, Brussels.

Commission of the EC (1992a), 'The Community Regions: A General Report on the Issues Facing European Society', *Eurobarometer*, No. 36.

Consolas, Nicolaos (1985), *Periferiaki Ikonomiki Politiki* [Regional Economic Policy], Athens: Ekdosis Papazisi.

Convention of Scottish Local Authorities, (1993), *Cost of Restructuring Local Government in Scotland*, Edinburgh: COSLA.

Council of Europe (1990), 'The Impact of the Completion of the Internal Market on Local and Regional Autonomy', *Studies and Texts Series, No. 12*, Strasbourg: Council of Europe Publishing and Documentation Service.

Crewe, Ivor (1974), 'Introduction: Studying Elites in Britain', in Ivor Crewe (ed.), *British Political Sociology Yearbook, Vol. 1: Elites in Western Democracy*, London: Croom Helm.

Crewe, Ivor (1992a), 'Partisan Dealignment Ten Years On', in David Denver and Gordon Hands (eds), *Issues and Controversies in British Electoral Behaviour*, New York: Harvester Wheatsheaf.

Crewe, Ivor (1992b), 'The 1987 General Election', in David Denver and Gordon Hands (eds), *Issues and Controversies in British Electoral Behaviour*, New York: Harvester Wheatsheaf.

Crook, R. and Manor, J. (1995), 'Does Democratic Decentralisation Lead to Better Institutional Performance?: Comparing Four Asian and African Experiences', *Journal of Commonwealth and Comparative Politics*, XXXIII (3).

Council of Europe (1990), *The Impact of the Completion of the Internal Market on Local and Regional Autonomy*, Studies and Texts Series, No. 12, Strasbourg: Council of Europe Publishing and Documentation Service.

Della Porta, Donatella (1996), 'Actors in Corruption: Business Politicians in Italy', *International Social Science Journal*, 48/3, pp. 340–64.

Dendrinos, Dimitrios (1984), 'Regions, Antiregions and their Dynamic Stability: The U.S. Case', *Journal of Regional Science*, Vol. 24, No 1, pp.65–83.

Desmonds, King (1989), 'The New Right, the New Left and Local Government', in J. Stewart and G. Stoker (eds), *The Future of Local Government*, London: The Macmillan Press.

Despicht, Nigel (1980), 'Centre and Periphery in Europe', in J. DeBandt, P. Mandi and D. Seers (eds), *European Studies in Development*, London: The Macmillan Press.

Diamandouros, N. (1983), 'Greek Political Culture in Transition: Historical Origins, Evolution, Current Trends', in R. Clogg (ed.), *Greece in the 1980s*, London: Macmillan.

Donckels, Rick (1981), 'Theories of Regional Stagnation', in W. Buhr and P. Frierich (eds), *Lectures on Regional Stagnation*, Baden-Baden: Nomos Verlagesellschaft.

Drakos, George (1986), 'Economic Policy in Theory and Greek Practice', in G. Yannopoulos (ed.), *Greece and the EEC*, London: The Macmillan Press.

Dunford, Mick and Bencko, Georges (1991), 'Neo-Fordism or Post-Fordism? Some Conclusions and Further Remarks', in G. Bencko and M. Dunford (eds), *Industrial Change and Regional Development: The Transformation of New Industrial Spaces*, London: Belhaven Press.

Dunleavy, Patrick and O'Leary, Brendan (1987), *Theories of the State: The Politics of Liberal Democracy*, London: Macmillan.

Dupoirier, Elisabeth (1994), 'The First Regional Political Elites in France (1986–1992): A Profile', *Regional Politics and Policy*, Vol. 4, No. 3.

Economic and Social Committee of the European Communities (1981), *The Economic and Social Interest Groups of Greece*, Brussels: General Secretariat of the Economic and Social Committee of the European Communities.

El-Agraa, A.M. (1982), *International Economic Integration*, London: Macmillan.

El-Agraa, A.M. (ed.) (1990), *The Economics of the European Community*, Hemel Hempstead: Phillip Allan.

Emerson, Michael et al. (1988), *The Economics of 1992: The EC Commissions Assessment of the Economic Effects of Completing the Internal Market*, Oxford: Oxford University Press.

European Economic Research and Advisory Consortium (ERECO) (1993), *European Regional Prospects: Analysis and Forecasts to the Year 1997 for European Cities and Regions*, *Vol. 1*, Cambridge: Cambridge Econometrics Limited.

Errson, S., Janda, K. and Lane, J. (1985), 'Ecology of Party Strength in Western Europe: A Regional Analysis', *Comparative Political Studies*, Vol. 18, No. 2.

Etzioni-Halevy, Eva (1993), *The Elite Connection: Problems and Potential of Western Democracy*, Cambridge: Polity Press.

Europa Institute (1991), *The Single European Market and the Scottish Economy*, prepared for the Convention of the Scottish Local Authorities, Edinburgh: University of Edinburgh.

European Venture Capital Association (EVCA) (1987), *Venture Capital in Europe*, London: Peat Marwick McLintock.

Fakiolas, Rosetos (1987), 'Interest Groups: An Overview', in Kevin Featherstone and Dimitrios Katsoudas (eds), *Political Change in Greece: Before and After the Colonels*, London: Croom Helm.

Fassin, Yves and Nathusius, Klaus (1989), 'Europe's Venture Capital Industry is Already Prepared for 1992', *European Management Journal*, Vol. 7, No. 2, June.

Fayerweather, J. (1982), 'Elite Attitudes Towards Multinational Firms', in J. Fayerweather (ed.), *Host National Attitudes Towards Multinational Corporations*, New York: Praeger.

Featherstone, K. (1987), 'Introduction', in Kevin Featherstone and Dimitrios Katsoudas (eds), *Political Change in Greece: Before and After the Colonels*, London: Croom Helm.

Featherstone, K. (1990), 'The "Party-State" in Greece and the Fall of Papandreou', *West European Politics*, Vol. 13, pp.101–16.

Featherstone, M. (ed.) (1990), *Global Culture. Nationalism, Globalisation and Modernity*, London: Sage.

Feathersone, K. and Katsoulas, Dimitrios (eds) (1987), *Political Change in Greece: Before and After the Colonels*, London: Croom Helm.

Featherstone, K. and Sonntag, N. (1984), 'Problems of Political Integration: Looking Towards the 1984 European Election', *Journal of Common Market Studies*, Vol. XXII, No. 3, March.

Fiedler, Fred E. (1971), *Leadership*, Morristown, NJ: General Learning Press.

Fields, James and Schuman, Howard (1976), 'Public Beliefs About the Beliefs of the Public', *Public Opinion Quarterly*, Vol. 40 (1976–77), pp.427–48.

Finer, S.E. (1966), 'Introduction', in *Wilfredo Pareto: Sociological Writings*, trans. D. Mirfin and ed. S.E. Finer, London: Pall Mall Press.

Fowler, Floyd J. (1988), *Survey Research Methods*, California: Sage Publications.

Galbraith, J.K. (1967), *The New Industrial State*, Signet: New York.

Garmise, Shari (1996), *Region Building: The Emergence of Multi-Level Governance in the UK*, paper presented at the 24th Joint Session of Workshops of ECPR in Oslo, mimeo.

Gaster, Lucy (1991), *Quality at the Front Line*, Bristol: School for Advanced Urban Studies.

Gellner, E. (1977), 'Patrons and Clients', in E. Gellner and J. Waterbury (eds), *Patrons and Clients in Mediterranean Societies*, London: Duckworth.

Gellner, E. and Waterbury, J. (eds) (1977), *Patrons and Clients in Mediterranean Societies*, London: Duckworth.

General Register Office for Scotland (1993), *1991 Census: Strathclyde Region*, Edinburgh: HMSO.

George, Stephen (1983), 'Regional Policy', in J. Lodge (ed.), *Institutions and Policies of the European Community*, London: Francis Pinter.

George, Stephen (1985), *Politics and Policy in the European Community*, Oxford: Clarendon Press.

George, Stephen (1990), 'Britain and the European Community', *European Access*, Vol. 2, No. 6, December.

Georgiou, G. (1993), 'From Policy to Action: The Implementation of European Community Regional Programmes in Greece', *Regional Politics and Policy*, Vol. 3, No. 2.

Geroski, Paul (1989), 'On Diversity and Scale – Extant Firms and Extinct Goods?', *Sloan Management Review*, Vol. 31, No. 1, Fall.

Gerth, A.H. and Mills, C.W. (eds) (1991 [1948]), *From Max Weber: Essays in Sociology*, London: Routledge.

Giddens, A. (1979), *Central Problems in Social Theory: Action, Structure and Contradiction in Social Analysis*, London: Macmillan Press.

Giddens, A. (1990), *The Consequences of Modernity*, Cambridge: Polity Press.

Gilbert, E.W. (1960), 'The Idea of the Region', *Geography*, Vol. 45, pp.157–75.

Giner, Salvador (1986), 'Political Economy, Legitimation, and the State in Southern Europe', in G. O'Donnel, P. Schmitter and L. Whitehead (eds), *Transitions from Authoritarian Rule: Southern Europe*, Baltimore: The Johns Hopkins University Press.

Girch, H. (1949), 'Economic Union Between Nations and the Location of Industries', *Review of Economic Studies*, Vol. 17, pp. 87–97.

Glasgow City Council (1991), *The Response by Glasgow City Council to the Scottish Office Consultation Paper: The Structure of Local Government In Scotland, the Case for Change*, Glasgow: Glasgow City Council.

Glasgow City Council, Estates Department (1991), *City of Glasgow Directory of Companies 1991*, London: E.J. Burrow & Co.

Glasgow Development Agency and Glasgow City Council (1995), *Metropolitan Glasgow: The Comprehensive Guide to Glasgow's Economy*, Edinburgh: Insider Publications Ltd.

Gogel, Robert and Larreche, Jean-Claude (INSEAD) (1989), 'The Battlefield for 1992: Product Strength and Geographic Coverage', *European Management Journal*, Vol. 7, No. 2, June.

Gold, J.R. (1980), *An Introduction to Behavioural Geography*, Oxford: Oxford University Press.

Goldstone-Rosenthal, Glenda (1975), *The Men Behind the Decisions: Cases in European Policy Making*, Lexington, Mass.: Lexington Books.

Gordon, George (1985), 'The City of Glasgow', in J. Butt and G. Gordon (eds.), *Strathclyde: Changing Horizons*, Edinburgh: Scottish Academic Press.

Gould, P. and White, R. (1986 [1974]), *Mental Maps*, revised edn, London: Penguin Books [Allen & Unwin, London].

Haas, Ernest B. (1968), *The Uniting of Europe: Political, Social and Economic Forces 1950–1957*, 2nd edn, Stanford California: Stanford University Press.

Habermas, J. (1987), *The Philosophical Discourses of Modernity*, Cambridge: Polity Press.

Hadjimichalis, Costis (1983), 'Regional crisis: The State and Regional Social movements in Southern Europe', in Dudley Seers and Kjell Ostrom (eds), *The Crisis of the European Regions*, London: The Macmillan Press.

Hadjimichalis, C. and Vaiou, D. (1992), 'Intermediate Regions and Forms of Social Reproduction: Three Greek Cases', in G. Garofoli (ed.), *Endogenous Development and Southern Europe*, Aldershot: Avcbury.

Halkier, Henrik (1992), 'Development Agencies and Regional Policy: The Case of the Scottish Development Agency', *Regional Politics and Policy*, Vol. 2, No. 3.

Hardy, S., Hart, M., Albrechts, L. and Katos, A. (eds) (1995), *An Enlarged Europe: Regions in Competition?*, London: Regional Studies Association.

Harrington, Richard (1992), 'Regional Policy', in S. Bulmer, S. George and A. Scott (eds), *The United Kingdom and EC Membership Evaluated*, London: Pinter Publishers.

Harvie, Christopher (1994), *The Rise of Regional Europe*, London: Routledge.

Heath, A., Jowell, R. and Curtice, J. (1992), 'Partisan Dealignment Revisited', in David Denver and Gordon Hands (eds), *Issues and Controversies in British Electoral Behaviour*, New York: Harvester Wheatsheaf.

Heraclides, A. (1991), *The Self-determination of Minorities in International Politics*, London: Frank Cass.

Hertz, R. and Imber, J. (1995), *Studying Elites Using Qualitative Methods*, London: Sage Publications.

Herzfeld, M. (1985), *The Poetics of Manhood: Contest and Identity in a Cretan Mountain Village*, Princeton, NJ: Princeton University Press.

Heywood, Paul (1991), 'Spain's Next Five Years: A Political Risk Analysis', *The Economist Intelligence Unit· Political Risk Series*, London: The Economist Publications, April.

Heywood Paul (1994), 'Political Corruption in Modern Spain', in P. Heywood (ed.), *Distorting Democracy: Political Corruption in Spain, Italy and Malta*, CMS Occasional Paper No. 10, Centre for Mediterranean Studies: University of Bristol, December.

Hitiris, T. (1994), *European Community Economics*, Hemel Hempstead: Harvester Wheatsheaf.

Hitiris, T. and Zervoyianni, A. (1983), 'Monetary Integration in the European Community', in Juliet Lodge (ed.), *Institutions and Policies of the European Community*, London: Frances Pinter.

Hix, S. (1994), 'The Study of the European Community: The Challenge to Comparative Politics', *West European Politics*, Vol. 17, No. 1.

HMSO (1991), *Scottish Economic Bulletin*, No. 43, June.

Hobsbawm, E. (1983), 'Introduction: Inventing Traditions', in E. Hobsbawm and T. Ranger (eds), *The Invention of Tradition*, Cambridge: Cambridge University Press.

Hoffman-Lange, U. (1987), 'Surveying National Elites in the Federal Republic of Germany', in G. Moyser and M. Wagstaffe (eds), *Research Methods of Elite Studies*, London: Allen and Unwin.

Holland, Stuart (1980), *Uncommon Market: Capital, Class and Power in the European Community*, London: The Macmillan Press.

Hooghe, Liesbet (ed.) (1996), *Cohesion Policy and European Integration*, Oxford: Oxford University Press.

Hopkins, Adam (1977), *Crete: its Past, Present and People*, London: Faber and Faber.

Howard, Robert (1990), 'Can Small Business Help Countries Compete?', *Harvard Business Review*, Vol. 68, No. 6, November–December.

Huberman, A.M. and Miles, M. (1994), 'Data Management and Analysis Methods', in N. Denzin and Y. Lincoln (eds), *The Handbook of Qualitative Research*, Thousand Oaks, California: Sage.

Hunter, A. (1995), 'Local Knowledge and Local Power: Notes on the Ethnography of Local Community Elites', in R. Hertz and J. Imber (eds), *Studying Elites Using Qualitative Methods*, Thousand Oaks, California: Sage.

Hutton, W. (1995), 'Nova Scotia's Load of Globaloney', *The Guardian*, 18 June.

Hveem, Helge (1972), *International Relations and World Images: A Study of Norwegian Foreign Policy Elites*, Oslo: International Peace Research Institute.

ICC Business Publications (1989), *Regional Company Survey. County and Regional Profiles of Company Performance: Western Scotland*, 1st edn, Hampton: ICC Business Publications.

Illeris, Sven (1989), *Services and Regions in Europe* (Copyright: Commission of EC), Aldershot: Avebury.

Inglehart, Ronald (1990), *Culture Shift in Advanced Industrial Society*, Princeton, NJ: Princeton University Press.

Inter-Parliamentary Union (1992), 'Women and Political Power: Survey Carried out Among the 150 National Parliaments Existing as of 31 October 1991', Series *Reports & Documents*, No. 19, Geneva.

Jaros, Dean and Grant, Lawrence (1974), *Political Behaviour, Choices & Perspectives*, Oxford: Basil Blackwell.

Jeffery, Charlie (1995), 'Whither the Committee of the Regions? Reflections on the Committee's Opinion on the Revision of the Treaty of the European Union. A Documentary Survey', *Regional and Federal Studies*, Vol. 5, No. 2.

Jensen-Butler, Chris (1996), 'A Theoretical Framework for Analysis of Urban Economic Policy', in W. Lever and A. Bailly (eds), *The Spatial Impact of Economic Changes in Europe*, Aldershot: Avebury.

Jessop, B. (1996), 'The Entrepreneurial City: Re-imaging Localities, Redesigning Economic Governance, or Re-structuring Capital?', paper presented at an Institute of British Geographers' conference, University of Glasgow, mimeo.

Johanisson, B. and Spilling, O. (1983), *Strategies for Local and Regional Self Development*, Oslo: NordREFO.

John, Peter and Cole, Alistair (1996), 'Decision-Making Networks in Britain and France: A Sociometric Approach', PSA Annual Conference, Glasgow, April, mimeo.

Jones, Barry (1985), 'Conclusion: Regions in the European Community', in M. Keating and B. Jones (eds), *Regions in the European Community*, Oxford: Clarendon Press.

Jones, Barry (1995), 'Conclusion', in B. Jones and M. Keating (eds), *The European Union and the Regions*, Oxford: Clarendon Press.

Katz, R. (1993), 'Review Article: Making Democracy Work', *Italian Politics and Society*, Vol. 40, Fall.

Kavanagh, Dennis (1983), *Political Science and Political Behaviour*, London: George Allen & Unwin.

Keating, Michael (1988), *The City that Refused to Die. Glasgow: The Politics of Urban Regeneration*. Aberdeen: Aberdeen University Press.

Keating, Michael (1991), *Comparative Urban Politics: Power and the City in the United States, Canada, Britain and France*, Aldershot: Edward Elgar.

Keating, Michael (1992), 'Regional Autonomy in the Changing State Order: A Framework of Analysis', *Regional Politics and Policy*, Vol. 2, No. 3.

Keating, Michael (1996a), 'The Invention of Regions. Political Restructuring and Territorial Government in Western Europe', paper presented in the ECPR Joint Session of Workshops, Oslo, 29 March–3 April, mimeo.

Keating, Michael (1996b), *Nations Against the State: The New Politics of Nationalism in Quebec Catalonia and Scotland*, London: Macmillan Press.

Keating, Michael and Boyle, Robin (1986), *Remaking Urban Scotland: Strategies for Local Economic Development*, Edinburgh: Edinburgh University Press.

Keating, Michael and Jones, Barry (eds) (1985), *Regions in the European Community*, Oxford: Clarendon Press.

Keating, Michael and Waters, Nigel (1985), 'Scotland in the European Community', in M. Keating and B. Jones (eds), *Regions in the European Community*, Oxford: Clarendon Press.

Kefalas, Anthony and Mantzaris, Alexander (1986), 'The Greek Balance of Payments and Membership of the European Economic Community', in G. Yannopoulos (ed.), *Greece and the EEC*, London: The Macmillan Press.

Kellas, James (1989), *The Scottish Political System*, 4th edn, Cambridge University Press: Cambridge.

Kellas, James (1991), 'The Scottish and Welsh Offices as Territorial Managers', *Regional Politics and Policy*, Vol. 1, No. 1.

Kellas, James and Grant, G.J. (1980), *Modern Scotland*, revised edn, London: Allen and Unwin.

Keohane, R. and Nye, J. (1975), 'International Interdependence and Integration', in F.I. Greenstein and N.W. Polsby (eds), *International Politics*, New York: Addison-Wesley.

King, D. and Stoker, G. (eds) (1996), *Rethinking Local Democracy*, London: Macmillan.

King, R., Keohane, R. and Verba, S. (1994), *Designing Social Inquiry: Scientific Inference in Qualitative Research*, Princeton, New Jersey: Princeton University Press.

Kimble, G.H.T. (1951), 'The Inadequacy of the Regional Concept', in L.D. Stamp and S.W. Woolridge, *London Essays in Geography*, London: Longmans.

Klaassen, Leo H. (1987), 'Regional Dynamics', in L. van den Berg, L.S. Burns and L.H. Klaassen (eds), *Spatial Cycles*, Aldershot: Gower.

Klau, T. (1996), 'Europe Enters the Age of Regions', *European Voice*, 30 May, Vol. 2, No. 22.

Knoke, D. (1990), *Political Networks: The Structural Perspective*, Cambridge: Cambridge University Press.

Konsolas, Nikolaos (1985), *Periferiaki Economiki Politiki* [Regional Economic Policy], Athens: Ekdosis Papazisi.

Koutsiaras, N. (1993), *E Glossa Stin Economiki Epistimi Ke E Thesi Tis Ellinikis Glossas, Kimena Ergasias Ar 21* [Language in Economic Science and the Position of the Greek Language, Working Paper No. 21], May, Athens: Hellenic Centre for European Studies.

Kouvertaris, G.A. and Dobratz, B. (1984), 'Political Clientelism in Athens, Greece: A Three Paradigm Approach to Political Clientelism', *East European Quarterly*, Vol. 18, pp.35–59.

Krugman, Paul (1991), *Geography and Trade*, Cambridge, Mass.: MIT Press.

Krugman, Paul (1994), 'Competitiveness Does it Matter?', *Fortune*, 7 March, pp.71–4.

Krugman, Paul (1995), *Peddling Prosperity: Economic Sense and Nonsense in the Age of Diminished Expectations*, New York: W.W. Norton and Co.

Krugman, Paul and Venables, Anthony (1994), 'Globalisation and the Inequality of Nations', *CEPR discussion paper No 1015*, London: Centre for Economic Policy Research, September.

Kuhne, R and Ruck, M. (eds) (1993), *Regionale Elites Zwischen Diktatur und Demokratie: Baden und Wurtemberg 1930–1952* [Regional Elites between Dictatorship and Democracy: Baden and Wurtemberg 1930–1952], Munchen: Oldenbourg.

Kukawaka, Pierre and Tournon, Jean (1987), *The Council of Europe and Regionalism: The Regional Dimension in the Work of the Standing Conference of Local and Regional Authorities of Europe (CLRAE) 1957–85*, Strasbourg: Council of Europe Publication Section.

Laitin, David and Sole, Carlota (1989), 'Catalan Elites and Language Normalization', *The International Journal of Sociology and Social Policy*, Vol. 9, No. 4.

Lamboy, J.G. (1986), 'Locational Decisions and Regional Structure', in J.H.P. Paelnick (ed.), *Human Behaviour in Geographical Space*, Aldershot: Gower.

Lambrias, Panayotis (1987), 'The Integrated Programmes A Model for the Present and Prospects for the Future', *European Digest*, No. 55, August–September, pp.61–7, Luxembourg.

La Palombara, J. and Blank, D.S. (1976), *Multinational Corporations and National Elites: A Study in Tensions*, New York: The Conference Board Inc.

Lasch, Christopher (1995), *The Revolt of the Elites and the Betrayal of Democracy*, New York: W.W. Norton and Co.

Lasswell, H.D. (1950), *Politics: Who Gets What, When, How*, New York: Peter Smith.

Lasswell, H.D. (1965), 'Introduction: The Study of Political Elites', in *World Revolutionary Elites: Studies in Coercive Ideological Movements*, Cambridge Mass.: MIT Press.

Lasswell, H.D. and Kaplan, A. (1952), *Power and Society: A Framework for Political Inquiry*, London: Routledge and Kegan Paul Ltd.

Lecomte, P. (1994), 'Research Report: Rhones-Alpes Citizens in the Political System: An Emerging Regional Identity', *Regional Politics and Policy*, Vol. 4, No. 2.

Leonardi, R. and Garmise, S. (1992), 'Conclusions: Sub-National Elites and the European Community', *Regional Politics and Policy*, Vol. 2, Nos 1 and 2.

Lever, W.G. (1992), 'Local Authority Responses to Economic Change in West Central Scotland', *Urban Studies*, Vol. 29, No. 6.

Lever, W. G. (1993), 'Competition Within the European Urban System', *Urban Studies*, Vol. 30, No. 6.

Lever, William (1996), 'The European Regional Dimension', in W. Lever and A. Bailly (eds), *The Spatial Impact of Economic Changes in Europe*, Aldershot: Avebury.

Levy, Roger (1990), *Scottish Nationalism at the Crossroads*, Edinburgh: Scottish Academic Press.

Liarkovas, Panagiotis (1993), *Esroes Kefaleon, Antagonistikotita Ke Isozigio Trehuson Sinallagon Ston Europaiko Noto, Kimena Ergasias Ar 27* [Capital Movements, Competitiveness and the Balance of Current Payments in the European South], Working Paper No. 27, Athens: Hellenic Centre for European Studies, September.

Lindberg, Leon N. (1963), *The Political Dynamics of European Integration*, Stanford: Stanford University Press.

Lindblom, Charles E. (1990), *Inquiry and Change: The Troubled Attempt to Understand and Shape Society*, New Haven: Yale University Press.

Linklater, Andrew (1996), 'Citizenship and Sovereignty in the Post-Westphalian State', *European Journal of International Relations*, Vol. 2, No. 1.

Lodge, Juliet (1989), 'The Political Implications of 1992', *Politics*, Vol. 9 , No. 2 October.

Lodge, Juliet (1993), 'EC Policymaking: Institutional Dynamics', in J. Lodge (ed.), *The European Community and the Challenge of the Future*, 2nd edn, London: Pinter.

Lodge, Juliet (1995), *Crisis or Opportunity?: Institutional Affairs*, Discussion Paper of the Jean Monnet Group of Experts, Hull: Centre for European Union Studies, University of Hull.

Lucas, John (1994), 'The State Civil Society and Regional Elites: A Study of Three Associations in Kano Nigeria', *African Affairs*, Vol. 93, No. 370, January.

Lyrintzis, Ch. (1984), 'Political Parties in Post-Junta Greece: A Case of Bureaucratic Clientelism?', *West European Politics*, Vol. 7, pp.99–118.

MacCrone, David (1992), *Understanding Scotland: The Sociology of a Stateless Nation*, London: Routledge.

McAteer, Mark (1996), 'Third Tier of Bottom Tier? The Implications of Local Government Reorganisation for the Scottish Local Governance System', paper presented at the 24th Joint Sessions of Workshops, Oslo, March–April, mimeo.

McCrossan, Liz (1991), *A Handbook for Interviewers*, London: HMSO.

McDonald, J.F. (1979), *The Lack of Political Identity in English Regions: Evidence from MPs*, Paper No. 33, Centre for the Study of Public Policy, University of Strathclyde.

McGranahan, D.V. et al. (1972), *Contents and Measurement of Socioeconomic Development: A Stuff Study of the United Nations Research Institute for Social Development*, New York: Praeger Publishers.

Mackie, Thomas T. (1988), 'General Elections in Western Nations During 1987', *European Journal of Political Research*, Vol. 16, No. 5, September.

Mackie, Thomas T. (ed.) (1990), *Europe Votes 3: European Parliamentary Election Results*, Aldershot: Dartmouth Publishing Co.

Makridimitris, A. and Passas, A. (1993), *E Elliniki Diikisi ke o Sintonismos tis Evropaikis Politikis, Kimena Ergasias Ar. 20* [Greek Public Administration and the Co-ordination of European Policy, Working Papers No. 20], February, Athens: Hellenic Centre for European Studies.

Manassakis, Anna (1986), 'Greece and the European Monetary System', in G. Yannopoulos (ed.), *Greece and the EEC*, London: The Macmillan Press.

Manheim, Jarold and Rich, Richard (1991), *Empirical Political Analysis: Research Methods in Political Science*, 3rd edn, New York: Longman.

Manolikakis, I.G. (1963), *Meleti Oikonomikis ke Pnevmatikis Anaptixis tis Kritis* [Study of the Economic and Spiritual Development of Crete], Athens: Ekdosis Papazisi.

Marks, Gary (1993), 'Structural Policy and Multilevel Governance in the European Community', in A. Calfruny and G. Rosenthal (eds), *The State of the European Community*, New York: Lynne Rienner.

Marks, Gary, Nielsen, Françoise, Ray, Leonard and Salk, Jane (1996), 'Competencies, Cracks and Conflicts: Regional Mobilisation in the European Union', in Gary Marks, Fritz Scharpf, Philippe Schmitter and Wolfgang Streeck (eds), *Governance in the European Union*, London: Sage.

Marsh, David and R.A.W. Rhodes (eds) (1992), *Policy Networks in British Government*, Oxford: Clarendon Press.

Martin, D. (1991), *Europe: An Ever Closer Union*, Nottingham: Spokesman.

Ma Valles, Josep and Cuchillo Foix, Montserrat (1988), 'Decentralisation in Spain: A Review', *European Journal of Political Research*, Vol. 16, No. 4 July.

Mavromatis, I.E. (1989), *Economia Tis Kritis 1951–1981* [The Economy of Crete 1951–1981], Vol. A., K.G. Papageorgiou: Heraklion.

Mazey, S. and Richardson, J. (ed.) (1993), *Lobbying in the European Community*, Oxford: Oxford University Press.

Meisel, James H. (1962), *The Myth of the Ruling Class: Gaetano Mosca and the 'Elite'*, Michigan: Ann Arbor.

Meisel, James H. (ed.) (1965), *Pareto and Mosca*, New Jersey: Prentice Hall.

Midwinter, Arthur (1985), 'Local Government in Strathclyde', in J. Butt and G. Gordon (eds), *Strathclyde: Changing Horizons*, Edinburgh: Scottish Academic Press.

Midwinter, A. Keating, M. and Mitchell, J. (1991), *Politics and Public Policy in Scotland*, London: The Macmillan Press.

Miles, M. and Huberman, A.M. (1994), *Qualitative Data Analyses: An Expanded Sourcebook*, 2nd edn, Thousand Oaks, California: Sage.

Miller, William L. (1977), *Causal Modelling in Three Party Systems: Trichotomous Regression Studies of Scotland England and America*, Paper No. 10, Centre for the Study of Public Policy, University of Strathclyde.

Miller, William L. (1981), *The End of British Politics?: Scots and English Political Behaviour in the Seventies*, Oxford: Clarendon Press.

Miller, William L. (1983), *The Survey Method in the Social and Political Sciences*, London: Frances Pinter.

Miller, William L. (1992), 'Voting Behaviour in Scotland and Wales', in David Denver and Gordon Hands (eds), *Issues and Controversies in British Electoral Behaviour*, New York: Harvester Wheatsheaf.

Miller, William L. (ed.) (1995), *Alternatives to Freedom: Arguments and Opinions*, London: Longman.

Miller, William L., Timpson, A.M. and Lessnoff, M. (1996), *Political Culture in Contemporary Britain: People and Politicians, Principles and Practice*, Oxford: Clarendon, Oxford University Press.

Mills, C. Stewart (1956), *The Power Elite*, New York: Oxford.

Molle, Wilhelm (1986), Regional Impact of Welfare Policies in the European Community', in J.H. Paelinck (ed.), *Human Behaviour in Geographical Space*, Aldershot: Gower.

Molle, Wilhelm (1988), 'Regional Policy', in Peter Coffey (ed.), *Main Economic Policy Areas of the EEC – Towards 1992*, 2nd edn, Dordrecht: Kluwer Academic Publishers.

Molle, Wilhelm and Cappelin, Ricardo (eds) (1988), *Regional Impact of Community Policies in Europe*, Aldershot: Avebury.

Moore, C. (1991), 'Regional Government in the UK: Proposals and Prospects', *Regional Politics and Policy*, Vol. 1, No. 3, pp.223–41.

Morata, F. (1992), 'Regions and the European Community: A Comparative Analysis of Four Spanish Regions', *Regional Politics and Policy*, Vol. 2, Nos 1 and 2.

Mosca, Gaetano (1939), *The Ruling Class* (first published as *Elementi di Scienza Politica*), trans. H.D. Kahn, New York: McGraw Hill.

Mosca, Gaetano (1972 [1933]), *A Short History of Political Philosophy* (first published as *La Storia delle Dotrine Politiche*), trans. S. Koff, New York: Thomas Y. Cromwell.

Mouzelis, Nicos (1987), 'Continuitites and Discontinuities in Greek Politics: From Eleftherios Venizelos to Andreas Papandreou', in Kevin Featherstone and Dimitrios Katsoudas (eds), *Political Change in Greece Before and After the Colonels*, London: Croom Helm.

Moyser, George and Wagstaffe, Margaret (1987), 'Studying Elites: Theoretical and Methodical Issues', in G. Moyser and M. Wagstaffe (eds), *Research Methods for Elite Studies*, London: Allen & Unwin.

Murray, Robin (1991), *Local Space; Europe and the New Regionalism: Economic Practice and Policies for the 1990s*, February, South East Economic Development Strategy: Herts; Manchester: Centre for Local Economic Strategies.

Myrdal, Gunar (1957), *Economic Theory and Underdeveloped Regions*, London: Duckworth.

Myrdal, Gunar (1975), 'The Equality Issue in World Development', Nobel Memorial Lecture 1975, *The American Economic Review*, December.

Nairn, A.G. and Kirwan, F.X. (1985), 'The Economy of Strathclyde Region', in J. Butt and G. Gordon (eds), *Strathclyde Changing Horizons*, Edinburgh: Scottish Academic Press.

Nam, Ch.W. (1990), 'Factors Shaping Regional Competitiveness Revealed in the Theoretical and Empirical Investigations', in *An Empirical Assessment of Factors Shaping Regional Competitiveness in Problem Regions, Volume III*, Munchen: ifo-Institute fur Wirtschaftsforschung.

Nam, C.W., Nerb, G. and Russ, H. (1990), *An Empirical Assessment of Factors Shaping Regional Competitiveness in Problem Regions, Vol. I: Main Report*, Munchen: ifo-Institute fur Wirtschaftsforschung.

Nevin, E.T. (1990), 'Regional Policy', in A.M. El-Agraa (ed.), *The Economics of the EC*, 3rd edn, Hemel Hempstead: Philip Allan.

Nevite, Neil and Gibbins, Roger (1990), *New Elites in Old States: Ideologies in the Anglo-American Democracies*, Toronto: Oxford University Press.

Newman, S. (1994), 'Ethnoregional Parties: A Comparative Perspective', *Regional Politics and Policy*, Vol. 4, No. 1.

Nicol, Bill and Yuill, Douglas (1980), *Regional Problems and Policies in Europe: The Post War Experience*, Paper No. 53, Centre for the Study of Public Policy, University of Strathclyde.

Nie, N. and Verba, S. (1975), 'Political Participation', in F. Greenstein and N. Polsby (eds), *Handbook of Political Science* (8 vols), Boston, Massachusets: Addison-Wesley, Vol. 4, pp.1–74.

Nuttal, T. (1986), 'The Role of Local Authorities in Promoting the Creation or Operation of Small or Medium Sized Firms Within a General Policy of Endogenous Development', *Study Series: Local and Regional Authorities in Europe*, No. 35, Council of Europe: Strasbourg.

Office for Official Publications of the EC (1989), *Bulletin of the EC*, Vol. 22, No. 9, p.32, Luxembourg.

O'Halloran, Desmond H. (1986), 'GATT, Regional Integration and Economic Theory', *Administration*, Vol. 34, No. 4, pp.535–52, Institute of Public Administration, Dublin.

Ohmae, K. (1995a), 'Putting Global Logic First', in Kenichi Ohmae (ed.), *The Evolving Global Economy: Making Sense of the New World Order*, Boston, Mass.: Harvard Business School.

Ohmae, K. (1995b), *The End of the Nation State: The Rise of Regional Economies*, New York: The Free Press.

Organisation for Economic Cooperation and Development (OECD) (1981), *Regional Problems and Policies in Greece*, Paris: OECD.

Organisation of Economic Cooperation and Development (OECD) (1993), *OECD Economic Surveys 1992–1993: Greece*, Paris: OECD.

O'Sullivan, N. (1988), 'The Political Theory of Neo-Corporatism', in A. Cox and N. O'Sullivan (eds), *The Corporate State: Corporatism and the State Tradition in Western Europe*, Aldershot: Edward Elgar.

Paddison, Ronan (1995), *Restructuring Local Government: The Scottish Experience*, preview of paper in forthcoming publication circulated in October, University of Glasgow, mimeo.

Padoa-Schioppa, Antonio (1991), 'Notes on the Institutional Reform of the EEC and on Political Union', *The Federalist*, Vol. 33, No. 1, pp.62–72.

Padoa-Schioppa, Tommaso et al. (1987), *Efficiency Stability and Equity: A Strategy for the Evolution of the Economic System in the European Community*, Oxford University Press: Oxford.

Paelinck, J.H. (1986), 'A Consistent Model for Regional Sectoral Dynamics', in J. Paelinck (ed.), *Human Behaviour in Geographical Space*, Aldershot: Gower.

Page, Edward (1991), *Localism and Centralism in Europe: The Political and Legal Bases of Local Self-Government*, Oxford: Oxford University Press.

Pahl, R.E. and Winkler, J.T. (1974), 'The Economic Elite: Theory and Practice', in P. Stanworth and A. Giddens (eds), *Elites and Power in British Society*, Cambridge: Cambridge University Press, pp.102–22.

Papageorgiou, Fouli and Verney, Susannah (1992), 'Regional Planning and the Integrated Mediterranean Programmes in Greece', *Regional Politics and Policy*, Vol. 2, No. 1.

Pelkmans, Jacques (1984), *Market Integration in the European Community*, The Hague: Martinus Nijhoff Publishers.

Perulli, P. (1992), 'The Political Economy of a 'Mid-European Region: The Alpe Adria Community', in C. Crouch and D. Marquand (eds), *Towards Greater Europe? A Continent Without an Iron Curtain*, Oxford: Blackwell.

Petersen, Per Arnt (1989), 'Comparing Non-Voters in the USA and Norway: Permanence vs. Transience', *European Journal of Political Research*, Vol. 17, pp. 351–9.

Peterson, John (1994), 'Subsidiarity: A Definition to Suit any Vision', *Parliamentary Affairs*, Vol. 47, No. 1.

Peterson, John (1995), 'Policy Networks and European Union Policy Making: A Reply to Kassim', *West European Politics*, Vol. 18, No. 2, pp. 389–407.

Pickvance, Chris (1996), 'Urban and Regional Policy: The Political Dimension', in W. Lever and A. Bailly (eds), *The Spatial Impact of Economic Changes in Europe*, Aldershot: Avebury.

Pierros, Phillipos and Mpiri, Maria (1991), 'Pos Chrimatodoti e Evropaiki Kinotita tin Periferia ke tin Topiki Aftodiikisi' [How does the European Community Finance the Regions and Local Government], *Economicos Tachydromos*, Special Edition, Athens, 15 August, pp.39–58.

Pierson, Chris (1991), *Beyond the Welfare State?: The New Political Economy of Welfare*, Cambridge: Polity Press.

Pinder, David (1983), *Regional Economic Development and Policy: Theory and Practice in the European Community*, London: George Allen and Unwin.

Pinder, John (1989), 'The Single Market: A Step Towards European Union', in Juliet Lodge (ed.), *The European Community and the Challenge of the Future*, London: Pinter Publishers.

Poulantzas, Nicos (1973 [1968]), *Political Power and Social Classes* (first published as *Pouvoir Politique et Classes Sociales*), trans, and ed. T. O'Hagan, London: NLB and Sheed and Ward.

Preston, Jill (1992), 'Local Government', in Simon Bulmer, Stephen George and Andrew Scott (eds), *The United Kingdom and EC Membership Evaluated*, London: Pinter Publishers.

Prestwich, R. and Taylor, P. (1990), *Introduction to Regional and Urban Policy in the United Kingdom*, London: Longman.

Pridham, Geoffrey (1987), 'Interviewing Party-Political Elites in Italy', in G. Moyser and M. Wagstaffe (eds), *Research Methods for Elite Studies*, London: Allen & Unwin.

Protopapadakis, S (1987), *E Katastasi ke ta Provlimata tou Nomou Hanion* [The Condition and Problems of the Prefecture of Chania], Document f355.11/73/2896/ 25.9.87, paper presented at the School of National Defence of Greece, 25 September.

Pryce, Roy (ed.) (1987), *The Dynamics of European Union*, Kent: Croom Helm.

Puchala, Donald J. (1986), 'Domestic Politics and Regional Harmonization in the European Communities', *World Politics*, Vol. 27/4.

Putnam, Robert J. et al. (1993), *Making Democracy Work: Civic Traditions in Modern Italy*, Princeton: Princeton University Press.

Quelch, John A. and Buzzell, Robert D. (1989), 'Marketing Moves Through EC Crossroads', *Sloan Management Review*, Vol. 31, No. 1, Fall.

Rasmussen, Jesper (1992), *The Entrepreneurial Milieu: Enterprise Networks in Small Zimbabwean Towns*, Copenhagen: Roskilde University and Centre for Development Research.

Ravet, Vincent (1992), *Les politiques Regionales dans L'Opinion Publique*, Luxembourg: Commission of the EC.

Rencki, Georges (1987), 'Regional Policy and Social Solidarity', *European Digest*, No. 55, August/September.

Rhodes, R.A.W. and Marsh, D. (1992), 'New Directions in the Study of Policy Networks', *European Journal of Political Research*, Vol. 21, No. 1, pp.181–205.

Richards, T. and Richards, L. (1994), 'Using Computers in Qualitative Research', in N. Denzin and Y. Lincoln (eds), *The Handbook of Qualitative Research*, Thousand Oaks, California: Sage.

Rickets, Martin and Shoesmith, Edward (1990), *British Economic Opinion: A Survey of a Thousand Economists*, London: Institute of Economic Affairs.

Rietveld, Piet (1989), 'Infrastructure and Regional Development: A Survey of Multiregional Models', *Annals of Regional Science*, Vol. 23, No. 4.

Riker, William H. (1986), *The Art of Political Manipulation*, New Haven: Yale University Press.

Riker, William H. (1975), 'Federalism', in F.I. Greenstein and N.W. Polsby (eds), *Governmental Institutions and Process*, New York: Addison-Wesley.

Robert, J. (1985), *Regional Development Agencies and Peripheral Regions*, Strasbourg: Council of Europe.

Robson, Peter (1984), *The Economics of International Integration*, 2nd edn, London: George Allen and Unwin.

Rosamond, B. (1995), 'Mapping the European Condition: The Theory of Integration and the Integration of Theory', *European Journal of International Relations*, Vol. 1, No. 3.

Rosenau, J.S. (1992), 'Governance Order and Change in World Politics', in J.S. Rosenau and E.Q. Czempiel (eds), *Governance Without Government: Order and Change in World Politics*, Cambridge: Cambridge University Press.

Ross, Lee, Greene, David and House, Pamela (1977). 'The 'False Consensus Effect: An Egocentric Bias in Social Perception and Attribution Processes', *Journal of Experimental Social Psychology*, Vol. 13, pp.279–301.

Rossi, Peter, Wright, J. and Anderson, A. (1983), *Handbook of Survey Research*, New York: Academic Press.

Roumeliotis, Panayotis (1987), *E Enopeisi tis EOK: Provlimata ke Prooptikes* [The Unification of EC: Problems and Prospects], Athens: Ekdosis Papazisi.

Ruggie, J.G. (1993), 'Territoriality and Beyond: Problematizing Modernity in International Relations', *International Organisation*, Vol. 47, No. 1.

Rusbridge, R.J. (1990), *The Municipal Year Book and Public Services Directory: 1990*, London: Municipal Journal Ltd.

Sallez, A.L. (1986), 'Land Prices, Negotiators' Behaviour and Game Theory', in J.H. Paelinck (ed.), *Human Behaviour in Geographical Space*, Aldershot: Gower.

Samuelson, Paul and Nordhaus, William (1992), *Economics*, 14th edn, New York: McGraw Hill.

Sandholtz, Wayne and Zysman, John (1989), '1992: Recasting the European Bargain', *World Politics*, Vol. 42, No. 1, October.

Sassen, S. (1991), *The Global City: New York, London, Tokyo*, Princeton: Princeton University Press.

Scarbrough, Elinor (1995), 'Materialism-Postmaterialism Value Orientations', in J. van Deth and E. Scarbrough (eds), *The Impact of Values*, Oxford: Oxford University Press.

Schmitter, Philippe (1979), 'Still the Century of Corporatism?', in P. Schmitter and G. Lehmbruch (eds), *Trends Towards Corporatist Intermediation*, London: Sage.

Schmitter, Philippe (1982), 'Reflections on Where the Theory of Neo-Corporatism has Gone and Where the Praxis of Neo-Corporatism May be Going', in G. Lehmbruch and P. Schmitter (eds), *Patterns of Corporatist Policy-Making*, London: Sage.

Schmitter, Philippe (1986), 'An Introduction to Southern European Transitions from Authoritarian Rule: Italy, Greece, Portugal, Spain and Turkey', in G. O'Donnel, P. Schmitter and L. Whitehead (eds), *Transitions from Authoritarian Rule: Southern Europe*, Baltimore: The Johns Hopkins University Press.

Schumpeter, J.A. (1939), *Business Cycles*, 2 vols, New York: McGraw Hill.

Schwab, Peter and Frangos, George (1973), *Greece under the Junta*, New York: Facts on File Inc.

Scott, John (1991), *Social Network Analysis: A Handbook*, London: Sage Publications.

Scottish Constitutional Convention (1989), *Towards Scotland's Parliament: A Report to the Scottish People by the Scottish Constitutional Convention*, Edinburgh.

Scottish Office (1991), *The Structure of Local Governmet in Scotland: The Case for Change. Principles of the New System*, Edinburgh: Scottish Office.

Scottish Office (1992), *The Structure of Local Government in Scotland: The Case for Change. Summary of Responses*, Edinburgh: Scottish Office.

Scottish Office (1993), *Scotland in the Union: A Partnership for Good*, Edinburgh: Scottish Office.

Scottish National Party (1984), *SNP – Scotland's Voice in Europe: Manifesto of the Scottish National Party for the 1984 Elections to the European Parliament*, Edinburgh: SNP.

Scottish National Party (1992), *Recovery in Scotland, Make it Happen Now: How we Will Rebuild the Scottish Economy*, Edinburgh: SNP.

Secchi, Carlo (1980), 'The Effects of Enlargement on the EEC Periphery', in J. de Bandt, P. Mandi and D. Seers (eds), *European Studies in Development*, London: The Macmillan Press.

Seers, Dudley and Kjell, Ostrom (eds) (1983), *The Crisis of the European Regions*, London: The Macmillan Press.

Shaw, William et al. (1979), *Privacy and Confidentiality as Factors in Survey Response*, Washington DC: National Academy of Sciences.

Sheatsley, Paul (1983), 'Questionnaire Construction and Item Writing', in P.H. Rossi et al. (eds), *Handbook of Survey Research*, New York: Academic Press.

Slaven, A. and Kim, D. (1994), 'The Origins and Economic and Social Roles of Scottish Business Leaders 1860–1960', in by T. M. Devine (ed.), *Scottish Elites: Proceedings of the Scottish Historical Studies Seminar, University of Strathclyde 1991–1992*, Edinburgh: John Donald Publishers Ltd.

Smith, Andy (1996), 'Putting the Governance into Multi Level-Governance. Examples from French Translations of the Structural Funds', presented at the ECPR 24th Joint Session of Workshops, Oslo, March–April, mimeo.

Smith, Anthony (1986), *The Ethnic Origins of Nations*, Oxford: Blackwell.

Smith, Anthony (1995), *Nations and Nationalism in a Global Era*, Cambridge: Polity Press.

Smith, Neil (1988), 'The Region Is Dead! Long Live The Region!', *Political Geography Quarterly*, Vol. 7, No. 2, pp.141–52.

Sonntag, Niels and Featherstone, Kevin (1984) ,'Problems of Political Integration: Looking Towards the 1984 European Election', *Journal of Common Market Studies*, Vol. XXII, No. 3, March.

Sorman, Guy (1987), *La Nouvelle Richesse Des Nations*, Editions Fayard (Greek translation: *O Neos Plutos ton Ethnon*, Athens: Roes, 1988).

Sotiropoulos, Dimitrios A. (1994), 'Bureaucrats and Politicians: A Case Study of the Determinants of Perceptions of Conflict and Patronage in the Greek Bureaucracy under PASOK Rule, 1981–1989', *British Journal of Sociology*, Vol. 45, No. 3, September, pp.349–66.

Spinelli, Altiero (1972a), *The European Adventure: Tasks for the Enlarged Community*, London: Charles Knight & Co.

Spinelli, Altiero (1972b), 'European Union and the Resistance', in Ghita Ionescu (ed.), *The New Politics of European Integration*, London: The Macmillan Press.

Stewart, John (1989), 'A Future of Local Authorities as Local Government', in John Stewart and Gerry Stoker (eds), *The Future of Local Government*, London: The Macmillan Press.

Stoddart Report (1981), *A Committee of Inquiry into Local Government in Scotland*, Cmnd 8115, HMSO.

Stoker, Gerry (1989), 'Creating a Local Government for a Post-Fordist Society: The Thatcherite Project?', in John Stewart and Gerry Stoker (eds), *The Future of Local Government*, London: The Macmillan Press.

Storey, D.J. (1985), 'The Implications for Policy', in D.J. Storey (ed.), *Small Firms in Regional Economic Development: Britain Ireland and the United States*, Cambridge: Cambridge University Press.

Strathclyde Regional Council (1993), *Strathclyde Works. The Structure of Local Government in Scotland: Shaping the New Councils*, Glasgow: Strathclyde Regional Council.

Sweeney, Gerry P. (1987), *Innovation, Entrepreneurs and Regional Development*, London: Frances Pinter.

Swyngedouw, E. (1992), 'The Mammon Quest. Glocalisation, Interspatial Competition and the Monetary Order: The Construction of New Scales', in M. Dunford and G. Kafkalas (eds), *Cities and Regions in the New Europe*, New York: Belhaven Press.

Taft, Ronald (1955), 'The Ability to Judge People', *Psychological Bulletin*, Vol. 52, January.

Taggart, J.H. (1993), *Political Opinion about Scottish Multinational Subsidiaries*, Working Paper 93/5, Strathclyde International Business Unit, Glasgow: University of Strathclyde.

Tarrow, S. (1996), 'Making Social Science Work Across Space and Time: A Critical Reflection on Robert Putnam's *Making Democracy Work*', *American Political Science Review*, Vol. 90, No. 2.

Taylor, Garth D. (1983), 'Analyzing Qualitative Data', in P.H. Rossi et al. (eds), *Handbook of Survey Research*, New York: Academic Press.

Taylor, Paul (1983), *The Limits of European Integration*, London: Croom Helm.

The Economist (1991a), 'The World in Figures: Countries', *The World in 1992*, London: The Economist Publications.

The Economist (1991b), 'Regional Economy: Upside Down', *The Economist*, Vol. 324, No. 7772, 15 August, p.20.

The Economist (1992), 'Local Government: Subsidiarity Begins at Home', *The Economist*, Vol. 324, No. 7771, 8 August, pp.20–21.

Thomas, Patricia (1985), *The Aims and Outcomes of Social Policy Research*, London: Croom Helm.

Torre, Augusto de la and Kelly, Margaret R. (1992), *Regional Trade Arrangements*, Washington DC: International Monetary Fund.

Tsinisizelis, Michael (1988), *Odiporiko stin Eliniki Vivliographia se Themata EOK* [Survey of Greek Bibliography in EC Issues], Athens: Ekdosis Paratiritis.

Tsinisizelis, Michael (1993), 'Recent Political Science Writing in Greece', *European Journal of Political Research*, Vol. 23, No. 4.

Tsirkas, S. (1975), *Enimerosis ton Spudaston tis Scholis Ethnikis Aminis ipo Nomarhou S. Tsirkas (Hanion)* [Brief for the Students of the School of National Defence from Prefect S. Tsirkas (Chanion)], Chania, 17 February.

Tsoukalis, Loukas (1983), 'Money and the Process of Integration', in H. Wallace, W. Wallace, C. Webb (eds), *Policy Making in the European Community*, Chichester: John Wiley & Sons.

Tsoukalis, Loukas (1991), *The New European Economy: The Politics and Economics of Integration*, Oxford: Oxford University Press.

Tufte, Edward (1974), *Data Analysis for Politics and Policy*, Englewood Hills, NJ: Prentice-Hall.

Twitchett, C. and Twitchett, K. (1981), *Building Europe: Britain's Partners in the EEC*, London: Europa Publications.

Tzoannos, John (1986), 'Greek Shipping After the Accession of Greece to the European Economic Community', in G. Yannopoulos (ed.), *Greece and the EEC*, London: The Macmillan Press.

United Nations (1993), *From the Common Market to EC 92: Regional Economic Integration in the European Community and Transnational Corporations*, New York: United Nations.

Unwin, Tim (1992), *The Place of Geography*, New York: Longman.

Vaitsos, Constantine V. (1980a), 'The Role of Europe in North-South Relations', in J. de Bandt, P. Mandi and D. Seers (eds), *European Studies in Development*, London: The Macmillan Press.

Vaitsos, Constantine V. (1980b), 'Corporate Integration in World Production and Trade', in D. Seers and C. Vaitsos (eds), *Integration and Unequal Development: The Experience of the EEC*, London: The Macmillan Press.

Van der Knaap, Peter (1994), 'The Committee of the Regions: The Outset of a "Europe of the Regions?"', *Regional Politics and Policy*, Vol. 4, No. 2.

Van Deth, Jan W. and Scarbrough, E. (1995), 'The Concept of Values', in J. van Deth and E. Scarbrough (eds), *The Impact of Values*, Oxford: Oxford University Press.

Van Frausum, Yves (1986), 'The Macroeconomic Effects of Greece's Accession to the European Economic Community: An Evaluation With the Use of the Gracint Econometric Model', in G. Yannopoulos (ed.), *Greece and the EEC*, London. The Macmillan Press.

Vanhove, Norbert (1986), 'Tourism and Regional Economic Development', in J.H. Paelinck (ed.), *Human Development in Geographical Space*, Aldershot: Gower.

Vanhove, Norbert and Klaassen, Leo H. (1987), *Regional Policy: A European Approach*, 2nd edn, Aldershot: Avebury.

Vaus, D.A. de (1991), *Surveys in Social Research*, 3rd edn, London: University College London Press.

Vazquez Barquero, A. (1990), 'Local Development Initiatives Under Incipient Regional Autonomy: The Spanish Experience in the 1980s', in Walter B. Stohr (ed.), *Global Challenge and Local Response-Initiatives for Economic Regeneration in Contemporary Europe*, London and New York: Mansell Publishing.

Vazquez Barquero, A. (1992a), 'Local Development Initiatives Under Incipient Regional Autonomy: The Spanish Experience in the Eighties', in G. Garofoli (ed.), *Endogenous Development and Southern Europe*, Aldershot: Avebury.

Vazquez Barquero, A. (1992b), 'Local Development and Flexible Accumulation: Learning from History and Policy', in G. Garofoli (ed.), *Endogenous Development and Southern Europe*, Aldershot: Avebury.

Verba, Sidney and Nie, Norman H. (1972), *Participation in America: Political Democracy & Social Equality*, New York: Harper & Row.

Vergopoulos, Costas (1986), *E Apoanaptixi Simera: Dokimio Gia Ti Dinamiki Tis Stasimotitas stin Notia Evropi* [Negative Growth Today: A Thesis on Stationary Dynamics in Southern Europe], Athens: Exantas.

Verney, S. and Papageorgiou, F. (1992), 'Prefecture Councils in Greece: Decentralization in the European Community Context', *Regional Politics and Policy*, Vol. 2, No. 1, pp.109–38.

Voloudakis, Evangelos and Efstathios, Panourgias (1984), *Periferiaki Katanomi tu Ethniku Isodimatos to 1981: Diahronikes Metavoles* [Regional Distribution of the National Product for 1981: Seasonal Changes], Athens: Bank of Greece.

Walker, G. and T. Gallagher (eds) (1990), *Sermons and Battle Hymns: Protestant Popular Culture in Modern Scotland*, Edinburgh: Edinburgh University Press.

Walker, J. (1985), *International Trade and the Scottish Economy: A 'Pattern' Model of the Published Data on Scottish Trade 1968–1979*, PhD thesis, University of Strathclyde.

Wallace, William (1983a), 'Less than a Federation, More than a Regime: The Community as Political System', in H. Wallace, W. Wallace, C. Webb (eds), *Policy Making in the European Community*, Chichester: John Wiley & Sons.

Wallace, William (1983b), 'Political Cooperation: Integration Through Intergovernmentalism', in H. Wallace, W. Wallace, C. Webb (eds), *Policy Making in the European Community*, Chichester: John Wiley & Sons.

Wallace, William (ed.) (1990), *The Dynamics of European Integration*, London: Pinter.

Wallace, William (1994), 'Theory and Practice in European Integration', in S. Bulmer and A. Scott (eds), *Economic and Political Integration in Europe: Internal Dynamics and Global Context*, Cambridge: Blackwell

Ward, Benjamin (1963), *Problems of Greek Regional Development*, Center for Economic Research, Research Monograph Series, Athens: Serbinis Press.

Wasserman, S. and Galaskiewicz, J. (eds) (1994), *Advances in Social Network Analysis*, London: Sage Publications.

Welsh, William (1979), *Leaders and Elites*, New York: Holt, Rinehart and Winston.

Whitley, Richard (1974), 'The City and Industry: The Directors of Large Companies, Their Characteristics and Connections', in Philip Stanworth and Anthony Giddens (eds), *Elites and Power in British Society*, Cambridge: Cambridge University Press.

Wiatr, Jerzy J. (1973), 'Political Elites and Political Leadership: Conceptual Problems and Selected Hypotheses for Comparative Research', *Indian Journal of Politics*, December.

Winkler, John (1987), 'The Fly on the Wall of the Inner Sanctum: Observing Company Directors at Work', in G. Moyser and M. Wagstaffe (eds), *Research Methods for Elite Studies*, London: Allen & Unwin.

Woodhouse, C.M. (1968), *Modern Greece: a Short History*, London: Faber and Faber.

Woodhouse, C.M. (1982), *Karamanlis: The Restorer of Greek Democracy*, New York: Oxford University Press.

Woodhouse, C.M. (1983), 'Greece and Europe', in R. Clogg (ed.), *Greece in the 1980s*, London: Macmillan.

Wright, M. (1991), 'The Comparative Analysis of Industrial Policies: Policy Networks and Sectoral Governance in Britain and France', *Staatswissenschaft und Staatspraxis*, Vol. 2, No. 4, pp.503–33.

Yannopoulos, G. (ed.) (1986a), *Greece and the EEC Integration and Convergence*, London: The Macmillan Press.

Yannopoulos, G. (1986b), 'Integration and Convergence: Lessons form Greece's Experience in the European Economic Community', in G. Yannopoulos (ed.), *Greece and the EEC: Integration and Convergence*, London: The Macmillan Press.

Yannopoulos, G. and Dunning, J.H. (1976), 'Multinational Enterprises and Regional Development: An Exploratory Paper', *Regional Studies*, Vol. 10, pp.389–99.

Yates, Frank (1953), *Sampling Methods for Censuses and Surveys*, 2nd edn, London: Charles Griffin and Co.

Young, Stephen, Hood, Neil and Peters, Ewen (1993), 'Multinational Enterprises and Regional Economic Development', *Strathclyde International Business Unit*, Working Paper 93/11, University of Strathclyde, Glasgow, June.

Yuill, Douglas Allen, Kevin et al. (1990), *European Regional Incentives*, 10th edn, London: Bawker-Saur.

Ziegenhagen, E. and Koutsoukis, K. (1992), *Political Conflict in Southern Europe: Regulation Regression and Morphogenesis*, New York: Praeger.

Newspapers and Periodical Publications

Cretan and Greek

Alithia	Cretan local newspaper
Chaniotica Nea	Cretan local newspaper
Chaniotiki Eleftherotypia	Cretan local newspaper
Ekonomikos Tachydromos	Weekly economic journal
Epilogi	Monthly economic journal
Ethnos tis Kyriakis	National Sunday newspaper
Kritiko Fos	Cretan local newspaper
Kyrikas Chanion	Cretan local newspaper
To Vima tis Kyriakis	national Sunday newspaper
Tourismos ke Ekonomia	monthly journal (special issue 'Crete and Tourism', June 1991, No. 155).

Scottish and UK

The Economist	Weekly economic journal
The European	European affairs weekly
Financial Times	Economic newspaper
The Glasgow Herald	Scottish newspaper
Scottish Economic Bulletin	HMSO Statistics on Scotland
The Scotsman	Scottish newspaper
Stathclyde Economic Trends	Published by the Strathclyde Regional Council

European Commission/European Union

Eurobarometer	Public opinion statistics of EC and EU
Eurostat	Statistics of the EC and EU
Regio	Regional statistics of the EC and EU